Management for Professionals

Daniel F. Pinnow

Leadership -
What Really Matters

A Handbook on Systemic Leadership

 Springer

Daniel F. Pinnow
Akademie für Führungskräfte der Wirtschaft GmbH
88662 Überlingen
Germany
dpinnow@die-akademie.de

ISBN 978-3-642-20246-9   e-ISBN 978-3-642-20247-6
DOI 10.1007/978-3-642-20247-6
Springer Heidelberg Dordrecht London New York

Library of Congress Control Number: 2011932215

Cover design: estudio calamar, Berlin/Figueres

Printed on acid-free paper

Springer is part of Springer Science+Business Media (www.springer.com)

Everything good has been thought before one has only to try, to think it again. (Johann Wolfgang von Goethe)

Foreword

It is a great honor for me that my book has been translated into English as well as Chinese which makes the concept of systemic leadership accessible to an international audience. Furthermore, it shows how this concept is gaining momentum internationally. Although the cultural, social and historical premises are different in different regions of the world, the basic assumptions of systemic leadership concerning success and impact to be found in this book, especially in the second chapter, remain perfectly applicable all around the globe. Leadership is an art of creating a world that others would love to be a part of. This fundamental principle of leadership is valid worldwide. I am deeply convinced that we can only shape and bear this planet if executives focus on the aspects of appraisal, trust and network establishment and put less emphasis on authority and formal powers.

Acknowledgments for the 5th Edition

Executives and authors have much in common. They share the loneliness of being decision-makers as well as the impact of their words in public. Yet at least in one situation authors have an advantage: they receive more immediate and spontaneous feedback. Authors are grateful for both positive and negative feedback, and in most cases they are also glad to receive meaningful praise. As a matter of course I was very pleased about the favorable reception of the book "Führen – Worauf es wirklich ankommt" not only in relation to the coverage in the media and the management community but also with regard to the positive feedback I received from seminar participants, readers and colleagues. These very personal judgments, in combination with the awareness that a fifth edition in a short timeframe proved to be essential, are also significant indications for the success of the book.

The Chinese translation and publication of the existing book by the renowned publisher "China Machine Press" in May 2008 was a great honor for me. The first edition sold out in just 6 months, a clear indication of how managers value the importance of leadership in China. For the translation into Chinese the publisher had no need to adjust the content or to add further explanations.

Although the cultural, social and historical premises are generally different in China, the basic assumptions of systemic leadership concerning success and impact to be found in this book, especially in the second chapter, remain perfectly applicable. Leadership is an art of creating a world that others would love to join in. This fundamental principle of leadership is valid for Europe, China and every other country and region in the world. I am deeply convinced that we can only shape and bear this planet if executives focus on the aspects of appraisal, trust and network establishment and put less emphasis on authority and formal powers.

Enjoy your reading!

Überlingen
November 2010

Daniel F. Pinnow

Acknowledgments

This book has only become a reality because of the support of many people. I would therefore like to take this opportunity to give my thanks to the consultants, trainers and members of the advisory program committee of the Academy for Leadership in Germany (Akademie für Führungskräfte der Wirtschaft GmbH Bad Harzburg & Überlingen), hereafter "the Academy," who encouraged me to present the approach of systemic leadership in-depth; to the seminar participants who helped us shape this approach again and again; and to the colleagues who helped me with their questions.

Prof. Peter Müller-Egloff, my systemic teacher, was particularly instrumental to the steady growth of this book, as was Alexander Höhn, my motivator and friend. I also owe thanks to my fellow trainer Marita Koske, my fellow in the seminar for top executives, for her perfectly complementary cooperation. I would like to thank journalist and consultant Dr. Bernhard Rosenberg and his wife Dagmar for their valuable assistance in editing and researching, as well as Dr. Lars-Peter Linke, representative of the Academy, who always provided open and critical feedback.

I am also grateful to all employees of the Academy: you put me to the test daily in my responsibilities as a manager and managing director.

Not least of all, I would like to thank the executives who attended my leadership seminars. You have always challenged me and encouraged me to write this book on leadership.

Überlingen
September 2005
        Daniel F. Pinnow

Contents

Introduction

Why another book on leadership? For many years now, if not decades, books concerning leadership have all put forth reasons why further books on leadership are necessary, from the point of view of the respective authors. Everything seems in fact to have already been thought, said and written. Indeed, from Sunzun and Macchiavelli, to Drucker and Mintzberg, to Malik and Sprenger: we can no longer count the volumes that fill the libraries.

Why not stop here, simply write my book by referring to the available literature? From my point of view, despite the abundance of information, the available literature lacks compact, applicable knowledge on this vitally important aspect of business management: "leadership."

Apparently, there is no lack of ideas and concepts, but a lack of implementation, application and action–especially for the "users," the executives. We are giants in terms of information but dwarves in terms of implementation. Leadership seems to be as bad and as problematic as it ever was. The number of complaints about bad managers and discouraged employees is increasing. According to the latest surveys, only one out of ten employees is actually loyal to his or her employer. Scores of executives attend seminars in order to learn the essence of good leadership. However, in daily business practice everything remains the same. Leadership is not only about listening and understanding; it is more about trial and error and implementation. I have the impression that nowadays the cooperative leadership style–having been popular for many years–is *still not* quite working, but beyond that, the advantages of the authoritarian leadership style are *no longer* working.

What is missing? There is clarity about what really works in practice, what is important and what have proven promising ideas that may become relevant. In addition, how many of the numerous publications from the many self-styled "gurus" can you use? Which sometimes neglected aspects are important for the modern leader? What leadership approaches are important and what is negligible? What do you need for your everyday management? What is new and yet already outdated, or already old but still of real value today?

Please don't misunderstand: I am not trying to claim to have written the ultimate book on leadership true to the motto: "Forget everything you have read and heard before. I have written the one, true, ultimate book on leadership." I would like to invite you to follow me on an unusual journey through the available literature. On this journey I will provide stations comprising my personal commentaries, evaluations, and additions. While subjective, these are based on 10 years of personal experience working with, training, and advising high-level personnel.

Herein, my contributions do not represent a specific paradigm. Instead, the goal is to examine aspects of leadership literature and select useful and remarkable facts. However, the best description for the primary approach is "systemic leading." Systemic leading is a rather broad approach focusing on relationships and encouraging development. It is pragmatic, and does not adhere to any particular ideological framework. Systemic leadership is open to the simultaneous validity of concepts and techniques from a wide range of paradigms. Connections as well as paradoxes are explored and related to everyday life. It includes the personal attributes, methodology, relationships, hard and soft factors, psychology, marketing and management that make up leadership. Furthermore, systemic leadership does not sell ready-made solutions, as there are none. In my opinion, "leading" means operating in such a way as to cultivate a world that people want to be part of.

Jointly with Alexander Höhn and Bernhard Rosenberger, I have presented a book entitled "Caution Development: What You Really Need to Know about Leadership and Change Management."–a first approach to systemic leadership (see Höhn 2003). Back then, the focus was on a lively dialogue with executives; now this title is mainly based on the systematic refurbishing of the existing management literature.

For this purpose and in this understanding this title is a contemporary, comprehensive book on leadership, from a non-academic perspective but taking academic research into account where relevant. My views are embedded in the knowledge and experience of other authors on management and will be complemented with practical examples, current surveys, and data. In this book, executives will find everything they need for working with their staff. This does not rule out certain "classics" authors being extensively referred to. These national and international writers are important keys to me and others and include Peter F. Drucker, Sumantra Ghoshal, Daniel Goleman, Manfred Kets de Vries, Fred Malik, Henry Mintzberg, Rosabeth Moss Kanter and Reinhard K. Sprenger.

At this time I would also like to pay a special compliment to the late Peter F. Drucker. I can only wholeheartedly support what the Frankfurter Allgemeine Zeitung (FAZ) wrote on the occasion of his 95th birthday. This "living legend of a mastermind" has indeed not only managed to capture the essence of leadership using (ostensibly) simple slogans, but to consider it from all sides. For example Drucker had already formulated the principle of "management by objectives" at a time when many of today's top managers were still in diapers. What I like about Drucker is not only his integrity, but also his calm and interdisciplinary approach. He takes into account not only lessons learned from the business school, but also from the social sciences. His claim that "leading above all means leading one person–yourself" has greatly influenced me and has become my personal motto as well.

I will begin by looking at the working conditions for managers (and staff) today. This is mainly about change becoming commonplace and how you as a manager can be forced to become a juggler of change in difficult times (Part I). Then I discuss the question of what core good leadership represents from different perspectives and according to different theories. I will guide the reader from the skills of leadership through the personality of the leader to the relationships and situations in the business environment in which leadership takes place (Part II).

Next I will "distil" nine essential principles from the approaches and lessons discussed before. These are, I feel, the functions, features, tools and styles of good, relationship-oriented leadership. This is especially the approach of systemic leadership as we use it in the seminars of the Academy and apply it in an overall context. It moves in the dynamic tension field between the "self" of the leader, the people led, and the organization. I refer to this as the "magic triangle" (Part III).

Finally, I will present some very effective leadership tools based on my own experience. They can improve your work just by using them frequently and consistently. The central instruments are the "employee conversation" and the establishment of a broad feedback culture within the company (Part IV). In closing, I would like to brief you in a "final word" on a few theories that I expect to determine the essence of leadership in the future.

A note on terminology: this book is about leaders. A good leader has more capabilities than just a manager. I deliberately emphasize this distinction. Other (cited) authors have their own definitions and may consider managers and leaders interchangeable; I do not share this view. I ask you to bear this in mind as you read.

Additionally: the term *Humankapital* ("human capital") was voted the non-word of the year 2004 in Germany. For many people, "human capital" sounds disrespectful towards human beings, reducing a person to his or her economic value. Yet in economic theory "human capital" describes exactly the opposite: the enhancement of human capability and willingness to perform, and the knowledge of each employee, which has become the most precious commodity in our time. Today the companies must take the needs and interests of the people working for them "into account." They must not squander their employees' strength and motivation, but promote them. Throughout this book, the term "human capital" is used and understood in this sense.

Chapter 1
Leadership in the Twenty-First Century
Leadership in the Crisis?

Who always does what he's always done, will only achieve what he has always achieved.

George Bernard Shaw

Leadership in the Twenty-first century means leading under intense conditions; today's markets and people are different than their counterparts of 20 years ago. Managers and employees are faced with new challenges, have other goals and interests, live in another environment, and they define themselves and their work differently than the generation before them did. Before getting to the topic of leading, I would first like to briefly outline the most important basic social and economic conditions. This can of course be nothing more than a general outline, as, beyond its increasing complexity and acceleration, the Twenty-first century is especially characterized by one trend: change.

1.1 The Only Constant Is Change

Every company experiences naturally slow, gradual modifications in the course of its history. However, there are also intense periods of change at irregular intervals, sparked by new technologies, competitors, legal conditions, economic developments, company acquisitions, or a change at the top of the organization. These intervals have become even shorter in the mobile, highly sophisticated knowledge society. In the Twenty-first century, change is no longer an exception but the rule, and the basic conditions for leadership are no longer traditional, reliable constants.

Leadership personnel are confronted with processes of change in two ways: on the one hand they must adapt to changes in their own duties and environment, on the other they have to initiate changes and act as agents of change in order to adapt the culture, the strategy and the structure of their organization to the new environmental conditions. Just like all other jugglers, they have to keep several balls in the air simultaneously, which calls for courage, alertness, skill and practice.

D.F. Pinnow, *Leadership - What Really Matters*, Management for Professionals, DOI 10.1007/978-3-642-20247-6_1, © Springer-Verlag Berlin Heidelberg 2011

"Leaders' work is now subject to such substantial and rapid changes that many managers have practically had to relearn their occupation. There is hardly anything familiar that they can hold on to, and so they see the hierarchy disappearing and with it the clear divisions into titles, duties, departments and even companies. They are confronted with extremely complex and interdependent questions and see how the traditional sources of power vanish and old incentives lose their charm" (Moss Kanter 1998, p. 52). This is how Moss Kanter, a professor at the Harvard Business School, has aptly outlined the current situation faced by most high-level personnel.

In order to untangle the chaos of sudden and long-term, planned and unplanned, tangible and subtle changes at the personal, internal, national and international levels, with which leading personnel are confronted today, I would like to consolidate these changes into the following few developmental trends, which are tightly interwoven and mutually influential.

1.1.1 Hitchhiking Through the Global Working World

In the future enterprises will no longer position themselves as German or European, but as globally acting companies. And this is true not only for the larger, but also for medium-size and small enterprises, as well as for individuals. Due to the Internet and global logistics worldwide cooperation is not limited to the traditional global players – it is also expected from more industries and branches and from the lower hierarchical levels of companies.

Globalization has seized the capital and product markets as well as the job market and will rapidly continue to develop. Today, the borders of countries and continents are broken daily, innumerably and unnoticed, when this is in the interest of matching supply and demand for goods and services or about the co-operation of virtual teams on projects. In the near future, these borders will disappear completely.

Furthermore, the old classification of the world into industrial and developing countries is not any longer valid in all areas. The demographic factor will considerably change the economic world in the coming years: the developed countries will suffer from under-population. In these countries, growth will no longer result from more people working or rising demand. Only increased productivity in the knowledge sector will still produce growth (see Drucker 2000).

The economic globalization does away with frontiers; however, the local cultures will continue to exist to a great extent. Up-to-date leadership has to consider this dualism. No gap should be allowed to form between global and local leadership or between thinking and acting, as in the often cited and quite accurate slogan "Think global, act local."

Doug Investor, the former CEO of Coca-Cola, described some years ago a development in the US economy, which we can now sense and will increasingly experience in the coming years in the European Union. "As economic borders come down, cultural barriers go up, presenting new challenges and opportunities in business." While barriers to and border controls for Southern and Eastern Europe are now defunct, new borders are being erected in the minds of many Germans. The reasons for this are, apart from differences in mentality and the innate human skepticism towards other and new things, above all the fear of production relocation and price dumping.

It is the responsibility of leaders to create a corporate culture that at the same time preserves the identity of the employees and opens their minds for cooperation with other companies, other countries and other cultures. It is about finding a form of business organization connecting internal market control – e.g. using profit centers – and internal career competition with the creation of an internal social network. Rolf Wunderer, former professor at the University of St. Gallen, calls this form of fair, cooperative competition "coopetition." True for the internal perspective, it is also valid for the manifold networked corporate world in its entirety.

Moreover, the game, rules and playing field, as well as the requirements for the players in worldwide competition have to be defined clearly and uniformly for global players in order to ensure that all may internalize the spirit of the game. Up-to-date leadership on both the international and the domestic level has to be person-oriented and emotion-oriented in order to maintain the balance between pragmatic, goal-oriented and result-oriented management (see Wunderer 2002, pp. 40–45).

Internationalization has led a substantial number of people to become bilingual. On the job, one may speak English, at home their native language. The corporate language also changes the corporate leadership, since language and communication are indispensable components of leadership.

1.1.2   Knowledge Is Economic Power

The agricultural society – the industrial society – the service society – the knowledge society: these are the stations of socioeconomic development. Technological development is the catalyst of the knowledge society and an engine for change, information being its fuel. Thus, modern organizations are knowledge organizations, and their employees are knowledge workers. Knowledge-based and information-based companies have a different structure and other ways of working and communicating than traditional companies, and accordingly have to be led differently.

Peter F. Drucker, the father of modern management, predicted that the information technology in knowledge companies will make nearly the entire middle management redundant, because these employees, who have to date largely been busy with collecting and passing on information without having real leadership authority or decision-making responsibilities, will be replaced by computer systems and internal information highways. In knowledge-based organizations specialists, who master their field better than their superiors, will communicate directly with the higher management. They need the organization only as a structure and/or platform, in order to unite their knowledge with that of other specialists and convert that knowledge into value.

Knowledge workers are constantly carrying their means of production with them and define themselves by means of them, and no longer identify with the organization where they are employed. They are mobile, individual, and cannot be managed or motivated in the traditional sense but only by a common goal, a vision, in which they participate autonomously, and by their integration into the information flow and decision-making processes (see Drucker 2000).

Further, I believe that knowledge workers come together time and again in new projects and teams. Thus, the importance of teamwork and project management will continue to increase – a topic that, though now offered in seminars, has by no means sunk in as a reality for functionaries still focused on their traditional insignia of power.

1.1.3 In the Vortex of Dynamics and Complexity

The innovation cycles will become shorter and will follow one after the other in rapid succession. The time for product development is shrinking. That means that the companies have to create an ideal climate for new, creative ideas, and have to offer incentives and space for their employees that enable them to think innovatively. The dilemma is: although the pressure to innovate is rising, leaders have to simultaneously take the pressure to succeed and to justify their own worth off the shoulders of their employees, as no one can be creative and innovative on demand. For many leaders, this is a new challenge.

The acceleration of work is also driven by the mounting internationalization and globalization and increasingly dense virtual networking. This means that along with the dynamics also the complexity of the work environment and of workers' activities is increasing. Information technologies go beyond the borders of departments, bringing suppliers and customers from the other end of the world into your office in a matter of seconds. More and more service processes that were previously processed sequentially are now run simultaneously. Heijo Rieckmann, a professor of organizational development, has dubbed this "infernal duo" of dynamics and complexity "dynaxity" (see Rieckmann 2003, p. 36).

A dynamic environment requires dynamic organizational structures and processes that promote employees' self-organization and individual dynamics. Traditional management tools such as targets and controlling are based on stable frameworks and structures. If the environment inside and outside the company, however, is ever-changing, control will not facilitate but only serve to hinder development. Thinking and acting in schematic terms such as "boss," "department" or "jurisdiction" will lead to a standstill in modern knowledge organizations. Therefore, the term "learning organization," chiefly introduced by Peter M. Senge of the Massachusetts Institute of Technology, is not only theoretically but also practically relevant (see Senge 1996).

1.1.4   The Loss of Security

The Twenty-first century is also characterized by the erosion of traditional social security systems and values. Institutions such as the family, churches, clubs, local communities and nations will lose their importance and their role as a source of a connecting, communal meaning of life. As the physicist Carl Friedrich von Weizsäcker has summarized it, "The period in which we live is one of growing uncertainty. Everything is slipping away: the moral standards, the traditional structures, the familiar forms and families, religion, technology, the economy. Even the canon of values itself is collapsing. The world in the framework of which we once understood others and ourselves no longer works. Our lease has expired, and its order is crumbling."

The family's place has been taken over by friends, peer groups, life companions – and not least by the company we work for. Leadership must be present and convey meaning. Executives cannot evade this task and this responsibility, whether they enjoy being providers of meaning or not. Unlike Fred Malik, head of the St. Gallen Management Centre, I – like many others – very much believe that work should be fun and performance should yield satisfaction, a truth that applies to employees and leaders alike.

A leader spends three quarters of his or her (active) life on work, i.e., on a very energy-consuming activity that requires his or her complete energy. That is why work has to give leaders something back, be it positive energy, motivation and a sense of achievement, recognition, fulfillment, joy or growth. The new generation of knowledge workers has replaced the old status symbols with these parameters as the benefits of work, and thus the entire leadership has changed. In the "War for Talent" big cars, an impressive title on their business card and fluffy carpets in their offices will not lead to victory, nor attract top people.

This highly skilled, educated, mobile, cosmopolitan, communicative, immensely intellectually flexible, and committed knowledge generation no longer lives to work, but works to live. Nevertheless the motto of the successful firm Gore (makers of "Gore-Tex") is: "Make money and have fun." More and more companies offer their employees the opportunity for joint leisure time, essentially becoming a substitute family of sorts. And this is true even for the era after the so-called New Economy.

But the companies too are suffering from the loss of security: "We are approaching times of major uncertainties, uncertainties of material and immaterial nature, uncertainties about our business partners, the loss of the company as a fixed and physically solid place of business, the loss of long-term perspectives, and of five-year plans, including career planning." (Sprenger 2000, pp. 18–24.) For many workers this uncertainty produces feelings of anxiety and of resignation, but it can also open great opportunities for the working world as a whole and for each individual.

Executives, too, are only human, and often experience the changes in organizational structures such as the flattening of hierarchies, the opening of departmental borders and the repositioning of employees as co-entrepreneurs as a loss of power.

They need to learn to live without traditional "crutches" such as their position, title and authority, and discover new sources of power.

Their authority and ability to implement their plans can no longer be based on the obedience of their subordinates or on their substantially greater knowledge, but now depend on the number of networks in which they hold central positions, and on their ability to create critical interfaces. As such, it is becoming increasingly important to scan the business environment for new ideas, opportunities and resources. In addition, due to globalization and digitalization the relevant internal and external environment is growing larger by the day (see Sprenger 2000, pp. 18–24).

1.1.4.1 Fleeing Forward

Not only have the boundaries of national markets vanished, but also the organization itself. Many companies define themselves no longer (solely) by the number of desks in an office building. This trend is confirmed by the rise of decentralized forms of employment such as telecommuting or home office, or by virtual teams. Many employees come into the office only sporadically and instead of a fixed workplace, they have just a desk cabinet on wheels, which they put wherever they find space. With the loss of the familiar place, a "strong fortress," the security deriving from the traditional source of loyalty and identification for the employees is gone.

Employees and managers are no longer married to their businesses. An average worker is employed by seven or eight employers in their lifetime, when in the past it was only one or two. The 25-year anniversaries where the boss hands over a gold pocket watch to his or her employee will be rare in the future. This future will be characterized by an army of individual specialists that move like nomads from one company to the next or from one job to another. The companies will focus on a small "inner core" of permanent employees and outsource a large part of the work or, when necessary, hire freelance specialists for certain projects.

1.1.4.2 The Nomads of the Business World

The classic "dependent" work will be replaced by new forms of self-employment. Reinhard K. Sprenger predicts the future of work as follows: "What counts in the end are the knowledge workers, their training and to a certain extent their price. (. . .) Not the labor of many, but the knowledge of a few will generate productivity. (. . .) This means for the individual: The most important capital of the future is his own head." (Sprenger 2000, p. 21). Formal expertise is no longer the decisive criterion; rather, it is the capability and willingness to perform. Given the current job market situation this vision of the "knowledge mercenary" hardly seems exaggerated.

This is of course also true for the management level. There will be more "hopping managers," leading an organization for a time and then looking for new challenges, development and career opportunities in order to move on. Today Munich, Bangkok next year, then off to Warsaw. Whether these adventurers provide good leadership or not remains unclear at this point. Yet what is indisputable is that with a practically unlimited choice of jobs and employees from the global pool of knowledge workers, the relationship between employees and leaders will be more relaxed, which makes effective leadership harder.

In Japan we observe another development, which would seem to contradict the increasing autonomy at first glance and has been going on for quite some time: the trend towards working in groups and teams. The highly complex tasks and problems that must be managed in increasingly shorter times require skills, abilities and a range of knowledge that an individual alone cannot master. Besides technical expertise social intelligence, i.e., the ability to communicate and to act quickly and to establish relationships with other people, will play a growing role in the future. The German slogan "Toll, Ein Anderer Machts" (great, somebody else is doing it) as a clever but cynical acronym for the word "team" will find less and less approval, even in central European countries.

1.1.5   From Egalitarianism to Individualism

In the social sector a trend can be observed that is best described by the term "individualization." The trend is increasingly focusing on the "I": your own retirement plan replaces the contract between the generations, being single takes the place of having a large family, individual careers supplant standard careers, and there is specialization instead of general knowledge, class instead of mass, self-definition rather than roles, ideology or political positions. "People today value their individuality, they are more confident, better educated, with more freedoms, and they grew up under conditions of internalized democracy. This evolution will also be reflected in the companies." (Sprenger 2001, pp. 82–83).

The global society of expertise, the international markets and the heterogeneous target groups force German companies to compete: they can only win if they succeed, not regarding people as mass resources, but as individuals with individual skills, attributes and very personal, unique potentials to be challenged and encouraged. This is not about creating a society of egoists or one-man businesses whose only goal in life is their own interests, in keeping with the principles of Darwinism. Rather, there should be an individualized, social network society, as Sprenger calls it (cf. E-Interview with Reinhard K. Sprenger, Competence Site 1/2004a).

A strong ego and self-interest are not fundamentally selfish and inconsiderate, and also produce creativity, freedom, personal commitment and personal responsibility for personal and professional success – characteristics that are destroyed by egalitarianism. The pursuit of individualism does not preclude the welfare of others, because: "Only the consciousness of being an individual in my individual specificity makes it possible to recognize the other as an individual as well." (E-interview with Reinhard K. Sprenger, Competence Site 1/2004a, b). Individualism is characterized by respect for and appreciation of the individual person and his or her achievements and talents and leads to a new pluralism of values. As such, strengthening a healthy degree of individualism strengthens cohesion and facilitates integration.

1.1.5.1 No Off-the-Shelf Customers

The internationalization of markets means that the target groups of organizations are heterogeneous in terms of their gender, age, education, culture, etc. As new customer structures and niche markets develop the supply will be more and more tailored to specific target groups, which happens at very high speed. Homogeneous, clearly defined and universal parameters divide into target groups in smaller and smaller units – even down to the individual – that expect to be offered tailored products and services, neither mass-produced or generic products.

Businesses need to adapt to the demands of these "parallel buyers" with multi-option buying behavior. Sometimes they shop via the Internet, sometimes they actually walk into a shop, sometimes they shop by phone. They buy their fruit at the corner store piece by piece, their suits at Armani but also stand in line at Aldi to buy a computer. The businesses must become flexible in terms of their service and production, advertising and PR. It is becoming increasingly difficult to make customers loyal to a company and a brand. Customers are also hard to categorize, as often one and the same person objects to consumerism but also purchases luxury goods; further, they are mobile and demanding, and thanks to the Internet well informed about the best offers and prices.

This challenge must be embraced by modern businesses and their top executives, the managers. Just as hospitals are not there for the doctors and nurses, but for the patients, companies do not exist for managers and the staff but for clients, as Peter F. Drucker aptly put it.

1.1.5.2 No Off-the-Shelf Employees

The knowledge worker requires completely new standards for leadership. Knowledge workers cannot be monitored but only supported. Every knowledge worker is also a manager, namely, his or her own manager. They need to independently motivate themselves and manage their time themselves, they know their goals, learn continuously and are prepared to have several careers.

Knowledge workers are defined by their contribution, i.e., they focus less on position and payment, but rather on their contribution to meeting the objectives of the company or the project. Management by objectives, leading with goals, seems to be the recipe for the management of such employees (see Drucker 2004, pp. 45–47). The problem is: there can be no standard recipe, as modern workers are extremely individualized.

In the future the success of a company will therefore depend on factors associated with people and not with organizational structures or capital developments. Such factors include commitment, creativity, entrepreneurship, courage, visionary thinking and emotional intelligence. Leadership can less and less be exercised by pressure and coercion. It has to offer the employees more freedom, more personal development and opportunities to participate. As such, the management of companies will increasingly resemble the leadership of volunteer organizations such as clubs or charities.

The traditional organizational structures and management lessons, however, are proving to be extremely resistant to change and prevent the systematic, comprehensive support of individual expertise. Since the 1950s they have shown little or no development and cannot cope with the radical and rapid changes of the Twenty-first century. The individual encounters standardized functions and procedures and outdated management practices in many companies that are still tailored to the authoritarian leadership of collectives. Individual leaders, on the other hand, know about the differences and use them. They utilize and promote the differences, instead of making their employees fit a mold.

Yet there is also great resentment, stubbornness, and fear directed at self-determination and personal responsibility among employees. Most of us have been raised and socialized in a European country where the state has taken the responsibility for the personal development and protection of its citizens. We feel it is perfectly fair to heap the consequences of our actions or inaction onto the community and make others responsible for our own happiness, starting with kindergarten, school and training, health insurance and unemployment, up to retirement. We are accustomed to being motivated by our superiors through material incentives or more leisure time.

"It's the many small disenfranchisements that come along in the guise of protection and welfare against which we must defend ourselves. In reality they destroy everything unique and valuable in the individual," criticizes Reinhard K. Sprenger. The executive can no longer think of his or her company and look for the "right" people for a given job, but must begin to consider the individual. He or she has to offer tailored roles that promote and put to best use individual needs and talents. Therefore it is essential to build the organization and its structures around the people. These flexible structures are not kept together by control from above, but by self-confidence and motivation (see Sprenger 2001, pp. 82–83).

1.1.5.3 No Off-the-Shelf Leadership

In the Twenty-first century, individualism also affects leadership in a third way. We must say goodbye to the marvelously simple conception of the clearly definable standard type of "successful manager." "Individual leadership permits itself to develop in its own way – and does the same for employees." (see Sprenger 2001, pp. 82–83). A manager should not lead in one strict style, but rather approach leadership as a process in which he or she is allowed to be human.

It is the individual needs and abilities of their very human employees upon which managers must orient themselves. And just as no two employees are alike, there are no universal criteria for "good managers," each one being a unique and inimitable personality. Additionally, good managers able to compete on the market now and in the future are in short supply. A survey of 225 managers conducted at the Academy in 2003 revealed the skills and abilities that are most important for leaders in the Twenty-first century. The results are as follows:

Readiness to delegate responsibilities to employees
The ability to solve problems as a team
Genuine interest in their employees
Enjoy independent work and major responsibilities
A high degree of self-motivation

The modern manager recognizes that one's role is not to direct the system from a position of power, but instead acts as an architect, working closely with their employees on and in the system. The manager develops and fosters an organizational culture that promotes individual development, direct responsibility, and self-initiative among employees. He or she intensively works to maintain internal and external communication networks. Sustainable leadership is concerned not only with money, data, or goods, but above all is concerned with people.

In addition, quality leadership requires a great deal of emotional intelligence and social skills, paired with visionary thinking and remarkable courage. In today's business climate, successful managers are agents of change who think progressively, focusing on the future. They involve their coworkers and subordinates in vital processes, rather than operating from an individualistic position of power.

Modern leadership requires shifting from the role of the boss to that of the partner. The managers of tomorrow – and today – must learn to display a certain degree of humility. They must also know how to be competitive in a way that fosters cooperation. They must be able to draw satisfaction from good results made possible by the efforts of the team as a whole, despite their own desire for personal success (see Moss Kanter 1998, p. 46).

Successful modern managers do not fear chaotic transitions or the unknown. They must have the heart and the understanding to utilize chaos, creative unrest and uncertainty as sources of new ideas overcome their previous experiential framework. At the same time, good leaders must possess the knowledge and the management tools to get their enterprises ready for changes in the present and adaptable to continuing change in the future.

1.2 Through the Valley of Tears

Right now is hardly the time to celebrate for most companies. Popular incentives of fruit baskets are scarce, and the free beverage dispensers are no longer refilled. Instead crisis meetings, cost-cutting programs, personnel downsizing in an effort to "shrink to a profitable size" prevail. The courageous motivational speakers have grown silent as a general sense of crisis consciousness becomes widespread. However, there are exceptions to the rule.

The valley of the tears the German economy now finds itself in after the New Economy seems to have no end, weighing heavily on the minds of employers, employees and investors, and practically immobilizing human resources development in many enterprises.

Needless to say, it is hardly the ideal time to try to gain the affection of your employees. However, there are no new ready-made solutions for leading in times of crisis, which makes it all the more important that we rediscover the fundamentals. Leading without the respect of your employees will not allow you to navigate your company and employees through the crisis, not even with the most sophisticated charts, rhetoric and HR management. Given the increasingly difficult conditions for leading, the charisma of a manager has taken on new meaning. More is demanded of leaders, who now more than ever are in the spotlight, simultaneously the harbingers of hope and the bogeyman.

In a study conducted at the Academy in 2003, 267 managers were surveyed regarding their current working situations. The results indicated that 80% put a special emphasis on soft factors (the keyword being "corporate climate"). For the majority, the manager's "people skills" are more crucial than his or her industry know-how and technical expertise. Approximately 60% think that their requirements have changed during the course of the economic downturn. Half of the managers claimed that employees' fear of losing their jobs makes everyday leadership more difficult. Nevertheless, 88% of managers with personnel responsibilities expressed satisfaction with their achievements as managers. We should however bear in mind that this is the self-perception of the managers, which – as will be shown – can deviate significantly from the perspectives of their employees (see Academy Study 2003).

Especially when the wind of the economic crisis is blowing hardest, leaders are in demand – even if strict numbers, crisis meetings, financial balances and pressure hardly leave time or space for genuine relations management. The argument: "Once we are through this, we will have more time for discussions and contacts again" is a dangerous killer phrase, because there might be no "later." The trust lost by adopting this attitude towards coworkers and customers is infinitely difficult to recover.

The result: German managers consider their companies to be in a general economic crisis, yet no one speaks of a general crisis of leadership. To a large extent, they agree that only authentic leadership can be successful leadership. The manager is not only important for the role he or she fulfills, but also important as an individual. Whoever wants to bring their company and its people through the crisis must commit to two maxims. Firstly, appreciation and respect cannot be reserved for when things are rosy, but are also and especially indispensable in times of crisis. And secondly, leading is more than delegating and monitoring tasks; it presupposes an individual with a dynamic personality capable of moving the workers under it.

1.2.1 The Paradoxes of Our Time

"Progress has brought us profit and efficiency, but the price we have to pay is a loss of meaning." This is the balance drawn by Charles Handy, the founding father of the London Business School, in his book "Die Fortschrittsfalle." Only a new understanding of work and organizations can restore meaning to a world that is governed by nine fundamental paradoxes. These paradoxes describe in a simplified and caricatured way our modern working world: its divided and contradictory nature, its dynamics and complexity. At the same time, they reflect the demands placed on modern leaders (see Handy 1995):

1. The paradox of intelligence:
   Employees are considered the most important resource, and intelligence is the new form of property. However, this property can neither be purchased nor sold; as such, the most important means of production lies in the hands of the employees.
2. The paradox of work:
   Most organizations respond to the challenge of efficiency with dismissals or wage cuts and thereby deprive themselves of their very basis: motivated brain power. Some say performance must come with a high price, while others believe it is priceless and that top performers cannot be lured by money.
3. The paradox of productivity:
   Productivity typically means more work with fewer people. But there is a limit to people's ability to perform, beyond which productivity begins to decrease due to the strain.
4. The paradox of time:
   Time is a scare commodity as well as a crucial factor in staying competitive. The issue of money also plays a role in this paradox. Some spend money in order to save time, while others invest time to save money.
5. The paradox of wealth:
   In affluent societies, birth rates are declining, as a result of which there will be a shrinking customer base in the future. Affluent countries must reach out to poorer countries that are simultaneously their low-wage competition in order to set growth in motion and cultivate new consumer bases.
6. The paradox of organization:
   Leadership no longer focuses strictly on the local or national level, but must compete on a global level in order to prosper. Employees are expected to be able to work both independently and together as a team. The challenge for today's leaders is to delegate and direct their personnel more efficiently and effectively; for the leaders of tomorrow it will lie in guiding their company on new courses in the global business world.
7. The paradox of aging:
   This paradox involves newer generations' tendency to differ from the preceding generations, which stems from their desire to set themselves apart from previous generations. The behavior of each following generation will then correspond to

the behavior of the generation directly preceding it (A → B → A). In other words: materialism follows post-materialism; then comes materialism again, and so on.

8. The paradox of individualism:
   This paradox was described best by C.G. Jung, who wrote that we must be with others in order to truly be our individual selves. "I" needs "we" in order to be able to be a perfect "I". I would like to add to the thought of Handy and Jung: due to the complexity of the today's world, "I" can only then become part of a genuine "we" if that "I" is whole.

9. The paradox of justice:
   Finally, the distribution of justice within a society arises. Should people receive what they need, or what they deserve?

For Charles Handy, the key to handling these paradoxes lies in a new definition of organization, work and capital. So organizations today are not comprised of rigid structures of rules and functions, superiors and subordinates, but are instead organized communities of equally valuable members. The capital of the modern organization is no longer monetary, but instead the capital consists of the knowledge and the abilities of people within the organization. However, leaders cannot expect those possessing this capital, their employees, to invest in increasing their mental wealth. Leaders must recognize potential, promote it, and put it to the best use.

According to Handy, the fundamental values of the working world of the Twenty-first century consist of a sense of continuity, a sense of solidarity, and a sense of moving forward towards a goal. The sense of continuity refers to the concept that people are links in a common chain, rather than individuals in the vortex of change they experience in the complexity and speed of today's world. Stability and reliability give people the necessary footing to master the paradoxes of our age. The sense of solidarity refers to workers experiencing feelings of affiliation and shared goals, rather than being driven by the need for individual success. Apart from continuity and solidarity, people also need a sense of direction, a vision of the future.

According to Handy, there is no perfect method for success in a world characterized by change. "The secret in a time of the paradox is to balance the past and future, allowing both to exist simultaneously in the present" (Handy 1995).

1.2.2 The "Return of Leadership"

Who is equipped to lead modern enterprises and people into the future? Without question, honesty tops the list of characteristics distinguishing a successful leader from most managers. Following closely behind are: the ability to inspire others, the ability to tolerate high-stress situations, social skills, charisma and the ability to form trust. While most managers doubt the wisdom of using authority and strict discipline in difficult times, the majority also admit that in a crisis they are often inclined to lead in an authoritarian way.

This is seen in practice time and time again. When problematic situations arise, many managers lose their sense of interdependence. Their vision becomes short-sighted, the focus shifts to the delegation of tasks, information sharing decreases and they start supervising everyone and everything. Yet it is in tough times that employees look for a strong leader who knows the way forward and who shouts out the longed-for "land ahoy!" This may be considered the "Return of Leadership." However, "leadership" has more than one meaning.

Stories abound of managers who become obsessed with control and self-promotion. For these managers, the threat of losing power is more overwhelming than their organization's concrete problems. Whether a company remains in crisis or recovers from economic difficulties depends considerably on the behavior of the person leading it. When, under these conditions, only superficial and not genuine leadership prevails, cracks will start to show. Workers become discontent and performance suffers, in part due to a refusal to "cave in" to the demanding manager. There is less focus on tasks and more on evasive maneuvers. For managers who tend to respond to crises with personnel reductions, this can have grave conse-quences: the best employees are the first to go.

1.3 An Invitation to Dance

In the information age, an organization capable of transforming itself is the best strategic weapon on the market (see Moss Kanter 1989). But especially for large concerns, which have been slowly cruising the seas of the world economy for generations like ocean liners a course correction, let alone a U-turn, is never a short maneuver. Managers must develop change structures. This is the primary task of future-oriented and relation-driven leaders. Quality leaders stand at the helm, in firm control of the wheel, looking ahead and promptly recognizing what is approaching.

It is not impossible to teach giants to dance, but it does require combining forces and concerted efforts (see Moss Kanter 1989). Or, to continue the metaphor of the ocean liner: a good, coordinated crew, heading out together on a new course. The change-oriented manager recognizes the importance of inspiring and engaging others to come together in innovative labors, to awaken their joy in innovation and overcome conservative attitudes.

Large enterprises, such as Johnson and Johnson, 3 M, Citibank and Aventis, have a certain advantage concerning change processes compared to smaller enterprises. For the branch giants the business runs nearly by itself – otherwise they would not be so successful. Those who must constantly worry about their daily business hardly have the time to push innovative ideas. The magic word is "uncoupling" the think tank from daily business (see Drucker 2002).

Change processes occur in three stages. Concrete change projects are the first stage, and involve the integration of employees and managers in the same team. Considerable progress can be made quickly. The integration of employees and managers is a validating and motivating experience for the former. Thus the climate fosters innovative ideas and their exploration.

The second stage involves comprehensive, central or long-term change programs that merge multiple levels of personnel and aim to modify the structural aspects of the organization and the organizational culture. On the third level the transformation-focused organization finally stands as an integrated whole, able to recognize problems within the system early and react quickly.

On all three levels, and in each phase of the change process, managers must combat narrow-mindedness, self-centeredness, dissatisfaction and pessimistic thinking in the minds and hearts of employees. Throughout it is necessary to effectively handle risk and uncertainty.

This does not mean that employees are encouraged to take unnecessary risks. Instead, the task is to encourage risks related to operating differently than before. Additionally, patience is called for when handling troublesome aspects of change processes, and it is essential that such issues be used as learning opportunities. Change must grow; an enterprise cannot change overnight. A conversion of existing platforms into stepping stones must unfold. Additionally, change must not be forced upon the environment. Workers must be given time for adjustment and room to accept changes. The maxim of the change process should, as Moss Kanter claims, be, "In the center everything may look like a failure."

Successful enterprises allow for the human element of the employees and the need to voluntarily accept and participate in change. "Change is always understood as closing the gaps. But too many change projects and programs are nothing more solutions or reversals coordinated in the past, instead of a formation of assets aligned for the future, which is characteristic of the transformable organization" (see Moss Kanter 1998, p. 17).

Transformable organizations are dynamic, open systems, enabling employees to develop and implement better ideas. In a sense, staff members become "idea scouts." Such organizations also offer fast and efficient internal and external feedback loops. Organizations capable of quality change transformations also have three crucial intangible assets: concepts, authority and connections.

These three net assets encompass imagination, courage, creativity, etiquette, diplomatic skills and trust, which are combined in emotional intelligence. People are companies' most valuable raw material, but call for effective utilization. Otherwise the best coworkers remain nothing more than potential.

More on the topic on managing change processes is included in Part III, where concrete directions are given.

1.3.1 Result: Leadership in the Age of "Dynaxity"

Leadership in the Twenty-first century means leaving the safe haven of traditional values. It means becoming adept at managing highly complex circumstances and dynamics. It means being mobile and open to change, and cooperating worldwide with most different, demanding and "free" individuals on the real and virtual levels. Lastly, it means regarding employees as valuable capital. Managers can no longer utilize control over others as their primary management technique, but have to engage in dynamic leadership methods.

The increasing dynamics and complexity (dynaxity) of products, services, structures, and processes in the business world cannot be handled simply by lining up and distributing tasks to mechanistic workers. We need individuals who can contribute their diversity of knowledge and individual talents to the solutions pool in ways that transcend traditional hierarchical levels.

Chapter 2
Occupation or Calling: What Makes for Good Leadership?

Management is the most creative of all arts, for its medium is human talent itself.

Robert S. McNamara

John F. Kennedy, Mahatma Gandhi and Sir Winston Churchill were exemplary leaders of nations. With regard to leading workers, Heidrick and Struggles ask, "What is good leadership?" This is a complex and highly philosophical question, which has been met with innumerable, often opposing answers from management schools and theory. Typically, leaders are evaluated concerning their practices, leading to more confusion than clarification.

A practical increase in value is offered by the question of what good leadership depends on. There is a mountain of management literature that can be referred to on this topic. Searching the literature for what is paramount to good leadership, four critical factors emerge: the craft of leadership, the leader, the relationship between leader and led and the leadership situation.

Included in the following sections are the most well-known and important aspects of the four factors. While comprehensive coverage of management theories is not included, the following discussion of these four factors is sufficient to guide those on the journey of perfecting their leadership skills.

The selection of concepts here serves as a basis and delineation of relationship-oriented leadership. I feel it would be counterproductive and narrow-minded to ignore the work performed and valuable existent findings in the broad field of leadership.

To give away the ending: all four answers to the question of which factors good leadership depends on are examined one by one. Yet these answers alone are not sufficient for practice. Otherwise there would hardly be such a wealth of management training, seminars and manuals. Thus we will ask ourselves: "What does good leadership depend on?" and examine the old and new approaches to leadership.

D.F. Pinnow, *Leadership - What Really Matters*, Management for Professionals,
DOI 10.1007/978-3-642-20247-6_2, © Springer-Verlag Berlin Heidelberg 2011

2.1   The Craft of Leadership

Good leadership depends on the leader having learned and mastered their craft.

This section involves a brief review of the traditional and outdated leadership methods at the workplace. In the beginning, the mechanistic age defined operations and culture within industries and organizations. The goal was to operate as smoothly and efficiently as possible, with workers' roles being strictly like those of machines. At about this time, beginning in the 1880s and lasting through the early 1900s, Frederick W. Taylor developed the theory of scientific management (see Taylor 1913), which was briefly influential in methods of operations within industries (see Taylor 1913). Work activities were analyzed and divided into individual tasks, which were easily learned and executed, in order to promote efficiency. As Taylor stated, "One works smarter instead of harder."

Other pioneers of management theories and practice include Thomas Watson of IBM, Robert E. Wood of Sears, and George Elton Mayo of the Harvard Business School.

In addition, Henri Fayol was instrumental in the development of administrative practices and defined five essential duties of managers: planning, organizing, instructing, coordinating and controlling operations (see Fayol 1916). Likewise, Max Weber was pioneering in regards to examining bureaucratic aspects of office duties and hierarchy (see Weber 1972). In modern management models the responsibilities are typically classified more precisely into six components: analysis of the initial situation, formulation of goals, definition of measures, allocation of funds, execution (implementation), and evaluation of results. Managers' duties tend to be divided into the categories of supervision, planning, decision-making and task delegation (see Thommen and Achleitner 2001, p. 834; Rühli 1996).

2.1.1   The Old School of Modern Management

The most important and visionary management theoretician was the late Peter F. Drucker. Most of today's discussions and practices concerning management and leadership incorporate his work. In the following I would like to present why I believe that Drucker provided a pool of valuable knowledge, especially for today's managers. To this end I will draw on several works by him that first appeared in the 1940s and have since been reprinted time and again – a sign of their timeliness and their considerable value (see summary of Drucker 2004 – the individual books can be found in the references).

Three examples suffice: in the 1940s Drucker wrote on the legitimacy of management – today everyone talks about "Corporate Governance." In the 1950s he wrote on leading with goals; "Management by Objectives" has long since been recognized as an important instrument. And he coined the term "knowledge workers" in the 1960s; now everyone speaks of intangible assets, knowledge work and the knowledge society. Drucker did not always have such near-prophetic accuracy (Drucker 2004, p. 9); he simply thought in larger contexts, which was his unique strength.

Drucker once described himself as a "social ecologist," as he analyzed management and leadership disciplines. He included not only the company and its stakeholders, but also the social context and historical aspects in his analysis.

Drucker blurred the boundaries between two cultures, the arts on the one hand and the natural sciences on the other, providing management as both an art and a science. He stressed both the technical as well as the humanistic side of management, as management was in his eyes both a profession and a calling. And Drucker also predicted that management would increasingly develop in the direction of the "human sciences." Today I would put it as follows: leadership is relationship management.

2.1.1.1   What Is Management?

Drucker stated that in the history of mankind, few functions have become as widely and quickly accepted as that of management. In less than 150 years, styles of management have completely changed the social and economic structures of industrialized countries. In more recent years, management has had less to do with the supervision of largely unskilled staff and more with that of "a community of extremely knowledgeable workers" (Drucker 2004, p. 20). The development of management has transformed knowledge from a social decoration and luxury into economical capital.

The fundamental function of management remains unchanged: enabling people to reach a common achievement through common values, goals and structures, and through further training to allow them to respond to changes. I feel that, for three reasons, this one of the best definitions of leadership:

First of all, managers must base their decisions on values. Secondly, leaders will always be developers of personnel. And thirdly, they must constantly direct processes of change.

In other publications, Drucker stressed that the major task of managers is to produce results that, because they are unspectacular, fade into oblivion. "The justification for the existence of the management lies in the organization's results" (Drucker 2004, p. 120). These results are outside of the company, in the business world with the customers and competitors. The only purpose of an enterprise is to find a customer who wants to purchase its goods or services. In the long run, the customer defines the activities of the enterprise, and at the same time its leadership. Therefore the profitability of an enterprise is only one factor, not the entire purpose, and focusing too much on profitability limits the activities of the enterprise. This is an important clarification in the age of shortsighted shareholder pursuits of strictly monetary gain.

Drucker claimed that "everything that concerns the achievements and results of an institution is the subject of management and lies within the responsibility of management. (. . .) It is thus one of the special tasks of management to administer the organization's resources with the resulting external relationships in mind. (. . .) The results as manifested in external relationships must be a central focus of management teams" (Drucker 1999a, p. 63).

Yet neither productivity nor financial performance alone can measure the achievements of an enterprise. A balanced scorecard is achieved by combining market positioning, the ability to innovate, productivity, quality, and workforce development. As Drucker succinctly stated, "the result of the activity of an enterprise is a satisfied customer."

Drucker further differentiated between eight key areas essential to obtaining quality results: marketing, innovation, human resources, financial resources, material resources (e.g. production plants), productivity, social responsibility, and a winning attitude. In addition Drucker believed that goals are not an unalterable fate, but point us in the right direction. They are not orders, but are more like a religious confession. They do not dictate how the future will unfold, but serve to guide the usage of an enterprise's means, and free the energy of the enterprise to design its own future (Drucker 2004, p. 51). If the management lacks the ability to assimilate lessons learned through the achievement of or failure to achieve goals, and if it does not value the employees, the company will not survive.

In order to obtain good results, all activities of a company must focus on its goals. Thus, we are concerned with the topic of management "by objectives," an innovative philosophy put forth by Drucker. This point is best illustrated by the story of three stonemasons (Drucker 2004), who were asked what they do. The first mason answered, "I earn my living expenses." The second explained, "My masonry work is the best in the country." And the third answered with brightly shining eyes, "I am building a cathedral."

What exactly are the crucial goals for managers? Each manager needs clearly defined objectives that coincide with those of the enterprise. This is true whether managers are leading production processes, or marketing, or heading the executive finance committee. However, this is often considered banal and is as such neglected, decades after Drucker first recommended the practice of aligning managers' goals with those of the enterprise.

Frequently the practice of "management by campaigns," makes it impossible to achieve objectives in a steady and balanced manner. Additionally, as pointed out by Drucker, "All parties involved seem to know and accept that 3 weeks after the campaign, all will return to the status quo" (Drucker 2004, p. 145). Nevertheless, new managers continue to utilize this approach. For Drucker, "management by campaigns is nothing but a safe haven for confusion and an admission of incompetence," i.e., it reveals that the management is incapable of planning.

In summary, the principle of "management by objectives" offers room for individual strengths, needs, and responsibility while directing efforts in a collective and common direction.

2.1.1.2   Leading Knowledge Workers

According to Drucker, human beings should be the central focus of management. The task of the management consists in bringing people together and facilitating the process of collective achievement. Only by doing so can results be obtained. Today we call this process "empowerment." Drucker further explained that an organization consists of individuals whose abilities and interests widely differ. Thus in all interactions, the management must not overlook effective communication or individual responsibility. In addition, all employees must be supported and encouraged in their personal development efforts. Specifically, Drucker stated, "each enterprise is both a learning and a training mechanism." This concept of a learning-oriented enterprise predates the popular work of Peter Senge.

Is there only one right way to lead people? Drucker made it clear: no, there isn't. Nevertheless – and he criticizes this several times – managers continue to search for "the" ultimate style of leadership. Drucker also cited Maslow, who theorized and demonstrated that different people must be led differently. Further, an individual employee must be led differently at different times. Thus Drucker revealed the absurdity of "X and Y" theory (in particular the either-or variant formulated by Douglas McGregor).

Drucker recognized a workforce trend that I have already briefly touched on in Chap. 1. In the last few decades, manual laborers have been replaced by employees whose capital is their knowledge. They are partners instead of subordinates and must be led as if they were voluntary coworkers. Drucker recognized that volunteers derive more satisfaction from their work than paid employees. Volunteers look for challenges, exciting tasks and opportunities to grow.

Intelligence, imagination and knowledge are important resources, but knowledge workers, who do not use physical strength or provide manual labor, must above all be effective. The knowledge worker, as Drucker described, produces ideas, information and knowledge. But the most important knowledge is worthless if not utilized. Based on this, the idea of effective leadership, which would later be taken up by Fredmund Malik, was born.

It is also important to consider that today's "superiors" have as a rule never worked in the positions of their personnel. As a result, each staff member knows more about his or her job details and duties than anyone else in the enterprise. Therefore, Drucker stressed that each knowledge worker is in also a manager, provided his or her contributions affect the efficiency and the results of the organization. And, given their superior knowledge of their duties, the knowledge workers are best suited to make the correct decisions. Drawing an analogy between the military and the modern economy, Drucker stated, "In guerilla warfare everyone is a manager." This alludes to the principle of direct responsibility put forth by Reinhard K. Sprenger. Drucker proposed that knowledge workers and managers are exposed to a similar reality, which is determined by several characteristics. For example, both groups have almost no control over their individual time. Other workers frequently seek their assistance, or take up their time in other ways. Potentially, this can strongly impact their effectiveness.

There is only one point on which I disagree with Drucker, who held that whether knowledge workers – and leaders – maintain good interpersonal relations or not does not depend on whether they have empathy for people, but only on whether they concentrate on contributing to the entrepreneurial success. I think this is misleading. Empathy is crucial, and concerns more than a warm hug or small talk; rather, it permeates situations and guides leaders in sensing how to lead the individual person – as Drucker also confirmed.

In modern knowledge organizations, Drucker described effective interpersonal relations as having four fundamental requirements. First of all, effective communication is essential. Here Drucker noted that effective communication is nearly impossible when based on a hierarchical relationship. "The more the superior is anxious to communicate to his or her subordinates, the more probable it becomes that subordinates misunderstand the information. They will not hear what was said, but only what they expected to hear" (Drucker 2004, p. 253). Knowledge workers must communicate with one another as equals in order to be able to share information and in order to accurately gauge the intended message.

Secondly, teamwork must be possible. According to Drucker, cooperation is not simply a matter of formal structure and scope of responsibility, but requires both horizontal communication and solid self-organization. Thirdly, individual self-development of managers and knowledge workers is necessary. And again, all must ask themselves: what is the most important contribution I can make to the performance of this organization? How do I need to develop myself further? Which standards do I set for myself? Therefore, fourthly, managers should promote the learning and development of others, including subordinates, colleagues, and superiors.

Drucker observed that we still know very little about self-development, a situation I hope to remedy with this handbook. Drucker focused less on the personality of the manager, or of the knowledge worker, but rather on topics such as time management, communication, innovation, education and effectiveness (see Drucker 2004, pp. 156–256).

2.1.1.3 Making Personnel Decisions

Managers spend the majority of their time and energy on leading employees and with general personnel-related decisions – and that's the way it should be. Even so, many of these personnel decisions will be incorrect. After the decisions are made and thoroughly examined, only approximately one third of them prove to be correct in the long run. What basic rules should upper-level management use in order to make good personnel decisions? The aforementioned Drucker (2004, p. 158) created the following, brilliant list:

If an employee does not master his/her tasks, then it is the manager's failure. The
  manager should maintain communication with employees to ensure success.
The manager is obligated to ensure that those in responsible positions at his or her
  company succeed.
The manager's most important decisions are personnel decisions. The effectiveness
  and efficiency of the company depend on selecting the right staff.

New or less experienced employees should not be left unsupervised when working
on important tasks; lack of proper supervision is an unnecessary risk. If the management deems the less experienced employee suitable for the task, supervision and communication are essential and should not be ignored.

Drucker states, "Personnel decisions and issues always draw a great deal of
attention and focus. If managed correctly, this attention and focus can be used as an
effective evaluation tool." A successful, confident management role model who
possesses leadership, communication and management skills will be an example for
other employees to emulate in order to achieve success in the company. It is important
that this role model is aware of his/her impact on other employees and that he/she is
diligent in correctly following company policies. Occasionally, breakdowns in communication and leadership will occur. It is imperative that the leader re-evaluates the
situation, using the breakdown as a learning tool. If the outcome or desired outcome
of the situation needs adjusting, the management will implement change. In order to
bridge the gap between levels of management and employees, the leader must uphold
a position of leadership and maintain communications to bring all employees together
to solve the problem. This type of leadership style empowers each employee and
he/she feels important and valued in the company.

2.1.1.4 The Internal Drive

In the "management by objectives" approach put forward by Drucker, "the self-
check system is possibly the most important tool of goal-directed management."
The self-check tool of leaders and employees leads to increased motivation, productivity and effectiveness because it creates the desire to perform best instead of
just being able to handle things. The leader has to not only know the goals but also
be able to evaluate his or her own work by considering these goals.

Drucker cites the example of General Electric, where travelling auditors regularly perform overall examinations for all branches of the corporation. The reports
are documented and sent not to the headquarters but to the local managers – both
so that the information can be used for self-check, and to demonstrate that the top
management trusts the staff. The widespread reporting practice in some German
companies proves that there is also another approach – and unfortunately, one often
used without much success.

According to Drucker the trouble starts when managers begin to dictate their
own behavior towards employees using a textbook. "In fact, anyone who is familiar
with modern corporate life has observed situations in which a manager, in trying to

avoid causing trouble with a change in behavior, turned a perfectly good relationship into a nightmare of embarrassment and misunderstanding" (Drucker 2004, p. 143). By striving desperately to always behave properly the manager is ultimately discredited; "natural" and "casual" employee relations become impossible. In my view, however, this does not represent a contradiction to the need to also conduct behavior-related training. This training must not consist of schematic recipes, but should help managers to develop their own leadership styles and to trust themselves and their employees. In Chap. 3 we will see how this can be implemented with the systemic approach.

As a "teacher for companies," Drucker felt that charity organizations in the U.S., such as the Boy Scouts, the Red Cross and major churches, take a leading position in the application of modern management practices, especially when it comes to the issues of strategy, leading teams effectively, and the motivation and productivity of knowledge workers.

For example, let's examine the issue of motivation: because the volunteers are not paid, they have to derive the satisfaction from their work, and this reward must be great enough to compensate for the lack of payment. What do employees require? A clear mission and comprehensive training. And they want recognition, responsibility, prospects and accountability. In other words: they need their performance to be measured against clearly defined and meaningful targets. Drucker believed that such voluntary organizations can provide valuable insights into how to utilize and motivate knowledge workers (Drucker 2004, p. 51).

Drucker came to the following conclusion: employees should not be "managed"; instead, the task must be to lead them. And the goal here is to use the specific strengths and skills of each employee productively. But this is only possible if the leader begins with himself or herself.

2.1.1.5 Leading Yourself

Drucker emphasized the "art" of "managing yourself": in today's knowledge economy it is all about whether someone knows his or her specific strengths, values and preferred ways of working (see Drucker 1999a, pp. 9–19). Here he approaches my specific concern, the first-person perspective of the manager (Drucker 2004, p. 257) and also deals with the management of our own strengths. A note on understanding: when he talks about "management" Drucker usually means what I call "leadership."

Drucker supported the thesis that a growing number of employees will have to manage themselves in the future. He initially views this issue more structurally and economically, in the sense that the knowledge workers need to be entrepreneurs and marketers of their own achievements. At this point however, Drucker's perspective falls short. Self-management is not just a question of self-promotion, but also of self-knowledge. Also, what I particularly feel to be missing here is the involvement of the manager, who is also a knowledge worker who needs to lead himself or herself. Their leadership quality and style depends on their own strengths and weaknesses.

In order to develop and maintain their own resources, here are some of Drucker's recommendations: first, a leader and/or knowledge worker needs to find out what his or her strengths are. "Most people believe they know what they are good at; usually they are wrong. People also tend to know what they are not good at – but in this respect the majority is also wrong." For Drucker, there is only one way to find out what your strengths are, an approach he referred to as "feedback analysis." This is how it works: whenever you make a key decision you write down what results you expect. After 12 months at the latest, review these expectations with regards to the actual results. In this way, within 2–3 years you can find out what your strengths truly are. Drucker claimed to have used this method himself for over 20 years.

This feedback analysis – which should not be confused with the classic oral feedback – allows us to make several conclusions, such as: concentrate on your strengths. Develop your strengths. Make sure to notice where your intellectual arrogance leads you to be ignorant. Try to get rid of your bad habits. Improve your manners. Waste as little effort as possible on trying to improve in areas where your expertise is limited.

To manage yourself you have to know your own values. Personal values must be compatible with the values of the organization; otherwise frustration is sure to arise. According to Drucker, there is rarely a conflict between the strengths and practices of a manager. But sometimes there is conflict between a person's values and their strengths. Finally, it is still important that people discover where they belong. In a large organization? In a small company? At the university? In business? This is another point that Drucker associates with the management of our own strengths.

Drucker felt that we were all on the way to becoming an "entrepreneurial society." Everyone – not just the executives – must increasingly take personal responsibility for his or her life-long learning, development and career. In this future society, the free market will have more of an effect on the exchange of information than on traditional commerce. The future growth sectors will be two areas of knowledge: health and education. "The most important thing, however, is that the next society will have a completely different social composition. It will be a knowledge society, where knowledge is represented in the work of the largest and most expensive group of employees. In fact, this transformation has already taken place in all industrialized countries" (Drucker 2004, p. 398).

2.1.1.6   The Principle of Responsibility

Drucker criticized much of the literature on management. He found it lacking and believed it did not ask difficult questions such as, "What is the responsibility of the management, who (specifically) is responsible, what is management based on and how is it evaluated?" Political issues also cause situations in management and must be evaluated and not disregarded. Drucker posed the question to the upper-level management and leadership team regarding stakeholder value vs. shareholder value. A stakeholder is an employee who may or may not have an interest or share in the enterprise. A shareholder is someone who actually owns stocks, shares or bonds in the enterprise. "A healthy enterprise, a healthy university or a healthy hospital cannot exist in society if the latter is ill. A healthy society is therefore in the interest of the management, even if the management is not to blame for the illness in the society," Drucker claimed.

According to Drucker, management has to deal with expected and unexpected issues and crises with equal fortitude, leadership and responsibility. He also asks the question of how the general public and/or specialized clients view the company. "The question is not whether we manage and lead our company effectively, but rather do our clients view our company as effective, efficient and customer service-oriented?" With stiff global competition, Drucker points out that an organization must maintain economic efficiency, attractive working conditions and great customer serve and satisfaction (Drucker 2004, p. 33).

Drucker called for simple, everyday honesty from the management. "Leadership issues may be subject to problems occurring in the organization, the employee's values, education and personal life." Therefore, not a new set of ethics is needed, but harsher penalties. And he also demands that leaders take the principle of *primum non nocere* – "first, do no harm" – to heart.

The three dimensions of management defined by Drucker are:

An organization – this refers to public and non-profit organizations such as hospitals, universities and businesses that meet a specific need and in the end produce economic performance.

An organization must stand for productive work and effective employees. Step one is to organize the work or service provided by the company. Step two is more difficult and involves matching the work or service to the employees.

A company has a social effect and social responsibility, which must be controlled by the upper-level management. In order to succeed and survive, a company must meet the society's needs for services. "A business does not exist for shareholders alone, but exists to offer market goods and services to the paying customer" (Drucker 2004, p. 33).

According to Drucker, the distinction between "management" and "entrepreneurship" is an artificial construct; both are needed at the same time.

2.1.1.7 Honest Work

If someone had asked the late Peter Drucker what the quality of leadership depends on, he would have answered hard work. Effective management will try to minimize the number of decisions to be made and focus solely on the most important ones. Drucker explained that though compromises must invariably be found, this should happen as rarely and as late in the decision-making process as possible, for fear of weakening the original goal. He also states the problem with many company mission statements: "they do not contain a roadmap for actual implementation" (Drucker 2004, p. 292).

Effective leaders are aware that it is not useful to start with the facts but with opinions in the shape of hypotheses. A good decision-making process always includes disagreement. Leaders should remain skeptical when an agreement is reached too quickly, claimed Drucker, because disagreement protects the manager from becoming a "prisoner of the organization" (Drucker 2004, p. 299). Furthermore, disagreement creates an opportunity for alternatives, and it stimulates the imagination. Therefore, according to Drucker, the effective decision-maker welcomes disagreement. On the other hand, there are some situations that will resolve themselves. Likewise, managers should not intervene if a development is indeed troublesome, but will likely have no consequences for the company. The effective decision-maker also works fast. He or she takes only a short time to reflect and then acts quickly, "whether they like it or not" (Drucker 2004, p. 304).

Drucker states the following aspects as success factors for effective leadership:

Good time management

Focused on the final outcome

Based on employees' strengths, instead of placing weaknesses in the center of the group

Making simple, well-founded decisions

The ability to analyze, define and make changes if needed

Setting goals which maintain the company's focus and standards

Being able to adjust and re-evaluate outcomes due to human error

The management as a role model of efficiency, effectiveness and productivity

The management must accept responsibility, positive or negative, for their employees

Accepting, not fearing, employees' strengths

Having the ability to open the minds and imaginations of employees; empowering employees

According to Drucker, in addition you have to earn people's trust: "Without trust there are no associates" (Drucker 2004, p. 316). Subordinates do not have to like their superior in order to trust him or her, nor is it necessary that they share his or her opinion. Trust stems from the belief that the boss means what he or she says, and is all about integrity.

Whether a manager has dedicated or two-faced, effective or mediocre employees, depends on the standards he or she stands for. The worst are those managers whose organizations collapse after they have left. Similarly harmful, managers who feel inadequate will always try to be to get rid of the most competent and therefore "dangerous" people in their surroundings.

Drucker demonstrated that management is more than just a collection of techniques, tricks, and analytical tools. Ultimately, it depends on a few essential principles. These factors amount to a combination of "hard" factors related to processes, structures, and quantified results and "soft" factors that involve building and maintaining relationships.

Drucker believed that a leader should not only to master certain skills, such as creating a balance sheet, running a meeting or preparing a budget, but also that he or she should uphold moral values and contribute certain personal traits and skills we now summarize under the term "emotional intelligence": empathy, responsibility, courage, honesty, modesty, and sociability.

As such, Drucker's comprehensive, holistic and forward-thinking leadership approach goes beyond the dimension of pure craftsmanship. He pursues a systemic, action-oriented approach with the basic message that leadership can be learned. At the same time, his approach also belongs to those that place the personality of the leader with his or her character traits, decisions and relationship to their employees in the center of good leadership. Thus, we will revisit Drucker's insights at various points in this book.

2.1.2 Management as Mass Profession

A recent and important representative of the "handicraft" who draws on Drucker's teachings is Fredmund Malik, a professor of Business Management and since 1984 head of the Malik Management Zentrum St. Gallen. Malik is an important thinker and teacher in terms of leadership, as his practical approach is focuses on a reduction to essentials and has a clear structure. It features the basic conditions and requirements of leadership activities without glorifying leadership as something nearly mystical. He also expressed the decisive test of leadership: effectiveness, thus providing a significant contribution to modern management practice. Therefore, I want to examine his approach to effective leadership in detail. Despite some differences, Malik and I agree on the basic premise that above all "leadership must be effective" and share an admiration for Peter F. Drucker. According to Malik, management is the "creative and moving body of a society and its institutions" (Malik 2001, p. 8). The productivity, innovation and prosperity of a society depend on good leadership. Essentially there is no longer any social sphere that does not require leadership. Five percent of the employed population today have management responsibilities within organizations; in areas such as computer science, finance and consulting this figure jumps to 20–25% and is rising. Management is thus the most important type of work in the modern mass society, according to Malik.

Because of this central importance the manager is frequently – and wrongly – hyped as a universal genius who has to fulfill a utopian list of requirements. He or she seems to be some cross between an ancient general, a Nobel laureate and an entertainer. This ideal manager of course does not exist. There are effective managers and real "performers," but they cannot be mass-produced in order to develop a consistent personality profile to emulate. They are all different: hardly surprising considering the fact that, as Malik reminds us, they are only human after all.

All effective leaders share the ability to master their profession. This means that they have certain principles that guide their actions. They perform their tasks by using certain tools with great professionalism and effectiveness, and they take responsibility. For Malik, as an element of professional leadership responsibility means being prepared to answer for our own actions and not abusing our personal power. Unlike the other three elements responsibility cannot be learned, nor is it a hereditary trait. Responsibility is a choice. Malik summarizes this point concisely: anyone who does not choose responsibility is not a manager, but a careerist.

2.1.2.1   The Principles

Principles are paramount and should be used along with leadership tools and the ability to ensure task development and fulfillment. Principles are "the core of managerial effectiveness" and "a must-have in every organizational culture" (Malik 2001, p. 65). In order to uphold business principles, a certain measure of self-discipline is necessary. Almost every employee can learn the principles of the business. An effective employee needs to have an insight into the meaning of his/her own occupation, its risks and pitfalls. He or she must also understand that one can learn how to learn. As an organization grows and expands, the leadership and managerial roles will also grow and expand. These roles will evolve, diverge, and change along with the growth of the company.

Malik defines the six principles of effective leadership as follows:

First Principle: Focus on Results
The thinking and acting of competent managers is oriented on results. Management is part of a business that demands its personnel to have intelligence, drive and skills for positive customer relationships. If these skills are in the right place, the organization's structure is well oriented and, if the results are evaluated, then the organization should prosper.

Malik stresses the simple importance of effectively working with employees. Today, complex management models and leadership theories are often blown out of proportion to the point of losing effectiveness. Malik states that above all leadership should be effective. Managers may tend to forget the basic rules of leadership when bombarded with new theories and techniques. Most will describe their job as 80% managerial duties and job stress, the remaining 20% consisting of setting and achieving goals. Those who are focused on the negative side (80%) forget to acknowledge and celebrate the 20%.

Frequently, results-driven theories are falsely regarded as a style of leadership. Yet results can be achieved with a variety of different styles of leadership. Malik states that managers should derive pleasure and fulfillment from their job, and that this fulfillment should not be solely attributed to external incentives. "One must be glad and believe work is a privilege – if work is interesting on the whole and for the majority of the time, a certain level of satisfaction will arise. It is unrealistic to expect more from a work environment than general satisfaction on a certain level" (Malik 2001, p. 81). If leadership training, good management and a healthy work environment can efficiently co-exist, the satisfaction and drive of the employees should follow.

Therefore one of the most important management tasks consists of training employees to function and think as individuals but also as a team or unit. Performance of duties and job awareness are indispensable for upper-level management, according to Malik. When working with quality staff, leadership instruction should be used only when necessary. Good managers, he feels, help their subordinates to celebrate their own accomplishments and effectiveness; they do not help them to enjoy their work, as this is of no consequence.

It is at this point that I have to disagree with Malik. Having fun at work is neither unimportant nor unrealistic. If work is not fun and enjoyable to some extent, then the employees are in the wrong place and will not mature and flourish into becoming productive, effective personnel. If an employee does not feel a connection, has no drive and no direct responsibility, then he/she will become bored and frustrated. Unhappy and unproductive members of staff are a waste of resources. A company often loses its best, long-term employees due to the lack of job morale, fulfillment, importance and empowerment. Naturally, work cannot always be fun. Not every facet of the job is exciting and it can often become routine; nonetheless, enjoying your work cannot be a privilege. "The self-care factors of each employee will differ and may be directly linked to the variance of job enjoyment and satisfaction" (see Herzberg 1959). Upper-level management must bring lifetime commitment and a great deal of energy to the job. In order for the employee to maintain balance in his/her life, the job must bring satisfaction in addition to the happiness gained from their life outside of the office.

Therefore I do not share Malik's belief, namely that there is no evidence that employees who enjoy what they do tend to produce better results. Observing the workplace on a daily basis proofs just the opposite. Someone who is passionate about what he or she does will deliver maximum performance. Capitalizing on these colleagues' enthusiasm at work will result in higher productivity. A 2004 study surveyed some 350 upper-level managers from different industries, who were asked what hindered them from producing maximum output at work.

54% stated insufficient communication.
42% claimed it was due to confusion as to areas of responsibility.
31% cited distrust between employees and management.

The factors that drive managers to achieve at the workplace (see Akademie-Studie 2004) are:

83%: enjoy what they do
72%: being their own boss
50%: appreciation from their superiors

As managers are only human, these results also tend to ring true for employees. The upper-level management has the unique responsibility to guide and lead employees to achieve their maximum potential. This may often be an uncomfortable task involving pushing the employees out of their comfort zone in order to achieve higher goals. Yet leading, instructing, encouraging and driving employees to reach their full potential and have fun doing it is a valuable and noble gift.

Research calls the condition of a worker completely merging with his or her own activities "flow": one forgets time and space, because one becomes completely absorbed in a task. In this condition one can easily work for extended periods of time and experience deep internal fulfillment and satisfaction. Flow occurs when the task is ideally suited to a person's abilities – it is neither too easy for them nor far too challenging. Good leadership can help employees to experience flow, making happiness and entrepreneurial success go hand in hand. Happy employees are more productive, more committed, and identify themselves more strongly with the enterprise. "Flow on the job is achieved when employees feel that they are working not merely for a salary but for something greater than themselves. Managers should strive to do more than squeeze the most out of every employee. Leaders must have the vision to place employees' emotional needs above market share and profitability" (Csikszentmihalyi 2004, p. 37).

In order to experience flow with the work being done, certain conditions must be met. Employees need clear goals that are attainable and that they can accept. They need feedback on their activities and must be able to concentrate on their tasks. In addition, they must follow their own schedule. As you see, many of these factors contradict Malik's fun-hostile work ethics. Later we will return to the necessary "fun factor" of work.

Second Principle: Contribution to the Organization
Leaders do not separate their tasks at work from their job position. They ask themselves what they can contribute with their knowledge, abilities and experience to make the job and tasks become one. Rank, status and privileges are important to upper-level management, but their contribution to the overall productivity of the company should be the most important thing. Malik regards this principle as a precondition for business efficiency and holistic thinking (in the sense of thinking of the whole), flat hierarchies and long-term motivation.

Frequently specialists see only their task, their reality but not the reality of the entire organization. "In this sense, a false sense of specialization is one of if not *the* most the substantial cause for the frequently lamented communication problems" (Malik 2001, p. 92). Specialists are particularly important resources in today's society, yet they must be integrated into the organization as a whole, put themselves in the positions of others and always be ready to share their contributions with the organization. The manager may be viewed as a conductor, while the employees are his or her orchestra. The soloists or specialists work together in order to reach harmony and unity in the orchestra or company. This task is referred to as "corporate restructuring." and means that the customer, the product, the company, the profit, the employees and the management all do their part to make business run smoothly.

Leaders are constantly asking themselves for their contribution to the organization as a whole. They must also answer their coworkers' question: "What is your contribution to the company?" In today's complex organizations, managers and their employees must work together to accomplish tasks and maintain productivity and efficiency. For Malik, contributing to the organization is the strongest driving power. "To make a larger, stronger organization, each individual must be motivated to contribute. This contribution and motivation must be independent from incentives or motivating behaviors" (Malik 2001, p. 95).

Third Principle: Concentration on Quality, not Quantity
The principle of managing one's organization or company effectively is of essential importance. Many companies divide their work forces drastically in order to become more productive but often lose leadership, cohesion and ultimately efficiency. In the end it is quality, not quantity, that is most important in ensuring a company's longevity and success. Effective leadership is only possible by focusing on a small number of carefully selected goals or opportunities. It is imperative that companies are networked and interactive in our highly technological world. Concentration on the keys to a successful business requires self-discipline and setting priorities. It also requires a clear, concise organizational structure.

From my own experience, I would also like to stress that "management by objectives" does not lead to success if there are too many goals and too many leaders, as the key to this management method is to have only a few, well-defined goals; further, the employees involved are knowledgeable and committed until the final product evolves. These goals are even reflected in the smallest tasks and at the lowest levels. Managers should be able to summarize their goals for the coming year on a half-page of paper.

Physical or manual labor requires little intellectual work. Yet reaching mental achievements or pursuing thought processes takes large, uninterrupted segments of time. At today's workplaces, management is constantly being interrupted and thought processes are rechanneled or put on hold. Time is one of our most precious resources and it is often insufficiently used or wasted by upper-level management. Malik poses the question, "What surgeon allows himself or herself to be interrupted by a telephone call during open heart surgery?" Many managers have difficulties suitably managing themselves and their own time. Their hours spent at work are long but often lack in productivity – a serious problem, as leadership always begins with leading ourselves.

Fourth Principle: Putting Strengths to Good Use
It is completely logical that one uses knowledge already present more efficiently than starting with zero and accruing new knowledge. Nevertheless, most managers do not follow this simple principle. Managers seek to minimize their employees' weaknesses rather than focusing on their strengths. "The principle of putting strengths to best use has enormous consequences for everything to do with people – for the selection and training of employees, filling vacancies, for performance reviews and for potential analysis" (Malik 2001, p. 114). Consistent evaluation of the employees' strengths may seem redundant to management, yet this evaluation will provide a slimmer, simpler and more efficient team of employees. Malik suggests that neglecting this evaluation and not focusing on employee strengths may have disastrous effects for organizations.

The acknowledgement and utilization of employees' strengths is based on the assumption that managers actually recognize them. People tend to see negatives or weaknesses more readily than they see positives or strengths in others or themselves.

Top-notch employees will recognize strengths and weaknesses and utilize both to enhance the organization. Effective management uses employees in a way that best fits their strengths; this is a win-win situation. If the management does not take interest in employees and how they work best, nothing will develop. Many employees will give their best without substantial motivation in order to satisfy the management. Malik states that individuals are intrinsically motivated to a certain extent to perform to high levels of expectation. Nonetheless, positive feedback must play a role in this scenario in order to maintain high levels of performance.

Occasionally organizations or employees seek to change workers' personalities. "The task of management is to take employees just as they are in order to find out their strengths within the organization. They can then become active, achieve success and obtain positive results. No other approach can be justified, morally or economically" (Malik 2001, p. 123). As a leader, I must offer a corporate vision that will both move the business forward and promote employees' development; these two aspects are mutually beneficial.

Fifth Principle: Trust
"In the final analysis, leadership comes down to trust, which may be influenced by leadership style, motivational structure and corporate culture" (Malik 2001, p. 137). Malik explains that some upper-level managers who do everything wrong according to the textbook nonetheless create good working climates and are financially successful. If a manager succeeds in creating and maintaining trust in their immediate environment, then their authority will be robust and reliable. When mistakes are made, employees often doubt their managers. Yet if trust has been established, the harm done will be minimal.

How does one reach employees to gain their trust and confidence? Malik lists simple but effective rules for developing trust. First of all, looking from the outside or from the top down, employees' errors are their manager's errors. Internally, errors must be dealt with by means of constructive criticism and if need be punishments. This information must also be passed along the chain of command to ensure the error has been corrected. Secondly, the manager's errors are the manager's errors, with no exceptions. All managers must be mature enough to admit their mistakes. Thirdly, successes of employees belong to the employees. Unfortunately, superiors often adorn themselves with others' successes. This behavior will drastically diminish the positive feedback for the employee and be detrimental to the entire organization. Fourthly, the manager's successes are the team's successes, at least with good managers.

Trust must be cultivated in order for it to be taken seriously by employees. In addition, managers must also genuinely believe in the trust system. They (the management) have to fulfill obligations and not just play out roles. Malik addresses a point of good leadership that is important to me: the authenticity of the personality. Trust is the both the beginning and the ending of the study and will be discussed in detail later on. Another criterion for trust rests in integrity and its close relationship with authenticity. For employees, this means: reliability, consistency and a lack of procrastination. At the same time it is important to ensure that the basis of trust is not shaken by negative employees, warns Malik. Effective employees and managers must quickly rid themselves of negative employees. These employees can poison the working environment, something that cannot be balanced out, regardless of how good their performance is. When Malik speaks of trust, he means not "blind" but "justified" trust, meaning trusting everyone in such a way as they would wish to be trusted. If trust is abused, then the negative consequences will be inevitable and far-reaching.

Sixth Principle: A Positive Attitude

Malik does not see management as a system of settling problems or issues. More important than solving problems, good leaders should recognize the signs of trouble and assist before real problems can develop. "The principle of thinking positively has the function of directing the attention of the management toward taking chances" (Malik 2001, p. 154). This view corresponds to my concept of good leaders having a plan of action ready for any eventuality. A positive attitude, together with a plan of action, can lead to new successes.

Positive thinking and preparedness allow us to act on possibilities, not just impossibilities. Effective employees learn to think constructively. They see difficulties as challenges and meet them head-on. They always ask themselves, "What opportunities does this problem present?" and overcome their frustration using their own strengths. Employees motivate themselves to continue to be successful in the organization; they do not wait for someone else to motivate them or pull them out of the trenches. The principle of positive thinking leads employees to give their best in any situation. The adverse situation is no excuse for reaching one's own limitations and not being able to carry out the plan. Positive thinking is not an innate talent; anyone can learn it. Mental training is effective, since it can affect emotions, attitudes and our interpretation or evaluation of events and circumstances. There are many different methods of mental training, and everyone must find the system that works best for his or her organization.

According to Malik these six principles form a set of behavioral rules to establish effective, professional management. They can be easily learned by all employees and up to a certain degree can serve to fill in any gaps in the leadership structure. Leadership and management theories can be evaluated, implemented and modified as needed to suit the organization's structure.

2.1.2.2 The Tasks

Malik divides the central tasks of the upper-level management into specific tasks for employees and for the management. While tasks of the management are similar in most societies, they also require specialized knowledge, as well as various teaching methods for different cultures, industries and enterprises. Modern knowledge-based and information-based organizations are more sensitive to classical industry and management errors, making it all the more important that managers control their personal visions and act on the company's visions. Effective managers fulfill the same tasks as others, but in a different way, as Malik has examined in detail:

First Task: Providing Goals
"The first task of effective management is to provide goals" (Malik 2001, p. 174). According to Malik, it is less crucial whether the goals are assigned or agreed upon. Leading with goals is one of the most essential duties of management and was described by Drucker as early as 1955. Yet the "leading by objectives" approach often fails, the reasons being that no two managers will follow exactly the same principles, and that defining goals and duties and redefining them to meet all employees' needs is highly work-intensive.

Other stumbling blocks managers may encounter consist in having to put all of their time and effort into their work and neither looking ahead nor being creative. Beyond that, as Malik laments, employees are often insufficiently informed of the organization's principles. In organizations there are many different kinds of goals. Malik suggests understanding management objectives as leading with individual wisdom. It is important to first concentrate on the six management principles, then the goals. The goals should be clear, concise and relate directly to the company. Effective managers set clear priorities and ensure that no roadblocks arise to derail their attainment. Drucker makes the point as follows: "Effective executives DO examine goals and prepare an emergency plan for all projects" (Drucker 1955).
The definition of the goal and the decisions regarding it once went hand in hand; this is no longer true. The annual review of goals and objectives is the best time to re-evaluate and streamline goals and objectives that may be outdated. It is effective in ridding the company of unfinished, labor-intensive tasks and aspects of the leadership or a management system that may impede employees efficiently completing a task.

Each goal should be quantifiable and must be examined in regular intervals. The absolute minimum qualification of the goal is the time restraint or timeline. Also, the anticipated end product should be defined as clearly as possible: for example, not only "to increase sales" but to do so by 20% within 12 months. Approached in this manner, success becomes something the employees and the organization can grasp. Malik reminds us that a difficult situation may be short term, but the goals must be able to turn around projects from negative to positive, fuse together disparate aspects and assist in times of leadership crisis. In addition, short-term goals must be broken down into smaller sub-goals in order to make them concise and attainable. These sub-goals will also be easier to handle, thus thwarting possible chaos. Apart from a date and specific guidelines for the goal to be achieved, the employee/s must also be given credit for the accomplishment of the task. Malik reminds us that the most effective goals are personal goals.

Second Task: Organizing
Effective employees do not wait for someone else to organize or implement a plan; they do it themselves. "The structuring of the organization and almost all institutions in society becomes one of the most important topics of all time; it is a contagious issue with no solutions in the near future" (Malik 2001, p. 191).

The changes taking place in the economy and society force us to consider the structures of organizations in shorter time frames than we once did. A large number of managers pursue a strategy of constant reorganizing and restructuring; therefore things are in constant motion. This frantic, constant reorganization produces lethargy and fear among the employees, who are moved back and forth like pieces in a chess game. People can adapt to changes, but also need periods of stability and peace. Otherwise the productivity and the company will suffer.

Malik has also examined this problem, which will be dealt with in more detail in Chap. 3. "Organizational changes are comparable to invasive surgery without proper anesthesia. Good surgeons know that one does not cut without need or without anesthesia" (Malik 2001, p. 192). As with effective surgeons, effective managers also possess these skills. They reorganize only if change is truly needed, not just for the sake of change. If it is necessary, effective managers will notify the employees of the change and the new guidelines. Organizations are not lifeless, abstract things. They are like individuals, which Malik feels is best illustrated in three basic questions: How do we organize ourselves so that customer service and satisfaction is the most important topic? How do we organize ourselves so that our employees are sufficiently paid and receive proper feedback? How do we organize ourselves so that the management is paid and receives feedback? The organization must successfully answer these questions in order to thrive. Badly managed organizations have clear symptoms, such as breeding poor management, having too many meetings, and overwhelming their personnel with too many tasks, coupled with unclear directions or plans. Malik also lists another symptom, though I do not agree with him on this point: widely "spread-out" working. Here I feel he misses the mark, as interlaced and interdisciplinary thinking and working have become a necessity in the modern world. The reasons for this are described in Chap. 1.

Third Task: Decision-Making
Decisions are a substantial aspect of leadership. Whoever is capable of making decisions is a manager, regardless of their title and position; whoever is not capable of doing so, is not a manager, which is why it is a sad truth that there are many impostors who hold executive positions in Germany.

Most managers ignore information too readily before making a decision. They believe they have the ability to recognize what the problem is and the type of action needed. Yet major decisions with far-reaching consequences must be viewed from a variety of sources free from vague assumptions. If the problem is misunderstood, a correct decision cannot be made. A dangerous illusion is that the best mangers make many fast decisions. The opposite is true. Good managers will make few decisions, and these will be based on due reflection, not intuition, states Malik. They are aware that decision-making may bring about unwanted consequences, namely, more work and expense than if the problem and decision had thoroughly been thought through beforehand.

It is of course also possible to decide on an issue too slowly and thus immobilize the organization. There is no absolute certainty; as it is impossible to consider all information and outcomes, a certain element of risk will always remain. Above all,

Malik recommends due deliberation with regard to two kinds of decisions: person-nel decisions and decisions affecting remuneration systems.

What is even more important than the decision is its implementation. Effective management stresses the use of proper decision-making tools such as follow-up and follow-through. "In the beginning of the decision-making process it must be considered which people will be confronted with the decision's implementation. One has to let those employees know, so that they are prepared for potential scrutiny and can handle all issues of the process efficiently" (Malik 2001, p. 209). Resolutions are made reality by means of timely execution and responsible employees.

1. Disagreements regarding a task or decision must always be discussed openly. Effective managers should also be suspect when a consensus is too quickly reached, as this often means certain aspects have either been ignored or misunderstood. Malik offers the following seven steps to aid in decision-making:
2. The precise identification of the problem
3. The specification of the requirements the decision must fulfill
4. Working out all alternatives
5. The analysis of the risks and consequences for each alternative and the definition of the framework conditions
6. The solution
7. Implementation of the decision, including the use of feedback, follow-up and follow-through
8. A multiple-party or multiple-employee decision style is characteristic of most companies. From an ideological point of view or for the purposes of motivation, the decision-making process must use all possible knowledge within the com-pany, as Malik points out. As such, the persons playing key roles in the implementation of the decision should be able to participate in the process. In this way, a holistic and multi-layered understanding of the problem and its possible solutions is ensured. Yet the decision itself must ultimately still be made by the manager who will bear responsibility for it.

Fourth Task: Supervising

The most unpopular and most disputed task is, according to Malik, that of supervi-sion. Many management personnel shy away from supervision, and it also seems to have gone out of style. Nonetheless, the management bears responsibility and therefore must examine whether decisions are implemented effectively. All situations have to be taken into account to decide if the strategy is acceptable or needs to be changed. The manager can be compared to the captain of a ship. The captain is accountable for all crew members (employees), the course charted and for the ship's arriving at its destination in a timely manner. While it is true that supervision can be harmful to motivation, it certainly doesn't have to. Though in the eyes of many employees, supervision is a nuisance perpetrated by their superiors, ideally it should be an indication of the latter's interest and sense of responsibility. A detailed report or evaluation cannot replace a personal inspection. Furthermore, supervising does not mean doing away with personal independence; it means examining whether independence is used correctly and ideally whether there is enough of it. To avoid friction, it is best to perform supervision in the form of an institutionalized self-check, though doing so still does not completely do away with the need for supervision on the part of the manager.

Too much supervision can create a climate of distrust and resistance, thus causing an enormous waste of time and money. Malik suggests minimizing supervision and situations involving monitoring to a bare minimum. When it is possible, one should work with statistically valid samples and concentrate on meaningful parameters for quality assurance. In addition, systemic supervision must ensure that problems are recognized as early as possible. Supervision must always be related to the individual employee. Developing a style of using supervision to assist each employee is similar to developing a unique communication style for each of them. Each employee, from veteran to rookie, must be approached differently. I would like to add that good supervision and good leadership can be effectively used to administer the self-check method and also to lead by asking questions. Note, too, that effective questions should not be limited to the management; all employees should also have the right to ask questions.

Fifth Task: Developing the Potential of Your Staff

People are the most important aspect of the organization. Therefore, managers have the important task of cultivating and developing the potential of their employees. "Even the best human resource management team cannot replace the educational and development work performed by managers in an organization" (Malik 2001, pp. 247–263). Like many others I have my problems with the term "educational work" here, because it is the task of parents and teachers to educate young people, not that of managers. Employees are not children and should not be treated as if they were. Employees have experience in their specialization and may very well have more detailed knowledge than their superiors. Further, everything concerning employees has to happen on an individual level, not the level of the group. The organization is ideally a learning environment for employees in the sense that it gives them opportunities to learn and grow. Even if at school, all children are essentially forced to learn in the same way, as adults each will find his or her preferred style, which may be: learning by listening, learning by doing, by observing or by reading. Some learn more from mistakes and some more from successes. Many upper-level management development programs forget the important point that everyone learns in a different way. Malik states four substantial elements that must be considered by the management with regard to the development of their employees: the task, existing strengths, the superiors and the placement. To me this point is also important because of human nature. Individuals have the ability to develop further, and they also need suggestions, chances, challenges and alternatives. They must leave their comfort zone in order to learn and discover new talents.

In a society of constant change and ever-shorter innovative cycles, people are no longer staying on the job, understanding and practicing the same activity time and again. Operational sequences and authority structures change, companies and markets change and individuals are more mobile and flexible than they were 20 years ago. Employees must receive effective leadership to assist them with the possible fear of beginning a new job or career. People have to learn throughout their lives and be flexible. "The development of individuals must be uncoupled, if it is to be effective, from moving up the corporate ladder. The opportunity to make an achievement and assume responsibility must be the center of attention" (Malik 2001, p. 251). This achievement must also be a challenge, because individuals can then achieve more than their potential. The goal of challenging employees to go beyond their comfort zone and expand their potential should be practiced across the board, from entry-level to management-level positions.

Malik very accurately states that, in order to develop employees' potential, we must ask something of them and not offer them something. Employees wish to be challenged and rewarded appropriately rather than being stressed; they demand structure with little reward. Although the development of employees and a company are different, they do have something in common, as both must be task-oriented, involve forming a concrete task plan, and focus on qualifications. For Malik, management without the fulfillment of these five tasks cannot function or obtain satisfying results in the long run. They form the core of the manager's occupation. Additional tasks can be added if they represent progress and do not water down the job. Many other activities can be summarized under these five tasks but may decrease the value of communication and motivation.

Malik does not rank enthusiasm and inspiration of employees among the central tasks of management. However my own experience shows that these two factors are of great importance if leadership is to succeed. In Chap. 3, I will justify this in detail and provide support from additional authors. A style of management that excludes interpersonal relations and feelings, as well as the personal leadership style, is flawed. Likewise, Malik does not include motivating, informing and communicating as essential tasks. Also improvement and change are shared with management and leadership, but are used for special tasks only. However the execution of these management tasks when under pressure to innovate requires special efforts and special skills – like an alpine first ascent.

According to Malik, we have too little concrete information concerning motivation to classify it as a management task. "The whole motivation topic is like a bottomless pit. On the surface, everything seems to make good sense. But once you really start with this topic, you lose all frame of reference" (Malik 2001, p. 271). Today we know a lot about motivation, partly due to the research of Reinhard K. Sprenger and Frederick Herzberg, but if one is unwilling to leave the safe and narrow confines of the rational and jump into the "bottomless pit" of the psychological, many valuable insights are lost.

In this regard Malik does his readers no favors by withholding valuable knowledge and practical insights, only because he personally feels they are redundant. And he attempts to steer clear of the larger part of the "iceberg" (see Sect. 3.1.1), namely those aspects of leadership that lie below the surface: he assumes that motivation will tend to itself if the manager masters the fundamentals, tasks and

leadership tasks					
conferences	supplying goals	organizing	decision-making	controlling, measuring, evaluating	human resources development
communication					
basic principles of effective leadership					
communication					
reports and written communication	job design and assignment control	individual work methods	budgets and budgeting	assessing performance	systematic removal of garbage
leadership tools					

Fig. 2.1 The leader's tools (*Source*: Malik 2001)

tools Malik himself has recommended. He even suggests doing away with the term "motivation" entirely. Sprenger would also agree with Malik on this point, although for other reasons.

For Malik, management is a teaching occupation, like many others: "As one can see, management must only be learned once, provided it is correctly and professionally done. Once it has been learned, one can apply it step-by-step to more difficult problems and complex situations. That is not to say, however, that one has ever learned all there is to know when it comes to management" (Malik 2001, p. 274) (Fig. 2.1).

2.1.2.3 The Tools

In order to perform their duties, effective managers must possess a certain set of tools. Mastering certain tools, along with the tasks involved, defines an occupation. Mastering tools takes practice and dedication; however, Malik adds, it also requires a certain degree of talent. So perhaps it's not just a question of technique?

Malik describes seven tools consistently used by all upper-level managers in every organization: the meeting, the report, job design and assignment control, the personal working methods, the budget, the performance review, and the systematic disposal of useless things. Superficially the tools appear quite simple, but they are necessary for the work of both service and knowledge organizations. By properly using these tools, managers can master a much larger volume of complex work.

First Tool: The Meeting
Most managers spend 60% of their time in meetings. Most admit that the majority of the time spent in meetings is not productive, and that the meetings are run

inefficiently. Improving the effectiveness of meetings begins with recognizing their redundancy. In recent years, increasing amounts of work are performed by teams rather than individuals, resulting in a significant increase in the number of meetings required. Yet in many cases, meetings are unnecessary. According to Malik, smoothly working teams are characterized by a reduced need to meet.

Many upper-level managers call for meetings like a reflex every time a new situation arises, a decision has to be made, or simply as part of the work routine. This "meeting mania" is an ingenious means of wasting time. The actual work tends to be accomplished before or after, but rarely during meetings. Typically, the time needed to prepare for quality meetings is also underestimated, which results in unstructured meetings with little information exchange and insufficient information to make the right decisions.

The most important component of a quality meeting is the agenda. No meeting should be held without an agenda. Furthermore, the agenda should be coordinated with the key participants, though the manager should make the final decision as to what content is addressed. A good agenda includes a limited number of important topics.

Managers must moderate the meeting in order to keep discussions on track. Additionally, they must do so in a way that all positions are presented in order to transfer information and guarantee that alternatives are available at the point when decisions are made. Furthermore, they have the responsibility of ensuring the systematic examination of material presented by attendees. Meetings have only one purpose – producing results. Malik warns that meetings are not for the purpose of socializing, even though employees' relationships have a large influence on the quality of meetings. Some organizations minimize time spent in meetings by having the participants stand rather than sit, an idea I support.

The only meeting that does not require an agenda is the annual employee interview. In this kind of meeting, it is important that no topics are given, and that the leader provides only broadly formulated questions to be openly discussed. Otherwise, they should primarily closely listen to the employees' feelings and attitudes, while encouraging them to participate. This type of meeting serves to foster the development of working relationships within the organization. Good managers value this type of meeting and put it on their agenda. Personally it never would have occurred to me to consider a discussion with a coworker as a form of meeting, though I do agree with Malik concerning the open nature of discussions. Although no agenda is required, preparation for the meeting is still essential. This will be covered more thoroughly in Chap. 4.

Second Tool: The Report
According to Fredmund Malik, the written word is an effective tool, a fact that telecommunications and electronic means of communication will not change. "All forms of working made possible by modern modes of communication rise and fall with the rules and discipline for professional reports" (Malik 2001, p. 302).

Writing forces us to think more thoroughly, to outline and summarize. Whether reports, minutes, memoranda, business letters or offers, all must be oriented on the addressee rather than meeting the needs of the author. The central question is: What is the purpose of this report, in terms of its impact on the recipient? First, he or she must understand the content, and secondly steps of action must be clearly outlined. In order for reports to do the most good, managers must write the content in the briefest, most succinct manner possible, maintain formality, and write with the addressee in mind. For example, lawyers rather prefer text only, engineers prefer diagrams, financial experts prefer tables, etc. Whether reports are written in traditional paper form or formulated in emails, attention to proper grammar, word choice, punctuation and logical structure is required. Although this sounds banal, everyday written communication is often unbelievably deficient concerning these matters. The very purpose of reports and documents is to facilitate communication; thus they must be completely comprehensible. Therefore, upper-level managers must be conscientious and avoid widespread bad habits such as: referencing without citing, over-using charts with arbitrary symbols, vague interpretations that cause confusion rather than provide clarity, and presenting in landscape format.

Third Tool: Job Design and Assignment Control
Reaching goals effectively calls for the correct organization of the tasks and assignments for each coworker. Therefore Malik defines job design and assignment control, i.e., the controlling the placement and utilization of people, as the third essential tool. But in many organizations, job design is completely underdeveloped if existent at all. "Incorrect or not thoroughly formulated job design is one of the main sources of de-motivation, discontent, poor productivity and poor use of resources" (Malik 2001, p. 306).

Malik believes that the most common error within organizations is to have insufficient expectations of job roles; most workers have limited tasks and responsibilities that do not allow them to fulfill their potential. Jobs must allow people the room to function according to their capacity. "One should stretch oneself daily in some way, and thereby slowly increase the daily quota of performance. This alone leads to the development of people who use their internal strengths and hidden abilities and moves them to actively think about effective working" (Malik 2001, p. 307). I want to emphasize this: people do not have to feel a sense of mediocrity with regard to their work or bore themselves to death. Any worker who constantly watches the clock or spends time surfing the Internet while on the job has an unchallenging job.

Today's businesses commonly utilize flat hierarchies. The result is that employees and managers are no longer monitored by their superiors but instead in terms of the fulfillment of their duties – yet another important reason why the job must be appropriately inclusive in terms of the range of duties. Sometime job scopes can be too large and be excessively demanding, with requirements that are impossible to fulfill for any person, such as blending sales and marketing into one job. Malik calls such assignments "killer jobs."

The lack of appropriate assignment delegation or "employment control" in German enterprises is for Malik one of the main causes for the lack of turnover, weakness and lack of effectiveness. Here again Drucker (and later Warren Bennis) astutely made the following distinction: efficiency involves doing things right; effectiveness is doing the right things (see Drucker 1955). For Malik, the "assignment" means the employee's key task. As such, the term is more specific and situation-bound than a pure job description, and goes beyond pure job design. The assignment is the task with the highest priority at the given time.

For some employees the nature of their assignment is clear, and they work accordingly. Managers must ensure others are aware of what their key tasks are. They must focus on developing the assignment and providing a written description, particularly in complex cases and during times of rapid organizational change. The best employees must be entrusted with the highest priority activities, which is the objective of effective assignment control.

A good example of involves the budgeting and goal-setting that take place near the end of a business period. Six to 8 weeks before the end of the period the manager must personally see to it that employees are completing their respective high-priority tasks; he or she should also reduce the amount of routine tasks and less important assignments for their best employees during this period. These activities are delegated to the second or third best employee. According to Malik, in this way, a sense of "shared commitment" is established, with each person helping the other to accomplish important tasks. Effective managers train their employees to independently recognize priorities and respond accordingly.

Fourth Tool: Personal Working Methods
"Personal working methods are extraordinarily important for managers; nothing else affects their performance so directly and comprehensively. The results and success of managers depend above all else on these methods" (Malik 2001, p. 325). Talent, experience and expertise are useless if good methods are lacking, according to Malik. Appropriate work methods also safeguard against burnout, as they make a healthy work-life balance possible. The development of individual working methods is hardly a waste of time; on the contrary, a great deal of time can be saved as a result, the operational concept being: "Don't work harder, work smarter."

The concrete makeup of working methods depends on many different factors. These include the manager's personality, the basic working conditions, the nature of the industry, the kind of activity carried out by the organization, the corporate culture, their position within the organization, the existing infrastructure, travel requirements, their age, and their supervisor's expectations. Therefore, it is critical that working methods be reviewed at regular intervals. It is important to frequently ask oneself: Do my working methods still fit my tasks, priorities and the conditions of the enterprise?

From his own life experience as well as his professional studies, Malik has seen the benefits of correct methods. With such methods, a person can accomplish more and larger tasks without compromising their health, neglecting partnerships, becoming a slave to their work and missing out on other aspects of life. Initial questions like the following are important: How do I want to use 5,800 h per year of time being awake? How much of my time do I want to dedicate to my occupation, my family, my health, and my hobbies? How much time should I have for my personal recreation? What do I want to stop doing? Without making clear decisions, life just goes by, and fulfillment will not be achieved.

It is worthwhile to break down long-term goals into stages and to schedule important basic functions far in advance. Just as in the case of meeting agendas, one's time should never be scheduled in a way that there is no room for inevitable unexpected developments. In the daily agenda, it is better to plan an equal time share for the expected daily task and unexpected interruptions. Since the flow of material to the "in" box of a desk never ceases, and the computer of a manager provides ever-more requirements, an effective manager needs a system for processing the continuous inputs, states Malik. The basis of such a system relies on the art of delegating, and the ability to differentiate between what initially seems urgent and what is truly important.

The effective upper-level manager masters both classical and modern communication technologies. This means he or she is able to anticipate which medium is most appropriate, whether telephone, fax, letter or email. He or she prepares for telephone calls and keeps them short, works with text templates and dictating machines when the communication concerns text production. In addition, their personal working methods may require the employment of a secretary, a resubmission system, realistic "to do" lists, reliable checklists, as well as clear routines that ensure professionalism, productivity and smoothly running operations.

Fredmund Malik also includes the systematic maintenance of relationships in the category of working methods. I believe it has a higher value, as I will show in the course of this book. Maintaining relationships is not only a means but also a goal of organizing labor. More still: to a great extent, leadership consists in creating and maintaining relationships.

Fifth Tool: The Budget and Budgeting
The budget is one of managers' more sophisticated tools. Yet, according to Malik unfortunately no all university graduates with a degree in Economics are prepared to create a budget, let alone newcomers from other fields. Due to this inability and an aversion to numbers, many managers pass on this important tool to someone else. However, managers who do not have a solid grasp of budgets are unreliable, uninformed and can be easily manipulated.

The late Peter F. Drucker was one of the few who regarded the budget as a management tool rather than an accounting instrument. Due to the fact that the manager is responsible for work units such as profit centers, divisions or subsidiaries, they should establish the budget as one of their own tools.

The budget helps experienced managers to organize and plan their work; at the same time, it helps inexperienced managers to become acquainted with their new duties. As Malik states, "It is the best instrument for the productive utilization of key resources, in particular human resources; for this reason, the budget is the only tool that allows resources to be productive" (Malik 2001, p. 348). Malik emphasizes that budgets are the basis for effective and good communication because the budget clarifies what must be communicated in order to meet objectives. Yet I feel this is an extremely narrow understanding of communication, as if employees only dealt with budgetary questions and budget-related tasks. There are of course plenty of other topics discussed between people cooperating on a job than the budget! Further, it gives the impression that those who are not conversant with budgeting should be left out of communications, as they can't participate anyway!

But returning to Malik, the basis for an effective budget is the answer to the question: "What results do we want to obtain in our primary fields?" A budget is not a computer forecast, he warns, but an effort to bring to fruition long-term projects, objectives, strategies, innovations and changes.

Sixth Tool: The Performance Review

Many managers see the performance review critically and use it only halfheartedly, considering it largely useless. This is due to the dreadful bureaucracy involved in typical evaluation systems. According to Malik these systems tend to fail to meet the needs of the management for quality performance review methods. He dislikes most performance review measures, as they were developed by psychologists, whose main focus is on disorders and deficits. Therefore, the standard criteria are not aligned with the needs of the workplace, where Malik believes that the strength and continuity of relationships should be emphasized.

A meaningful performance review must be individualized and consider the character traits of the person reviewed, as well as tasks that person is responsible for. A "one size fits all" system is inappropriate and lacks fairness for the individual. Thus most reviews list and rate criteria describing activities that are inappropriate: sometimes the employee cannot demonstrate his or her competence, or does not use their abilities in their job. Further, two individuals performing the same job will never perform in exactly the same way. Here is an example from sales: one employee reaches her sales goals thanks to her considerable expertise, but another employee reaches his sales figures goals because he is particularly friendly and can better judge the customers' needs. Hence the problem of the highly popular pseudo-quantification of non-quantifiable values arises, which Malik criticizes as providing only an illusion of objectivity and accuracy.

Instead of just using any given scheme, managers should trust their own judgment in selecting the system used, basing it on the following questions: "What is needed in this unique, concrete position, in this concrete enterprise and in this concrete situation? What are the specific strengths of the employee, and how can the tasks be constructed to optimally bring out that employee's strengths?" In this way a realistic picture of performance develops. The ability to judge needed here is something that can be improved and trained; being able to assess people is no "voodoo," but results from good observation.

A problem that goes hand in hand with the use of standard criteria is the definition of standard profiles based on average performance. We just select the proper pigeonhole and insert the employee – a very convenient practice and one with no apparent consequences for the parties involved. Thus the upper-level management is spared the embarrassment of having to justify a bad evaluation or having to reward a particularly good evaluation with a promotion or wage increase.

But these meaningless, cookie-cutter evaluations are detrimental for everyone involved: the employee, who does not receive sufficient feedback to develop further; the management, which does not gain feedback to improve its own work; and the company itself, which cannot thrive with predominantly unmotivated, mediocre employees. Genuine performers want to know where they stand in regards to their performance. Malik believes that, for them, accurate and appropriate evaluations provide them both incentives to perform and indications of their personal success.

Good managers do not evaluate their employees only once a year. They constantly note the achievements of the people with whom they work. They notice how employees behave and consider such matters as how the employee reacts in everyday situations in which honesty, integrity, and backbone are required, and how male and female coworkers relate to each other. Using these puzzle pieces, they develop an overall view of the employee that is much more accurate.

Seventh Tool: Systematic Disposal
The last tool Malik mentions is often not put into practice, but inarguably important: organizations need – just like organisms do – systems and processes to free themselves from things that are old and superfluous. Such system makes the difference between trim, efficient, fast enterprises and fat, inefficient, slow ones. Organizations have, like people, habits that accumulate and carry along much unnecessary weight.

The idea of the "systematic disposal of garbage" goes back to Peter F. Drucker. The point of departure is the consideration: What would we not we start with, if we weren't already in the middle of it? And, what do we have to separate ourselves from and let go of? What do we need to stop doing? Effective managers ask themselves these questions regarding products, markets, customers and technologies at least every three years (unless they are engaged in change processes, in which case this should take place more frequently). All other aspects of business such as administrative practices, computer systems, lists, reports and meetings should be reviewed once a year. Malik reported that the consistent application of this way of thinking transformed General Electric from a tragically slow-to-act and bureaucratic business into one of the best led, most vital and profitable ones in the world. The critical decision was for the organization to withdraw itself from all endeavors in which it was not first or second in the world market.

To summarize Malik's review of the "systematic disposal of garbage": it has at least three consequences. First of all, it is the key component of business process redesign and essential to effectively reducing management to an appropriate level. Secondly, this disposal is necessary for effective change management and for promoting effective innovation. Thirdly, it is necessary in order to address and identify the core of an institution, to define its fundamental business and aims, and to develop its mission (Malik 2001, p. 377).

This disposal is also the fastest and easiest way to increase the personal effectiveness of a manager and his or her employees, allowing managers to better focus on the crucial work, save time and use resources more efficiently. After some initial hesitation, good employees will acknowledge the wastefulness in their departments, and are best suited to determining how operational sequences and structures can be simplified.

These seven tools and their professional implementation bridge the gap between efficiency and effectiveness. For Malik, "the descriptive principles and tasks determine what 'the right things' are, whereas these tools are the prerequisite for doing them right."

2.1.2.4   Profession Without Training

According to Malik, managers do not necessarily have to be natural born leaders, but leadership can be learned like every other career aspect. Upper-level managers must receive in-depth training on the first three elements, i.e., on the principles, tasks and tools. The knowledge necessary for good leadership can be acquired with normal intelligence and sufficient practice.

At the same time, Malik emphasizes that management is an occupation without standardized training. Novice managers mostly have a purely academic career and know only the theory of running a company. The remainder of their experience is gained on the job, following the principle of trial and error. However, each error can have bitter consequences, most often at the expense of the organization. According to Malik, someone who has a competent boss as mentor and role model at the beginning of their career is lucky. The new generation of managers has already been collecting relevant leadership experience since childhood. For example, many participated in sports clubs, were involved with youth organizations or were class president. All these methods of learning are lengthy and involve little systematic learning, but are nevertheless useful. In other occupations, it would be inconceivable to rely on this kind of learning.

According to Malik, the heart of effective leadership is not the manager's personality. As such, he believes that "not the selection of managers, but rather their training should be the primary focus. Managers are not chosen, but need to be made, educated and formed" (Malik 2001, p. 45). Malik regards the idea of the natural born manager as an illusion. "One uses character traits to gauge potential for achievement. Yet there is no proof of any such connection; indeed, history has clearly disproved it," says Malik in apodictically, though he does not go on to offer further support of his statement (Malik 2001, p. 33).

Malik only goes so far as to concede that not everyone can lead well, and that there are certain traits that make leadership easier for some. In order to manage best, and to accomplish the most difficult managerial tasks, one needs more than job related skills. Talent, skill, luck and experience are also needed, as Malik admits. I consider this marginalization of personality to be ill advised, which leads me to my main criticism of Malik: he neglects the subtle but important impact of the personalities of leaders and employees, which includes their character traits, feelings and relationships.

In brief: if the chemistry is not right and emotional intelligence is lacking, all of the tools and principles described above will not yield positive results. Although one may perform well professionally in the short term, there will not be long-term success. Such leaders will most likely be able to keep their businesses afloat, but they will likely to be swept along by the vortex of innovation and change without ever arriving at a new destination. To successfully manage change, leaders must be able to feel and take away their employees' fears, to inspire them with energy and confidence – abilities that Malik considers unnecessary or unimportant.

Indeed, in his eyes inspiration and enthusiasm are only for charlatans: "I see two ways of thinking that illustrate misdirected and harmful views of management particularly well. In its most general form, the first can be called the 'pursuit of happiness,' and the second is the concept of the 'great leader'" (Malik 2001, p. 27).

In this context he also criticizes the "'psychologizing' of management" and states that the practical effectiveness of the instruments taken from the field of therapy is doubtful. For him, it boils down to the dominance of focus on the pathological, to the deleterious concentration on conflicts, relationship problems and neuroses. However, the work of Manfred Kets de Vries clearly shows that Malik's criticism is not warranted, and that the psychological aspect of leadership is of central importance in practice, something that has also been impressively confirmed by the successes of the systemic leadership training offered by the Academy.

My second fundamental point of criticism is that Malik primarily refers to the American military as examples of good management. I consider the analogy dubious at best. Employees are not soldiers drilled for obedience. Armies are, unlike modern organizations, strictly hierarchical. In times of war soldiers can be drafted into service if they do not join the army voluntarily. In the business world, the best talents join organizations of their own free will. These are two main reasons why Malik's military model hardly suits today's younger management.

2.1.3   A Question of Style

Now let us look into the style of leadership, because style is frequently provided as the answer to the question of what constitutes good leadership. What is the correct style of leadership? This question is as old as the profession itself, and there have been innumerable attempts at categorization attempts, the majority of which will not be dealt with here. There is no single correct style of leadership; instead, just as a golfer bases their choice of club on the particular situation, good leaders select individual aspects from various leadership styles to best suit their needs.

In the past, the choice of leadership style chiefly depended on the personal values and authority of the management and on the level of leadership. Today, additional factors are relevant for choice of leadership style: economic factors, time limits, the complexity of tasks, corporate culture and the value orientation of the parties involved.

2.1.3.1 The Choice of Style

In the 1970s Victor H. Vroom and Philip W. Yetton, researchers at the University of Michigan, developed a leadership model (see Vroom/Yetton 1973), identifying five possible styles for upper-level management which differ from each other in the degree of the employees' involvement. The styles range from a completely authoritarian style to the complete transfer of decision-making power to the employees. Between these two extremes, there is a model in which leaders receive all necessary information from their employees in order to make decisions based on the information provided; a model involving the discussion of problems with individual employees and taking their suggestions into account before making decisions; and finally a model incorporating open group discussions, with employees helping to make decisions.

Apart from these five styles of leadership, Vroom and Yetton differentiate between seven organizational, technical and task-oriented aspects of situations that determine the style of decision-making; however, these aspects are of little use in practice and therefore will not be discussed here. Vroom and Yetton's approach is normative. This means that it prescribes how managers should proceed in order to meet certain company goals. Objectives of the manager or employee are disregarded, as are questions of decisions' coordination, enforcement and monitoring – this is problematic, as just because a manager knows which leadership style would be correct in theory, there is no guarantee that he or she can effectively implement it (see Neuberger 2002, p. 501 ff).

I also find other aspects of this approach disturbing, as it reduces managers to machines, programming them to automatically select leadership style Z in situation XY; as such, the only contribution of managers is their assessment of the situation. But this is (thankfully) not how the leading of individuals by individuals works. Each manager has a unique and individual style of leadership that cannot be neatly defined and is never identical to that of another upper-level manager, even in the same situation.

2.1.3.2 Classic Leadership Styles

The classical leadership styles involve the authoritarian style, in which the manager has control over everything while the subordinates cannot give any input, the patriarchal and advisory styles, and the cooperative style, where the leader serves as the coordinator and moderator for decisions made as a group (Fig. 2.2).

However, this description of leadership styles as a linear continuum is not sufficient to illustrate the variety of alternatives observable in daily practice. Apart from the level of control over decision-making, other characteristics of leadership styles can be identified. These include the level of participation of upper-level managers in work group processes; the degree to which managers bindingly assign tasks; the level of control used by managers; the frequency with which they make decisions

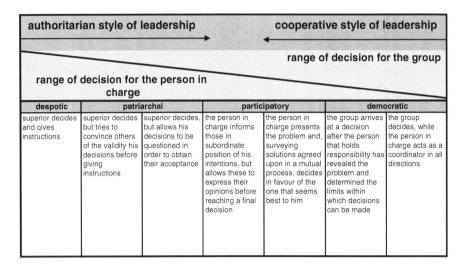

Fig. 2.2 Leadership styles (*Source*: Thommen and Achleitner 2001)

independently; and lastly, the extent to which the manager succeeds in motivating those he or she leads (see Heinen 1998, p. 227).

2.1.3.3 Styles of Leadership with EQ

Still another factor can be used to differentiate between leadership styles: the emotional intelligence of the managers. Daniel Goleman has made exciting findings on this topic that I would like to review here, as I believe they are state-of-the-art with regard to the topic of leadership styles. After interviewing more than 400 upper-level managers, Goleman identified 6 main styles of leadership. He also demonstrated that successful managers do not lead with a particular style, but are able to be flexible in utilizing different styles that call on them to activate various aspects of their emotional intelligence (see Goleman 2000, pp. 27–38).

The first of the six styles, the *authoritarian* style, is in most cases ineffective, as it harms the working climate and effectively "paralyzes" the employees. They do not feel any sense of responsibility, as they only carry out instructions and do not work on their own initiative. Therefore, their commitment steadily declines. There are however situations in which quick decisions and consistent "follow-through" are needed; one scenario would be the threat of a hostile takeover. In such cases, the authoritarian style of leadership might be a good option.

Secondly, there is the *authoritative* style of leadership. "Authoritative leaders are visionaries; they motivate the people by clearly showing them how their work contributes to the realization of the company's broader vision. Those who work for such leaders know that their work counts, and why" (Goleman 2000, p. 30). The manager provides the frameworks and goals, but does not limit the freedom or direct responsibility of the employees. Note that this style of leadership is not recommended for leading in cooperation with a team that consists of experienced workers. The leader may seem to be too dominant, which could decrease the quality of the relationships between colleagues.

In the third style of leadership, the *affiliative* style, the focus is clearly placed on those you work with and their feelings. Here the major task of the manager is to foster harmony and strong emotional connections. The employees are greatly appreciated and receive positive feedback. The drawback of this style is that under-achievement remains largely uncorrected, and there is no quick process for perfor-mance improvement or leadership assistance available for managers. Yet they should implement the affiliative style if they need to produce harmony, improve communication, or strengthen their team's fighting spirit.

The fourth style of leadership is the *democratic* style, which has a number of advantages. Utilizing this style, upper-level managers spend considerable time with their employees building trust, respect and commitment. The dangers of this style are that endless discussions can go in circles without resulting in firm agreements, and postponing decisions can result in conflicts. The democratic style is ineffective if managers and employees are not qualified or sufficiently informed to make the right decisions. This style obtains the best results when new ideas and guidelines are needed from other employees, e.g. with regard to implementing the corporate vision.

The fifth kind of leadership style, *achievement-oriented* leadership, should be used rather sparingly. When highly demanding bosses implement this style, employees can easily be crushed by over-planning and unrealistic goals. At the same time, flexibility and responsibility are reduced to merely carrying out assigned tasks. This style of leadership is appropriate only for highly motivated, competent employees who do not need guidance or coordination (Fig. 2.3).

The sixth type, the *coaching* style, is rarely used, as it can be extremely time-consuming and take a great deal of energy. According to Goleman, "It aims primarily at the personal development of the individual and only indirectly at the completion of concrete work tasks. Coaching nevertheless improves results, because it allows a sequential dialog and improves the working climate" (Goleman 2000, p. 35). Coaching is particularly successful when employees are aware of their weaknesses and want to improve their performance. Later on in this book, I will place greater emphasis on the possibilities presented by the coaching style of leadership.

Goleman's studies indicate that a manager's success increases with the number of styles of leadership he or she is able to utilize effectively. A manager's effec-tiveness depends on the particular situation and which leadership style he or she chooses. Highly competent upper-level managers correctly align their behavior to the situation not by behaving mechanically, but by reacting flexibly. Within minutes they recognize what style of leadership will have the most influence on others in the given situation, and adapt their style accordingly to obtain optimal results. Unsuccessful managers in contrast give the impression of pursuing a "just do what I do" approach.

	authoritarian	authoritative	affiliative	democratic	achievement-oriented	coaching
modus operandi of the leadership style	expects orders to be carried out immediately	stimulates people to realize a vision	creating a sense of harmony and emotional ties	reaching consensus through participatory measures	high standards of achievement	prepares colleagues for the future: "Give it a try!"
brief characterization of the style	"Do what I tell you!"	"Come along with me!"	"It's the people that count."	"What do you think of this?"	"Do things the way I do them – right away!"	encouragement of others, empathy, self-critical attitude
underlying skills related to emotional intelligence	zest for action, drive, self-control	self-confidence, empathy, catalyst for change	empathy, ability to create positive relationships and to communicate well	cooperation, being in charge of teams, communicative skills	diligence, success-orientation, energy	to support a colleague, advance his performance or develop long-term strengths
in what situations does this style work best	during a crisis in order to effect a turnaround or with problematic co-workers	in cases where change necessitates a new vision or when a clear direction is needed	reestablishing rapport within a team and motivating people under stress	to obtain commitment and consensus and procure contributions from valuable colleagues	whenever a highly motivated, efficient team has to come up with quick results	
general effect on the atmosphere	negative	clearest, positive	positive	positive	negative	positive

Fig. 2.3 Overview of the six leadership styles (*Source*: Goleman 2000)

2.1.3.4 "Management By" – Type Approaches

The numerous "management by ..." models also provide valuable insights into how managers lead, though they do so from a different perspective: they do not concentrate on the type or style of managers, but on what techniques and methods are used. As there are already countless management concepts and the number is still growing, I will only present the four most important variants. The others are extensions of or variations on these four concepts:

Firstly, in *management by delegation* decision-making tasks, responsibilities and authority are delegated as much as possible throughout the hierarchy. The responsibility of the manager is limited to providing supervision. This management principle developed naturally from the progressive division of labor in modern society. In Germany this has been propagated since 1962, when Reinhard Höhn developed the Harzburger Model. Höhn, a professor of State and Administrative Law at the Universities of Heidelberg and Berlin, as well as founder of the *Akademie für Führungskräfte der Wirtschaft* ("Academy for Corporate Managers") in Bad Harzburg (1956), defined the German understanding of leadership in management in Germany with this model, primarily in the 1960s, but also throughout the 1970s and until the mid 1980s. This model provides companies with effective methods for organizing and monitoring bureaucratic processes by means of establishing operational sequences in day-to-day business. The Harzburger Model provides accurate knowledge for managers on how to lead by delegating responsibility to employees and to their corresponding positions. The model also includes guidelines on how to lead, monitoring progress, agreeing on objectives, employee discussions, etc. Yet like all models, this was an idealized depiction of human behavior. Unable to cope with the complex reality of that behavior, this model is currently considered less relevant (see Höhn 1980).

The second management concept worth mentioning is *management by exception*. Following this approach, the management intervenes only when there are extenuating circumstances. As such, employees work on their own and are independently responsible, until and unless certain limits are exceeded or unpredictable events require the intervention of the management.

The third major concept, *management by objectives*, refers to the following: the managers and the employees work together to agree upon goals for all levels within the hierarchy. However, no rules are specified for the achievement of objectives. The person responsible for the respective task decides on the rules and on the resources to use. This concept, which is based on the division of labor and the delegation of responsibility, was developed by Drucker and is still valid today, enjoying considerable success.

Lastly, *management by systems* refers to a leadership method aiming for the integration of all subsystems within the company, using computer-assisted information, planning and control systems to optimize leadership and production processes.

Aside from these classics, there are numerous other "management by" schools of thought, such as: management by results, management by motivation, and management by participation.

These principles are often the butt of jokes, resulting in fanciful and fictional leadership styles. Some examples include "management by helicopter," in which managers swoop in, whirl up considerable dust, and then fly away again. Or there is "management by mushrooms": the employees are kept in the dark, every now and then someone comes to cover them with a load of fertilizer, and as soon as one raises their head, it's promptly cut off.

Managing Quietly

Against the rushing river of leadership trends, and against the scientific dissection of the leadership phenomenon, the university professor and best-selling author Henry Mintzberg has provided his noteworthy thesis that "management swims quietly." The central tenet of his work is the belief that people are of primary importance, not shareholder value, and his approach is intended to present an alternative to what he has accurately described as "management by barking around."

Mintzberg is of the opinion that managers benefit more from tried and proven traits like common sense and social responsibility than from the wealth of new talents being touted. "Managing quietly" describes a calm, persistent and unspectacular style, that constantly keeps the company on (or steers it back to) the right course, allowing it to remain strong and stable even in times of crisis. According to this approach managers have a protective function, preventing problems rather than solving them.

Mintzberg sees the urgent need for managers to liberate themselves "from all the fuss about management techniques and great men, and turn to a deeper understanding. We need more thoughtful managers, who are involved more extensively in processes and procedures" (Mintzberg 1999). The requirements of good leadership and the fundamental needs and interests of employees and customers, he feels, are timeless.

I consider this approach both groundbreaking and effective. In companies and leadership seminars alike, there is too much hot air, too much showbiz and too much hectic energy. Yet knowledge, quiet reflection and selfless service for the good of a common cause are what we need. To me leading also means serving, being humble, and being able to step back in situations where your employees know best. Executives should learn to listen to their own instincts in order to sense the moods of others, to empathize and see the bigger picture, instead of only awaiting their grand entrance.

The Five Managerial Mindsets

Based on this desire for much less "ado about nothing" and more well-considered behavior, and based on his own practical experience working with managers, Henry Mintzberg developed the concept of the five managerial mindsets (see Gosling and Mintzberg 2004, pp. 46–59).

The point of departure for this approach is the following premise: managers' daily work is often complex and confusing. In order to find their way and overcome the mounting demands placed on them, they must master five different ways of approaching problems – or mindsets – and be able to combine them to create the "big picture." It is not Mintzberg's goal to preach the "one, true" way of dealing with problems; instead he recommends that they orient their thinking on five core points: analysis, action, reflection, cooperation and being worldly.

Taken together, these aspects provide a framework opening new perspectives and allowing managers to better interpret the world (within the company and beyond) around them. Each mindset has its own focus or goal. The reflective mindset deals with managing your own ego; the analytic mindset examines the management of organizations. The collaborative mindset is based on the management of relationships, the worldly mindset on the management of contexts, and the action mindset on managing changes.

1. The reflective mindset
   Today's decision-makers attend seminars in droves. These seminars tend to have the ambiance of an adventure vacation or survival camp. Mintzberg argues that managers do not need this type of atmosphere in order to develop. Likewise a boot camp is not needed, because boot camps only teach people to March and

obey, not to stop and think. And that is precisely what managers need to do today: stop, take a breath and reflect.

Events can only become experiences if they are processed and reflected upon, explains Mintzberg. If the true meaning is not grasped, the managers become thoughtless and shortsighted. Enterprises need employees and managers with a wider range of vision. The Latin verb *reflectere* literally means "to turn back." Our attention must first focus inward, and only later outward. Managers must look inward and back, in order to gain the perspective needed to focus forward. Vision does not come from nowhere, but is the product of the collected and reflected experiences of the past.

2. The analytic mindset

No organization can exist without analysis, because the organizational structure is analytic by nature. Analyzing allows us to break down complex phenomena into their individual parts. The goal of the analytic mindset is to identify the important aspects of structures while filtering out the unimportant ones. The purpose is not to simplify complex decisions but to maintain the complexity without losing the ability to act.

In our enterprises too much is analyzed using the wrong methods, according to Mintzberg. For example, a marketing manager may become so consumed with defining the potential market group that she misses a sales opportunity. Managers must break out of this narrow interpretation and look beyond the figures, questioning and digging beyond conventional analysis.

3. The worldly mindset

The trend of globalization suggests a certain standardization of business at the international level. On closer examination it is hardly monotonous, and in fact consists of many different individual worlds. Mintzberg recommends that managers be globally aware and acquire both theoretical and practical knowledge of societies worldwide. Global activities are not a prerequisite for a worldly mindset, and a global project or a job with one global player does not automatically establish such a mindset. Managers must leave their offices and spend time where products are manufactured, customers are served and employees are recruited. They have to get to know the environments, customs and cultures of other people in order to better understand their own world. By adopting a worldly mindset, Mintzberg encourages managers to constantly investigate different cultures in order to return to their home country and integrate the knowledge gained. In this manner, the other world can become a mirror of the manager's own world. This mindset also serves to place the reflecting mindset, which revolves around the manager and his or her own world, in the correct context.

4. The collaborative mindset

Mintzberg feels that Western managers often have a limited perspective. Too often, they regard employees as independent actors, or as assets that can be shifted and redistributed as needed. However, the goal must be to manage relationships between people – in teams and projects, within and across departments, and in external alliances – rather than managing individuals.

Therefore, the collaborative mindset calls for breaking with the heroic style of management and implementing a more approachable on. Managers practicing this style spend more time listening than talking; they interact with their employees and do not remain isolated in their respective roles. The collaborative manager is an insider, who gets involved and manages holistically. The manager gets involved, but does not make himself or herself the center of attention.

Implementing the collaborative mindset means transferring the responsibility and the initiative to employees, and means that employees regain the power over themselves and their work. As Mintzberg envisions the function of managers, they contribute structures to create the conditions and attitudes needed to complete tasks, but do not do everything themselves. In Japan this style of leadership is referred to as "leadership in the background"; Mintzberg calls it "managing quietly."

5. The action mindset

Mintzberg compares an enterprise with a carriage pulled by wild horses. These horses represent the emotions, ambitions and motives of people at the company. Keeping the course requires a lot of skills, such as changing directions. An action-oriented mindset means that the manager does not race the horses through a zigzag course with the help of a whip; instead they develop a feeling for the terrain and the distance ahead. The manager must know how to get the team through the terrain while maintaining the proper course.

Leading requires action. However, without significant consideration of the actions to be taken, acting can be dangerous. The insistence on action at the expense of reflection should be avoided in Mintzberg's view. Furthermore, striving for constant change is not effective in the long run. As Mintzberg states, the action mindset requires modesty, because in the long run a company is evaluated by the number of products it sells, and not by the number of changes it went through.

Mintzberg refers to the environment of constant change as anarchy. Changes cannot be successfully implemented without continuity and structure. The action-oriented mindset carefully considers what really has to be changed, and makes sure that everything else remains the same. The objective is not change for change's sake but to be ready, curious, watchful and eager to gain new experiences. In Chap. 3 this topic will be revisited in more detail. For the time being let me say that in my opinion, leading means managing changes on the one hand, and providing orientation and a sense of security on the other.

These five mindsets are not clearly definable categories; their boundaries are flexible. As Mintzberg describes it, the manager is a weaver who weaves together threads from the different mindsets. When a company's managers cooperate with each another in an analytic and worldly way, blending their reflected actions together, the basis for a successful organization has been provided. "Successful enterprises produce convincing results from the interwoven mindsets of their managers" (Gosling and Mintzberg 2004, p. 59).

2.1.3.5   No Style?

According to recent data, the majority of German managers (64%) utilize a cooperative style of leadership. Only 9% lead with an authoritarian style, i.e., without integrating employees in the decision-making process. However, the surveys also revealed that only 38% of employees have a role that includes interaction with managers, very clearly showing the limits of cooperation in practice (see Frankfurt Allgemeine Zeitung, August 18, 2003).

To briefly review this section, let us return to Peter F. Drucker, who emphasized the meaning of relationships within the leadership role and the necessity of promoting relationships as a priority. The expertise of having leadership skills alone is not sufficient if the manager lacks the ability to take the human nature of himself/herself and the employees into account. "Nevertheless, if a leader lacks character and integrity, experience and success will not save them. Lack of character spoils people, the most precious production factor in any enterprise. It spoils the spirit of the company, along with its performance" (Drucker 1956, p. 198).

Malik in turn believes the influence of the leader should not be taken lightly. Quality leadership is not simply a matter of skill. There is a growing camp of theoreticians and practitioners who have come to recognize that the leader's personality, their character traits, way of thinking and feeling, and decisions are crucial to effective leadership.

2.2   The Leader

Good leadership depends largely on the personality of the leader.

The majority of theories and approaches defining good leadership are – some of them more, some less – based on the personality of the leader. According to these concepts, their character traits and properties, charisma, thinking and behavior, goals and decisions are crucial to the nature and success of leadership. These facets constitute one subset of personal-based leadership approaches – the other sub-group focuses on the personality of the employee and its influence on the leadership process, which we will come back to later.

2.2.1   Character Traits

Either you are a leader or not – this is the position of the trait-oriented approaches in a nutshell. Leadership cannot be acquired or learned, except for some techniques or some basic business management knowledge. Here, the proponents of the character-based approaches contradict very clearly those who see leadership as something that can be taught to anybody, believing instead that anyone who has certain personality traits such as commitment, responsibility, intelligence, discernment, adaptability and interpersonal skills, decisiveness, joy in taking action, and charisma can become a leader.

Interest in character's role in leadership is as old as history itself; history has always centered on prominent leaders, decision makers and rulers. Yet the difficulty with applying leadership concepts to the realm of business is twofold. Firstly, one and the same basic character trait can often go by different names according to different people. Secondly, the evaluation of the characteristics of others is invariably subjective. Therefore, reducing quality leadership to key characteristics is often shortsighted and ultimately simplistic.

Time Magazine and CNN recently conducted an analysis of the world's most influential business leaders. Out of the top 25 managers, 11 are Americans and 4 are women. Only 2 of the top 25 managers are from Germany: Wolfgang Bernhard (Volkswagen, formerly DaimlerChrysler) and Gunter Thielen (Bertelsmann). Both were included in the section "Profit Maximizers"; further sections included "Innovators" and "Heavy Hitters." All of the managers in the study have set worldwide standards of leadership. The most influential manager was reported to be Jeffrey Immelt, Chairman of the Board of General Electric (see www.t-online-business.de, December 14, 2004). The diversity of these leaders vividly illustrates the fact that the possible character traits for top managers can be both arbitrary and endless.

2.2.2 Charismatic Leadership

One trait that consistently appears throughout history concerning the personality of leaders is charisma. At the beginning of the twentieth century, Max Weber's sociological work intensively focused on the phenomenon of charismatic leadership. Weber differentiated between three types of leadership – rational, traditional, and charismatic – which are also relevant to our search for the foundation of good leadership.

The term "charisma" originates from Greek and means "gift of grace." According to Weber charisma is a sort of magic, superhuman and rare quality that, when possessed by a leader, can radiate through an entire organization. Those who study charismatic personalities have recognized that the employees of such leaders become extremely loyal and find it difficult to part from their leaders. As Weber describes, charismatic leaders must consider the long-term wellbeing of those they lead, while at the same time creating a new order and orientation within the arena they work in. In and of itself, charisma is not actually focused on economic benefit (see Weber 1972, p. 140 ff.).

Anyone who has ever met a charismatic person has felt this energy, but it tends to defy description. Nevertheless we will seek to more clearly define charisma:

charismatic managers convincingly lead people in such a way that their employees derive both a sense that their work is worthwhile and an increased quality of life from that work. These leaders are role models others emulate. Charismatic managers inspire their employees to pursue more ambitious motives and goals. They trust those they lead and show them their appreciation. In this way, they foster feelings of self-worth and self-confidence among their employees, strengthening their motivation in turn.

So far this sounds ideal. But charismatic leadership also has a shady side. When charisma turns negative, such leaders are dubbed fanatics. They promote blind obedience, dependence, and are egocentric. Such leaders exhibit arrogance, arbitrariness, abuse power, overestimate their own abilities, and are narcissistic. In modern democratic society and modern economies this can be fatal, because dependence entwined with power results in too much control and limited functioning; the power of fanatics is not sustainable in the long term. Nevertheless, in times of crisis the call for powerful leaders arises, as people seek leaders who seem to be able to solve any problem. Manfred Kets de Vries also agrees that charisma is an important characteristic of a good manager, but needs a second component. "Managers play two roles, the charismatic and the architectural. With charisma, they produce the vision of a better future, inspire and empower their employees. As architects, they concern themselves with the structure of the organization, control mechanisms and systems of recognition" (Kets de Vries, 2002, p. 223). Charisma alone is not sufficient; the authority to concretely implement change is also necessary.

Peter F. Drucker did not believe that charisma and good leadership necessarily go hand in hand. If a manager has a charismatic personality and is a good leader at the same time, this is ideal. But one does not automatically come with the other. In his writings, Drucker recalled the three most notorious charismatic leaders of the past century – Stalin, Hitler and Mao, none of whom was characterized by an exemplary style of leadership. In the past century, the world has also seen extraordinarily effective leaders – Dwight D. Eisenhower, George Mars and Harry Truman – who possessed as much charisma "as a mackerel," as Drucker dryly noted. Konrad Adenauer, Abraham Lincoln and Winston Churchill were not particularly charismatic either. However, John F. Kennedy possessed charisma exceeding that of nearly every other US President. According to Drucker, charisma can actually be detrimental at times, because it may result in the "illusion of infallibility," and decrease flexibility, whereas both will decrease capacity for change (see Drucker 1967).

I would go not so far as Drucker, as I know several successful managers who are charismatic. We can safely assume that charisma is quite important, but neither necessary nor sufficient for a manager's success. However, charisma can facilitate leadership in certain contexts and situations if it is paired with a genuine interest in others and not focused on self-promotion. When properly utilized, charisma can ignite the flame of enthusiasm, maintain a focus on the positive, and increase productivity.

2.2.3 Skills

Manfred Kets de Vries has formulated a relatively new interactive guide of personal characteristics essential for managers. His perspective postulates that the individual style of leadership consists of an "internal script" of the central needs and perceptions of the individual, and of their skills. Successful managers possess skills in three main categories. The first includes personal skills such as the orientation on success, self-assurance, energy and efficiency. The second category consists of social skills such as influence, political awareness and empathy. The third category is home to cognitive skills such as conceptual thinking, analytical abilities and the ability to see the big picture.

For Kets de Vries the following characteristics are also indispensable for leaders:

Directness: A manager must his/her own head and know how to meet his/her goals. Such leaders are dominant, energetic and highly meritocratic. They have the ability to move others to take risks or try something new.

Receptivity: A good leader is always open to new ideas and experiences.

Ability to get along: Effective leaders are pleasant people, nice and cooperative in their personal relations, flexible and amiable. They are good team players and can see the good side of every situation.

Reliability: A good leader is someone you can rely on. They have a conscience and delivers what they promise.

Analytical intelligence: Most good managers possess above-average analytical intelligence and can think strategically.

Emotional intelligence: Successful managers can control their own emotions and correctly interpret those of others. They can realistically evaluate their own strengths and weaknesses and are emotionally stable. They establish and maintain relationships easily (see de Vries 2004, p. 189 ff).

In addition to the work of Kets de Vries, I would like to add some timeless virtues from my own point of view: attention to detail, persistence and perseverance, consistency, respect, discipline, modesty and a sense of responsibility. These characteristics are not subject to trends in leadership styles. They are as valid today as they were a hundred years ago, although they may require slightly updated definitions as times and work environments change.

Helmut Maucher, former CEO of Nestlé, once claimed that managers must pay attention to strengthening characteristics such as sense of responsibility, reliability and long-term thinking. It seems that in Germany there has been a pervasive lack of trust in the political and economic elite. This perception was supported by the results of a survey conducted by the Emnid Institute on behalf of the World Economic Forum, which indicated that 70% of the Germans polled believed the management of their company was dishonest – the most negative image of managers in Western Europe. The population's distrust of managers in Germany is as bad as in developing countries such as Albania or Costa Rica. In France only 22% shared this

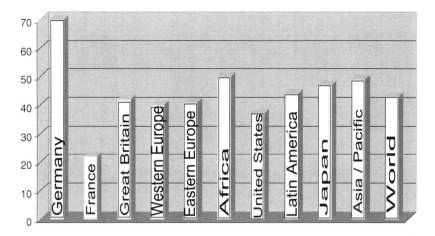

Fig. 2.4 Distrust towards executives by country/region (*Source*: The Emnid Survey in: Die Welt, November 19, 2004)

sentiment, in Great Britain 42%, and in the USA 37% (see Die Welt, November 19, 2004) (Fig. 2.4).

2.2.4 Conduct

The starting point here is the acceptance that the conduct of managers determines their style of leadership, their relationships with colleagues and subordinates, and their effect on others. In turn, their conduct is also shaped by their corporate culture. In the enterprise, certain positions and roles are assigned to managers. Therefore success depends on to what extent expectations are met, which factors work against managers, and to what extent the assigned role is compatible with their self-perceptions. Leadership positions are if you will a blank space in the social system, which is to be filled and occupied by a person.

2.2.4.1 Role Plays

The role of the leader brings with it a certain list of procedural instructions and creates a certain role, which should not be confused with the personality of the individual who assumes it. "Roles are on the one hand cognitive interpretation patterns, which involve 'reading' or understanding a situation. On the other hand they are normative demands" (Neuberger 2002, p. 314). Roles schematize and simplify social relations, as they convey what is expected of others. However, they also convey conflicts between people, and between the personality and the role.

George Graen has provided a valuable contribution to role theory by examining the dovetailing of role taking and role making in work groups. Graen does not regard roles as rigid corsets, which the managers are obligated to fit into. Instead, he sees the role of the leader as a system of flexible agreements negotiated between superiors and subordinates (see Graen 1976, pp. 1201–1246).

The role theory clarifies how much the requirements of managers and their positions can differ and provides insights concerning the connections between the individual and the group. It is therefore useful for leadership practices, particularly with regard to personnel evaluations, leadership analysis, training courses and the creation of strategic models.

Currently, managers are expected to perform the role of coaches for their employees, and are also frequently expected to be active in their personnel's development. However, each of these roles entails an entire set of requirements, a detailed analysis of which would be beyond the scope of this work.

2.2.4.2   Types and Typologies

Managers cannot be distinguished only by their roles, but also by their leadership behavior. Michael Maccoby differentiates between four managerial archetypes: the *specialist*, the *jungle warrior*, the *company man (or woman)* and the *playmaker* (see Maccoby 1977).

The *specialist* is rational, economical, quiet, modest and sincere. For the *jungle warrior*, the job is a struggle where the winners destroy the losers, according to the motto "kill or be killed." He or she is proud to be feared and thinks like a social Darwinist. The *company man or woman* is solely defined by being part of the larger, protective community. Such managers submit to the company and lionize those in power. At the same time they care very much about the feelings of the people around them. The *playmaker* is constantly energized, driven by an effort to keep things going. He or she is interested only in the implementation and thinks in operating results only, is in constant competition with everyone and everything, and eventually ends up burning out.

Another typology was created by the Augsburg professor of Psychology Oswald Neuberger, based on his questionnaire describing the conduct of supervisors. He identified six pairs of extreme leadership types: friendly colleague versus adjutant, go-it-alone versus do-it-together, he/she who drives versus he/she who lets go, keeper of order/controller versus monitor/coordinator, boss versus partner, and protector versus intermediary (Neuberger 2002, pp. 83–409). I feel the names speak for themselves and do not need to be explained further. In principle, it should be noted that the type perspective is an extended form of the character traits perspective, as behind a certain type of leader there is always – explicitly or not – a certain set of traits.

2.2.4.3   Person and Duties

The psychologists Robert S. Blake and Jane S. Mouton differentiated between two fundamental kinds of leadership behavior in the 1960s. Person-oriented leadership behavior stresses individuals living and working together at the company; duties-oriented behavior in contrast is only concerned with efficient production (see Blake and Mouton 1980).

Blake and Mouton's "Managerial Grid" portrays the two behavioral dimensions graphically on a nine-level scale. The four extremes mark the corner points of the grid:

A manager who worries only about the production, with no concern for his or her employees.

A manager whose employees spend a good deal of time talking and celebrating, but get little work accomplished.

An inhuman slave driver focused strictly on performance while discouraging and/or preventing social contact.

A popular boss, who creates a warm interpersonal climate, inspires others and gets motivated, maximum performance from his or her employees (Fig. 2.5).

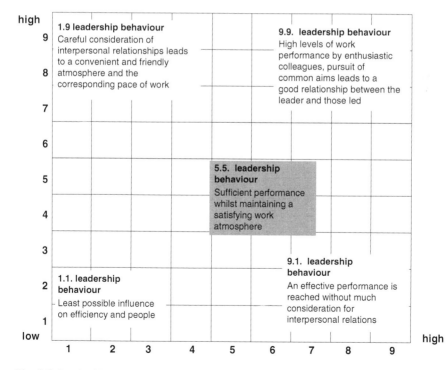

Fig. 2.5 Leadership conduct according to the Managerial Grid (Blake and Mouton) (*Source*: Staehle 1989)

In addition Jim Kouzes, a lecturer, researcher and chairman of the Tom Peter Company in the US, states that success particularly depends on the activities of managers. He outlines five specific types of conduct that managers can display in order to facilitate performance among employees:

Managers should constantly analyze outcomes for continuous process improvement.
Managers should put forth a cohesive, participative and inspiring vision of the future.
Managers should empower others by promoting cooperation and emphasizing the individual strengths of others.
Managers should live out the vision and values of the organization and serve as role models for others.
Managers should strengthen employees feeling of self-worth by recognizing their contributions and by celebrating those who are passionately committed to the wellbeing of the enterprise.

Each generation of managers must redefine these five types of conduct based on its own economic, social and cultural context. Nevertheless, these types stay valid over time (see Kouzes 2002).

Exploring the work of Blake and Mouton, and even more the work of Kouzes and Mintzberg (see Sect. 2.2.1), the following becomes obvious: it is critically important that managers behave in a socially aware manner and connect well with others. As such, the concept of "emotional intelligence" deserves careful consideration.

2.2.5 Emotional Intelligence

In our modern, democratic and individualized society, in which successful managers are characterized by a broad range of personality traits and styles of leadership, all seem to agree that managers' greatest duty is the management of relationships. Successful managers have a high degree of emotional intelligence, or "EQ". Daniel Goleman established the concept of EQ in the mid 1990s. Managers with high EQ engage in self-reflection, are motivated, have empathy and have solid social skills (see Goleman 1999b, pp. 27–36, see also Goleman 1996, 1999a).

Self-reflection is the ability to recognize and understand one's own feelings and drives while also recognizing their impact on others. People with substantial self-reflection express themselves with self-assurance, have a realistic self-image and generally have a sense of humor about themselves. By self-reflection, Goleman refers to the ability to manage one's impulses appropriately and to refrain from acting without considering the consequences. In other words, self-reflection means "thinking before acting." Characteristics of a person with a high level of introspection are integrity, trustworthiness and openness to diversity and change. Motivation means devotion to work for reasons beyond money and status. Motivation implies an inclination to pursue goals with energy and perseverance, with a strong will to succeed, a healthy portion of optimism, and commitment. Empathy refers to the ability to understand the feelings of others by experiencing those feelings oneself, without necessarily having had the same experience. When a person is empathetic, they treat others in a kind and considerate manner. Finally, social skills are the "culmination of emotional intelligence," (Goleman, p. 36) and are the result of engaging in the other four components. Conversely, only social skills allow managers to effectively use their emotional intelligence.

Goleman's concept of EQ explains why highly intelligent managers with outstanding training fail, while others who possess average intelligence and solid but by no means outstanding technical skills are able to climb the corporate ladder. Emotional intelligence is indispensable for successful leadership because only individuals who understand the feelings of others in the way that they understand their own can accurately steer employees in the right direction. According to Goleman, managers with high EQ exceed the annual sales targets of lower EQ managers by over 20%.

Goleman's work was monumental for the growth of high-quality leadership, but has been underutilized for the most part. In my opinion, EQ is the most important contribution to leadership approaches and practice in the past 10 years. Furthermore, EQ can be trained and acquired, but it is a difficult and lengthy process. Typical seminars and training programs focus on specialized knowledge, logical thinking and leadership techniques; they do not tend to facilitate the development of EQ. However, new methods of developing EQ, social skills, and relationships skills are evolving (see Chaps. 3 and 4).

2.2.5.1   Achieving Emotional Intelligence

Manfred Kets de Vries has also intensively explored the topic of emotional intelligence and contends that emotional intelligence is just as important in the business world as logical mathematical intelligence. "A high EQ frequently triumphs over high IQ" (de Vries 2002, p. 37). He refers to the origin of the term "emotion" as deriving from the Latin word *movere* ("moving down"), and feelings do move people in the workplace as well as in other areas of life: to paraphrase, numerous organizations understand that a gram of feelings is worth more than a ton of facts.

Unlike our IQ, which remains relatively stable from age 20 until old age, the EQ develops over our lifespan as we gain experience. People can therefore increase their EQ by the following steps. The first step on the way to emotional intelligence, and thus to effective leadership, is introspection. "A person who knows himself or herself is not impulsive and does not constantly blame others," Manfred Kets de Vries states (see de Vries 2002, p. 39). In his seminars, Kets de Vries encounters time and time again managers who have lost touch with their own feelings, as in: "I don't know how I feel. My wife tells me." Such managers' behavior and level of adjustment have blurred the border between genuine feelings and feelings expected by others. When this happens, the authenticity of a manager can diminish and be replaced by a caricature of the perfect manager. These managers become blind to their own feelings and do not notice what is obvious to others.

The second step in the development of emotional intelligence is learning to control one's feelings. Managers must explore, recognize and take responsibility for the entire spectrum of their true feelings. When we gain access to our internal processes, we can use them to motivate ourselves. For people leading others, it is crucial that they control their emotions and behavior. "Managers who are not in control of their emotions may, for example, allow the annoyance to accumulate to the point of rage, which can produce a whole cascade of effects penetrating the lowest levels of their organization," (de Vries 2002, p. 40). An effective manager is able to transform feelings such as annoyance, frustration and fear into constructive activity rather than giving in to spontaneous reactions.

The third step involves learning to recognize the feelings of those around us, and learning to deal with such feelings in an emotionally intelligent way. Managers must learn to accurately perceive the emotions of others, and feel these emotions as the others feel them – in other words, they must have empathy. For Kets de Vries, emotional intelligence consists of three central abilities that good managers continuously develop: active listening, effective nonverbal communication, and empathy.

Active listening does not consist only of hearing the words spoken, but on grasping the whole meaning of what is being communicated. Managers must be "all ears," without the exaggerated nodding that accompanies pseudo-listening. They must not simply sit and wait for their own turn to talk, or be preoccupied with other duties they must attend to. While listening actively, the listener concentrates solely on the discussion. From time to time, the listener briefly takes stock of what he or she has heard; and the meaning derived from the communication, in order to avoid any misunderstandings. The process of active listening also incorporates inquiries and feedback regarding the feelings of the speaker. Another important component of emotional intelligence, according to Kets de Vries, is attention to nonverbal behavior that occurs simultaneously to verbal expression during conversations. Examples of nonverbal behavior include: mimicking, gesturing, eye contact, volume and speed of speech, etc. All such behaviors occur and are interpreted on an almost unconscious level.

The spectrum of emotions that human beings are capable of is extremely broad, and each emotional condition has both positive and negative aspects. For example, annoyance is a negatively classified feeling because it robs us of our energy and alienates us from the source of the annoyance. Yet, annoyance can have a positive impact in that it boosts our sense of self-worth when we feel we are in the right. At the same time, "positive" emotions like joy and love, while pleasant, can also lead to arrogance and (unrealistically) high expectations that inevitably lead to disappointment.

Kets de Vries further claims that those with pronounced emotional intelligence will have more intense human relationships; the ability to motivate themselves and others; a more active, innovative and creative approaches to problem-solving; more efficient styles of leadership; will be better at handling stress; and will have fewer difficulties adapting to changes, as they are at peace with themselves. The higher on the career ladder the leader is, the more important emotional intelligence becomes, and the less important technical abilities are, as Kets de Vries claims (Goleman has made similar observations). This claim directly contradicts the work of Fredmund Malik. Kets de Vries recognizes that one ascends due to technical abilities, but as soon as one advances to a certain level, emotional intelligence becomes the critical factor for continued success: EQ makes the difference between successful and stagnant careers.

Possessing a high EQ does not necessarily mean that a person is always nice to others or that they allow their feelings to dictate all of their decisions and activities. Rather, having a high EQ means that one can accurately assess oneself and others, accepts differences in people and appropriately utilizes the feelings of his or her fellow men. It may be easier and more comfortable to increase regular IQ by systematically pulling information from one's fund of knowledge and activating more effective cognitive thought processes than to work on emotional sensitivity and acknowledge the emotional experiences of others. But the effort pays off. As stated in the literature, "The dividends are considerable: a high EQ allows us to make better decisions, to have more appropriate expectations of others, and to have fewer disappointing experiences" (de Vries 2002, p. 47).

2.2.6   Decisions

Apart from personal characteristics, conduct, and emotional intelligence, the function of managers is ultimately to make decisions. Apart from delegating and supervising, above all leading means making decisions. In daily practice, a multiplicity of diverse decisions must be made such as: innovative decisions and routine ones, decisions with certain and uncertain outcomes, collective and individual, rational and irrational, conscious and unconscious, strategic and operational decisions.

Therefore, characteristics such as determination, courage, deliberation, a sense of responsibility and decisiveness are essential requirements for managers in order to generate and execute their ideas. And therefore a possible answer to the earlier question of what good leadership depends on is the ability to make the right decisions.

Decisions must be made with regard to goals, values, leadership style, working methods and retaining or dismissing employees. The speed and the certainty with which managers make decisions, and how closely the decisions meet company goals, the results for the company and the ramifications for the working climate all say much about the quality and effectiveness of the leader.

Genuine leadership decisions cannot be delegated because they are decisive in terms of the company's present and future. The big picture must remain in focus, with the consequences for the company as a whole in mind. Major leadership decisions include setting corporate goals, identifying measures necessary to achieve them, and allocating the appropriate resources.

Before managers can make decisions, various courses of action must be identified as well as the influence of the environmental conditions on the alternatives. Questions must be asked and answered: What is the impact on the customer? What is the effect on the competition? How will these decisions affect the market development? Based on the answers to such questions, managers determine the possible consequences of the courses of action and compare them to the established goals. In practice, decisions are not always made based on logical conclusions; social and emotional influences often play an important or even a decisive role. In particular, group dynamics can influence decisions. Group dynamics are comprised of the informal power structure and the relationships between coworkers on the same or on different levels of the organizational hierarchy. In addition, time pressure and incomplete information often interfere with the ability to make quality decisions.

2.2.6.1 Decisions Are Decisive

A study released by the personnel consultancy Heidrick & Struggles revealed that of 500 managers surveyed, 57% indicated that enjoying making decisions is the most important characteristic of managers. 49% rated strong communication skills as the second most important trait, while 34% ranked results orientation as the third most important characteristic of managers. The readiness and ability to make decisions and accountability were also identified as being important.

To reiterate, leaders still have one primary responsibility: to decide. After all important viewpoints and opinions have been heard, after the critical factors are all weighed, it is the managers' task to make the final decision. Leaders must be accountable for the decisions, responsible for their own actions, and accept any unintended negative consequences. Leaders must be willing to take calculated risks when necessary. Lastly, leaders must abide by their own good conscience, moral principles and personal integrity. Unfortunately, the media report incidents where managers fail with regard to the last aspect on an almost daily basis.

The management appraisals of the personnel consultancy Egon Zehnder International have systematically examined the technical and leadership skills of top German managers for many years. These top managers are praised for their specialized knowledge, which is competitive on the international market. Yet they are also criticized for their unwillingness to take risks. German managers rarely dare to engage in new tasks and challenges. What they are lacking is an appreciation of the big picture, along with strategic thinking. They also often lack a sense of adventure – and the readiness to assume personal responsibility is of precious little help when the general direction of the corporation as a whole is wrong (see Wirtschaftswoche, August 21, 2003).

Above all, German managers are specialists. However, specialists are often doubtful and do not hold on to bold visions. They tend to perceive errors or defeats as personal failures, and therefore do not take risks. Furthermore, they are imprisoned in hierarchies that stifle the progress of new generations of managers. Unfortunately, not much has changed in this regard in the past few decades.

Peter F. Drucker believed that good leaders make only a few, but important decisions in a systematic process. "Above all the confusion around the difference between effectiveness and efficiency leads to the fact that things are done right, instead of doing the right things" (Drucker 2000, p. 117). Only 20% of all decisions and processes account for 80% of entrepreneurial success. Successful managers concentrate on these few decisions.

However, successful managers are also characterized by the courage to openly admit the uncertainty of their decisions. They talk with colleagues openly about the fact that their decisions are not always crystal clear, and they discuss the process of decision-making. In doing so, they not only win the trust of their coworkers and employees, but also benefit from new sources of knowledge, ideas and strategies, providing them with more alternatives for the next round of decision-making.

Leadership decisions are influenced by conscious and unconscious, rational and irrational, objective and subjective factors. Consequently, selecting the best option is determined not only by the situational factors and their "fellow players," but also by managers' own experiences, goals and preferences. The decision-making process depends on several variables that in turn provide possible answers to our question about the nature of good leadership. In the following section, we will further explore the unconscious, irrational and subjective forces that continue to affect managers and their work.

2.2.7 The Dark Side

Hardly any author has so intensively focused on the connection between the individual and leadership as Manfred Kets de Vries. His work deals with observations of the individual in the role of leading as well as those being led, and offers concrete recommendations for managers. His studies have contributed considerably to the paradigm shift of current academic pursuits and everyday practice. Figure 2.6 illustrates the relationships Kets de Vries has observed.

To fully grasp the meaning of leadership, we must leave the plane of the directly observable and shift our attention to internal and social processes. In addition to the relationship between leaders and those they lead, it is important to explore the unconscious psychodynamic process and structures influencing the behavior of individuals. Without this complex analysis of organizations, it is difficult to understand the processes within them. And furthermore, "leadership tends to grasp only a three-dimensional view of life in an organization while not recognizing a further layer of unconscious anxieties, hopes and motives" (de Vries 2002, p. 17).

We can compare the organization with an iceberg (see also Sect. 3.1.1). Most management theorists analyze only the tip of the iceberg, and concern themselves with obvious, rational phenomena such as missions, visions, goals, strategies, tasks, roles, structures, processes, and systems of control and compensation. Naturally, these factors are important, but they represent only a small part of the organization. Like the largest part of the iceberg, the largest part of an organization is invisible

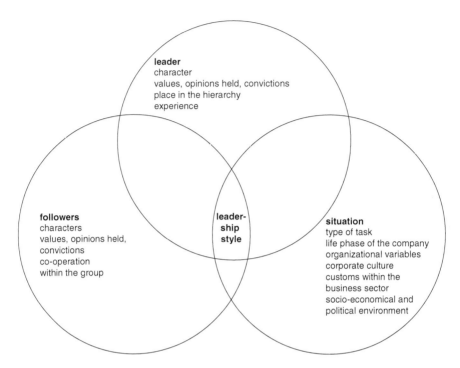

Fig. 2.6 The conflict fields of leadership (*Source*: de Vries 2002)

and therefore below the surface. Kets de Vries is interested in exactly these
processes. What are the underlying dynamics? What irrational variables feed
the organizational culture? What subconscious values influence and drive organizational structures? What relationship patterns influence the direction of decisions
and thereby the direction of the iceberg's motion?

de Vries' work is based on the clinical psychology paradigm. He uses concepts
from the fields of psychoanalysis, psychotherapy, developmental psychology, systematic family therapy and cognitive psychology to explain the conduct of people
in organizations and cites three reasons why this paradigm is useful (see de Vries
2002, pp. 21–50).

1. *Reality is not unconditionally identical to what we see.* Therefore, only those
   managers who can see new connections, remain open for different schemes of
   perception, and move past conventional ways of thinking will obtain extraordinary results. New points of view often lead to unexpected opportunities and
   surprising solutions.
2. *Every type of human behavior, no matter how irrational, has a reason.*
   According to Kets de Vries these reasons often originate in the subconscious.
   So many reactions are initially incomprehensible or unobservable at first sight
   that a more exact analysis is needed to reveal the basic mechanisms ("transfer
   mechanisms"). For example, a boss avoids direct confrontation with a colleague

because in his childhood he was always punished severely by his father for openly disagreeing.

We can compare these unconscious motives to "blind spots" in our personalities. We deny their existence because they cannot be easily controlled. In extreme forms, this "blindness" can become a personality disorder, like in the narcissistic personality type, which exhibits strong self-confidence; in the dependent type that overly relies on others; or in the type suffering from bipolar disorders, which exhibits strong mood swings. One finds these types of people on every level of every business. Insight is the first step towards improvement, but unfortunately the psyche has a wide array of defense mechanisms to protect itself. Some examples of defense mechanisms are: projection of one's own feelings onto other persons, denial of reality, venting aggression on a "harmless" replacement person rather than the problematic person, or conversion disorders (i.e. the transformation of mental conflicts into physical symptoms).

3. *We are all the product of our past.* This means that in addition to genetics, early environmental influences and individual experiences strongly shape people, who they are and how they function in the world. "In every man and in every woman there is a child stuck just under the surface," claims Kets de Vries. Being greatly influenced by experiences in our early childhood, we tend to repeat patterns of behavior in similar situations for much of the rest of our lives. The clinical paradigm helps us to begin paying more attention to our behavior, to be more aware of the connections between our past and present, and to decipher the reasons behind irrational behavior. Our emotional intelligence, which, as previously mentioned, is an essential characteristic of good managers, is also vital in such efforts.

Managing emotions is a decisive part of necessary leadership skills. Our moods, whether good or bad, extreme or moderate, grant us insights into our personalities. Such insights do not simply come naturally. We must fight for them by recognizing the internal dialogue and conflicting forces within ourselves. "It is the task of every person to understand these forces, but for people in positions of leadership, the responsibility has a special urgency," warns Kets de Vries. "The irony is that too little feeling produces consequences just as undesirable as too much. It is just as uncomfortable to live with a dumb fish as it is with a raging tiger" (de Vries 2002, p. 47).

2.2.7.1 The Central Relationship Conflict

To a great extent our behavior is based on relationship patterns, which our most deeply held convictions manifest themselves in. This behavior develops in our earliest childhood and is influenced by the messages we receive from others and from our environment. The concept of the central relationship conflict may be divided into three components: what we wish to derive from a relationship; our expectation of how others will react to our requests; and our conscious behavior and emotional responses to their reactions. Our unique relationship conflict makes us into the people we are.

"The central relationship conflict (CRC) permeates our private life and is the basis of repeated relationship conflicts. It also naturally influences everything we experience on the job. The CRC of leadership also determines the business culture and the decision-making within the organization" (de Vries 2002, p. 51). The recognition of one's own CRCs and those of others is complicated, because the past distorts the present. We transfer previous experiences with people to current relationships, influencing our behavior in the present. Our expectations become self-fulfilling prophecies. Kets de Vries notes, "Character is a form of memory. The internal drama of a person and the configuration of the essential personality features manifest themselves in it" (de Vries 2002, p. 26). Many managers neglect their inner experiences. They avoid examining their inner processes, do not pay attention to themselves and their feelings and in doing so, erect a "manic wall of protection." However, in this way they become prisoners of their own psyche and go through life without knowing what they are a slave to.

"Mental health requires that the individual has choices. Our internal drama rarely changes, and we cannot change certain preexisting internal processes, but we can decide how to respond to our central desires. We are the architects of our fate, the authors of our own script – or at least we can be" (de Vries 2002, p. 58).

2.2.7.2 In the Transference Trap

According to Kets de Vries the chief explanation for the failure of well-trained and highly motivated professionals is "transference." It decisively affects each human relationship and how we live together. The term "transference" is used because "none of our relationships is a new one; each is influenced by earlier relations. And the relations with the strongest long-term effects (. . .) are those of our first months of life. Therefore we treat persons in the present just as we did persons from the past. For example, we behave as children do with their parents and forget that in the meantime we've grown up" (de Vries 2002, p. 83).

Examples of transference at the workplace include situations like a boss asking his secretary for a small correction in a document, causing her to break into tears, or a young manager reacting strongly to the criticism of an experienced older colleague. The contact with authority, criticism and power in the family determines our later relationships to authoritarian, critical or powerful people, especially as we climb the career ladder. And especially managers tend to evoke transference processes in themselves and in others.

In Kets de Vries' diagnosis many managers suffer from transference, as they are practically addicted to receiving affirmations of their own worth. The parents were the first to provide this affirmation, and now colleagues have taken the place of parents. Leaders may speak of "constructive criticism," but the hierarchy can result in colleagues saying only what they believe the boss wants to hear. Praise and recognition can be mere hypocrisy and an effort to accommodate the speaker, as a result of which managers can soon find themselves surrounded by yes-men and lickspittles. Such double-layered communications lead to a fear of conflicts and lazy compromises, hinder initiative and innovation, weaken mutual trust and paralyze the decision-making process. Only a business culture that promotes open feedback on all levels can help to prevent such a climate. In the Roman Empire, when a victorious general marched through the triumphal arch there was a slave behind him on the chariot whispering in his ear: "Remember, Caesar, that you too are only human." Today good feedback systems fulfill the same purpose.

The 360° feedback system is one of the most effective means of eliciting quality feedback and necessary candor, and of encouraging dialogue. In this system, the participants provide feedback for coworkers at all levels – above, below, and on the same level of the participants. In addition, this approach serves as an early-warning system and sharpens the sensitivity to blind spots. In order to be effective, it must be guaranteed that no one gets punished, directly or indirectly, for his or her honesty. The managers must have the courage and the strength to hear unpleasant truths about themselves, and their employees must be encouraged to provide open feedback.

2.2.7.3 Necessary Narcissism

The concept of "narcissism" tends to mean being in love with oneself and being very egocentric. In developmental psychology, the "narcissistic phase" refers to the first three years of life, when the foundations of the personality are laid. In these early years, we are especially formed by our experiences, all we observe and feel, and our relationship to others and our environment.

The infant perceives pleasure through its body and bodily functions. The unavoidable frustrations of growing up can interfere with having this need met. For this reason, a child often creates an exaggerated and idealized picture of its parents. The remnants of this idealization are preserved for many years, and in later relationships. Narcissism is therefore an important drive for the individual. In moderation, it is necessary in order to develop a healthy sense of self-worth and independent identity. Narcissism and leadership are closely interwoven, as narcissism is a prerequisite for dominance, self-confidence and creativity.

On the other hand, too much or too little narcissism destroys a person's internal balance. Therefore, it is useful to distinguish between "constructive" and "reactive" narcissism. Constructive narcissism develops from sufficient care and support from parents and is the basis for stable self-confidence. Reactive narcissism is the consequence of lacking attention from the parents. People who lacked attention in early childhood become driven by the need to undo this insult and prove their worthiness to others ("Monte Cristo complex"). This is a detrimental but considerable part of what motivates some managers.

Those who have made it to the top often experience feelings of melancholy, sadness and emptiness. Whether CEO or marketing director, they all ask themselves whether it was worth all of the struggle, all the sacrifice, and all of the life energy they invested. Others fear the envy of competitors if they are successful. Not everyone can bear the "thin air at the top" and the solitude at the summit of power.

2.2.7.4   The Fish Rots from the Head Down

The strategy, structure and culture of an organization depend on the man or woman at the top, and not only on their conscious decisions and actions. A manager's unconscious and neurotic behavior can affect the entire organization. According to Kets de Vries, "in strongly centralized businesses – in which the decisions lay in the hands of one person or in the hands of a small but homogeneous group, the space between people and the organization is so narrow that every twitch quickly spreads downward. In organizations with decentralized structures, several different managers influence strategies and culture, as there is only a loose connection between leadership style and organization pathology" (de Vries 2002, p. 128).

Pathological organization styles often reflect the weakness of an individual and his or her neurotic behavior. Kets de Vries has distinguished between five types of organizations and personalities: the dramatic, the suspicious, the detached, the depressive and the compulsive.

1. Dramatic personalities and organizations

   Some managers behave like dramatists, wanting to impress others and receive maximum attention. These managers exaggerate their own achievements and capacities, and tend to be overly reactive. The costs of such strong narcissism are the loss of concentration and discipline. Superficially these managers can appear sincere, but they lack true empathy and attention for others. They exploit employees for their own purposes and bind them into relations of dependency. Conversely, dependent people feel magically drawn to dramatic bosses. They lionize their boss, ignore his or her faults, do not criticize – even if they should – and bask in his or her glory.

   Dramatic organizations are characterized by impulsiveness, hyperactivity, audacity, lack of restraint, diversification and centralization. At the same time they are often structured too simply, have no feedback structure and communicate in only one direction, from the top down. Instead of responding to the demands of the external market, the dramatic organization creates its own demand, which rarely leads to success.

2. Suspicious personalities and organizations

   Suspicious (in the sense of distrustful) personalities and organizations exhibit are marked by their paranoia, anxiety and extreme caution, a climate of suspicion, secrecy, envy and hostility. Suspicious managers are easily provoked and tend to make a mountain out of a molehill. They are narrow and callous, overly rational and hyper-vigilant.

   Organizations led by such managers are dominated by a hostile atmosphere. Most of the organization's energy is invested in uncovering enemies, and in preparing for anticipated attacks by those it believes to be enemies. Instead of open communication, backstabbing and espionage, including the trading of "secret" information and rumors, flourish. The personnel are supervised as closely as possible, and any subordinate who freely expresses his or her opinion is threatened with draconian punishment; the organization becomes a police state. The efficiency of suspicious organizations is hampered by their unmotivated employees, lack of information exchange and paralyzed decision-makers (de Vries 2002, pp. 85–131).

3. Detached personalities and organizations

The detached personality type can be seen in extremely distant managers who are selective in the company they keep and tend to be cool and disinterested. Managers of this type avoid social ties, isolate themselves, and have no need for exchange with others. If managers become so distant as to no longer recognize their own responsibilities, the management is delegated to the level just beneath them, absolving them from authority and responsibility. The managers in the second row become the real power players, using the vacuum at the top to lobby for their own interests.

In turn, power struggles and political discord arise, and the implementation of business values and aims falls by the wayside. Strategic decisions become gambits, resulting in breaches and gaps throughout the entire organization. This prevents effective coordination and communication. The individual players concentrate only on themselves, and not on their business, colleagues, customers or the market.

4. Depressive personalities and organizations

Every person experiences phases of dejection. Yet some regularly sink into hopelessness and sorrow, which characterizes the depressive personality. Depressive managers feel worthless, guilty, impotent and out-of-place, and therefore shy away from responsibility. They seek others to make decisions for them and then idealize these saviors. The feeling of powerlessness often produces feelings of anger and aggression directed at one's self.

Depressive managers are characterized by their incompetence and lack of drive and imagination. They are passive, unsure of their actions and even fear success, as it could spark envy in others. According to Kets de Vries the business culture that evolves under this type of manager, is that of the "self-insecure individual": the organization is characterized by negativity and lethargy. In the eyes of the depressive manager, the business is only a machine that needs minimal attention. Depressive enterprises are very conservative, resistant to change, and often become isolated, losing their orientation. They become locked in their routines and unable to implement change processes. Decisions are put off for so long that the necessary information is no longer useful, and the entire system stagnates.

5. Compulsive personalities and organizations

"Obsessive-compulsive personalities often fight their way to the top. Although they are real over-achievers in certain fields, the presence of such individuals can tend to have brutal consequences" (de Vries 2002, p. 138). Compulsive managers do not want to be on the same level as other persons or dependent on events; as such, they want to control everything and everyone. They view relationships only in terms of dominance and subordination – they are domineering towards subordinates and practically grovel in the presence of superiors.

The work of the compulsive manager is characterized by perfectionism, rigid opinions and over-the-top industriousness. Workaholics are always busy but rarely effective, as these managers lack vision, imagination and decisiveness. In compulsive personality organizations, an intense mistrust exists between the leaders and lower positions. The organization relies on formal directions, bureaucracy and direct supervision instead of trust and enthusiasm. Managers lead with complex rules systems instead of by personal example. Business policies are oriented towards the compulsive person at the top rather than towards objective requirements, and independent thinkers are quickly smothered. The heavily internal focus prevents decision-makers from considering the larger picture and thus stymies processes of renewal.

Dysfunctional leaders like these can steer businesses onto a vicious circle, starting with sinking employee morale, a high turnover rate, a high illness rate and low job satisfaction. All of this results in bad performance throughout the organization, sinking profits, increasing costs and decreasing share prices. The organization then responds by laying off employees, freezing salaries, reducing investments in training, and hiring temps, further eroding employee morale and bringing a new turn in the vicious circle. Manfred Kets de Vries convincingly shows how neurotic behavior on the part of the manager impacts their relationships with those they lead and thereby causes the business to fail. In the next chapter, we will examine precisely these interactions.

2.3 The Relationship Between Leader and Led

> Good leadership stands and falls with the people led.

As already stated, leadership is not only business management, but primarily consists in leading people. Leadership aims at achieving harmony between the potentially conflicting goals of the organization and the employees. Even the best manager will fail if their authority is not acknowledged by their employees. Manager and employees must have good "chemistry," and managers must also fit well with their own superiors and with customers.

For this reason numerous books covering the subject of leadership focus on those being led and their influence on the success of leadership. In the past few years, a major change has taken place that leadership practice is only slowly beginning to take into account.

2.3.1 From Subordinate to Associate

Leadership always depends on the people involved, i.e., it depends on certain basic assumptions about human nature. The way I deal with someone, how I evaluate their behavior and react to it, depends crucially on how I perceive them.

2.3.1.1   X or Y?

In the 1950s, management consultant Douglas McGregor defined two scientific theories regarding the position of managers and employees that clarify different positions of leadership: the X theory and the Y theory. They would later become the basis of countless leadership models (McGregor 1960).

According to the X theory, the average person has an innate aversion to work and tries to avoid it. Therefore most people usually have to be forced, directed and threatened with punishment in order to be motivated. The average person prefers to be taken by the hand and takes as little responsibility as possible, for they have little ambition and a considerable need for security. If a superior perceives their employees in this manner, he or she leads with an authoritarian, controlling leadership style.

In the Y theory McGregor outlined a more positive vision of man. According to the Y theory, the physical and intellectual effort of working is just as natural for a person as resting or playing. Given suitable conditions, a person will strive to take on responsibility, independently finding solutions to organizational problems based on his or her own initiative and creativity. Supervision and punishment are not the best ways to motivate a person. According to theory Y, people apply themselves voluntarily, and have the self-discipline and self-control needed to meet goals. A manager with this view of people gives them latitude, encourages commitment and individual responsibility, and includes employees in the decision-making process. Leaders with this view choose a participative and cooperative leadership style.

I feel it is fairly obvious that the X theory confuses cause and effect, forming a vicious circle. People only become stupid and irresponsible when they are granted no latitude to work autonomously. Such working climates are based on mistrust and create the breeding ground for this type of employee. Reversed, the Y theory sees people from a positive perspective, resulting in a desirable type of employee.

Is there a single correct method for leading people? According to Peter F. Drucker, there is not. Nevertheless there is the desire for one correct theory for leadership. However, Drucker was also a proponent of theory X and theory Y and further stated that, just as different employees must be led in different ways, the same employees must be led differently in different situations (Drucker 2004, p. 102).

2.3.1.2   The Human Resource

The capital-oriented management philosophy has had its day – according to strategy guru Sumantra Ghoshal (along with his colleague, Christopher Bartlett of the Harvard Business School), and I agree. Financial capital is no longer the resource of highest value to an organization, but it is rather the employees with their know-how and orientation on performance that are essential. We need to be aware that it is employees who provide the largest increase in value, we have to appreciate them as assets and recognize them as voluntary investors who give their knowledge, ideas, talents, and efforts to a business, and we have to stop viewing employees as subordinate cost factors (Bartlett and Ghoshal 2000, cf. also Ghoshal 2003, pp. 220–222).

Ghoshal wrote about the "bottleneck of human capital," which includes not only technical knowledge but the concept of emotional and social capital, reasons for competition in the future. For the paradigm shift from subordinate culture to a culture of associates places new strains on management and its training. Managers must be able to forge and maintain long-term relationships based on trust and reciprocity. This capacity represents an enormously important resource for the further development of businesses. The second skill that will become even more important in the future is energy. There are plenty of visions and lofty ideas, but the ability to translate these ideas into action is rare in everyday working life.

The human capital of a business takes into account on the one hand the knowledge of its employees, and on the other the social and emotional capacities of its managers. It is necessary to find the best management-employee match in order to generate knowledge and channel it into productivity and increasing business revenues. Companies must orient themselves on people, must mediate visions and values, and cultivate individual potential. Under these conditions extraordinary achievements are possible (Bartlett and Ghoshal 2000).

With the new paradigm of leadership, there are also changes in the "psychological contract," i.e., the unspoken, implicit obligations on the part of employees and employers alike concerning various issues. In the past, the employee's loyalty to a certain job was based on a paternalistic model. The new model moves back and forth between mutual dependence and individualism. In the information age, "employability" (being considered a lucrative employer) is more important than loyalty for businesses. The companies provide their employees with opportunities and development rather than security, and with partnership rather than dependence (de Vries 2002, p. 64). In this regard, Peter F. Drucker also contributed the idea of the "volunteer organization" (see Sect. 2.2.1).

On the other hand, there are of course also expectations placed on employees. As associates, employees must possess social, design and implementation skills. They must voluntarily and responsibly commit themselves and be ready for lifelong learning. Volkswagen designated this type of worker with the term "4-M employee," which indicates that one distinguishes oneself through multiple qualifications, mobility, cooperation and humanism (Wunderer 2002, pp. 40–45).

So much for the ideal image. In reality, however, we cannot increase the demands on employees to unreachable heights, but must define realistic goals in mission statements, as Reinhard K. Sprenger does. "'I will make at least one thing my own' in the sense of mastering one task or duty is also an appeal to the personal responsibility of the employees (here keeping in mind that almost every executive is also someone else's employee). While careers are losing their security and the future of businesses is becoming increasingly unpredictable, people can at least take responsibility for their own professional life. This applies to their choice of company, to their choice of position, and to how they choose to use the leeway within their position. This does not mean waiting for things to get better, fairer or more permissive on their own, or waiting for others to do something for you (see above); leeway is not there so that we can sit and wonder how things are done elsewhere, in situations that don't apply to us; it is there for us to conquer" (Sprenger 1999, p. 251).

The reverse applies to the expectations of the employees from the management. "The secret of efficiency is having an understanding of the people one works with and on whom one depends, so that one can profit from his or her strengths, ways of working and codes of values. Work relationships depend in equal measure on the person and on the work itself" (Drucker 1999, p. 16).

Though once only the management benefited from power struggles with its employees, this is no longer the case. Today the employees are in power even if they may not seem it at first glance. The employees possess power as they in a way "select" a manager by deciding for or against them and being cooperative or emotionally or literally refusing to work for them. Employees make this selection with their level of commitment to a manager. There are employees without managers, but no managers without employees (Sprenger 2002a, p. 160).

2.3.2 Motivation

The different ideas of human nature put forward in the X and Y theories and the work of Bartlett and Ghoshal illustrate the importance of motivation in the leadership process. Good leadership depends to a high degree on the readiness of staff members to commit to giving maximum performance and to reaching the business goals in cooperation with the management. Yet how can this readiness be established? What drives people? What are the goals and needs of the employees? Are people more easily prompted to action by extrinsic or intrinsic motivation? The social sciences, business sciences and psychology have been attempting to answer these questions for decades. Abraham H. Maslow's hierarchy of needs forms the starting point in our exploration of the findings of motivation research.

2.3.2.1 The Hierarchy of Needs

In 1943, Maslow developed a theory of motivation that included a model outlining individual goals and five categories of individual needs arranged in a hierarchical pyramid. The underlying concept is that the basic needs must be met first before the next level of the hierarchy can be met. These needs are categorized as physiological needs (hunger, thirst, sex drive, etc.); safety; love/belonging; esteem; and self-actualization. Note that nourishment is a primary need, while social contact and even esteem are considered secondary needs (Maslow 1943). In short: a hungry man has no conscience.

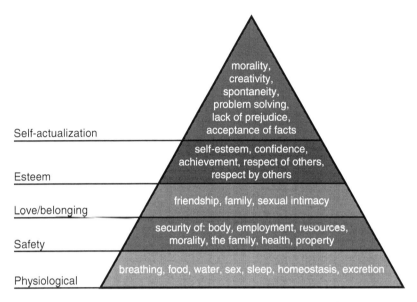

Fig. 2.7　The hierarchy of needs according to Maslow (*Source*: Maslow 1943)

According to Maslow, motivation functions along a simple equation: needs plus incentive equals the desired behavior. This conservative model is simple and clear, but it reduces the person to a bundle of needs. The model has been disputed for years, and criticized as at least being in need of supplementation. Nevertheless it is still used around the globe today as an important basis of employee motivation, which is why it is presented here (Fig. 2.7).

2.3.2.2　The Two-Factor Theory

In the 1950s and 1960s, Frederick Herzberg investigated the sources of employee motivation. Based on the insights gleaned, he developed the two-factor theory, which distinguishes between the factors that make people satisfied with their activities and those that produce alienation and lack of productivity.

If employees are asked why they are dissatisfied, in most cases they claim that it is because of their incompetent or unfair boss, insufficient salary or bad working environment. Yet these very same factors, even if they are absolutely idea, cannot motivate employees to work harder, which is why Herzberg dubbed them "hygiene factors." They must be acceptable; however this is not enough because they are extrinsic and are only indirectly connected with the activity itself. In contrast, "motivators" are all factors that satisfy employees' deeper needs to perform meaningful work, to realize their potential, to grow and to be appreciated for what they do. These factors are intrinsic and are related to the content and formulation of work.

As such, it is not the infamous "kick in the tail" in the sense of pressure, harassment and threats that motivates employees, nor is it necessarily the positive aspects of raises, shorter working hours, a company car or retirement benefits. Leaders cannot motivate employees by either cracking the whip or promising incentives, as Herzberg recognized very early in his studies. Motivation comes from business activities that mean something to the employees, activities that are varied and multifaceted (Herzberg 2003, pp. 30–62, 1959). The concept of "job enrichment" belongs to the classics on psychology of work and organizational psychology, but even now, 50 years later, Herzberg's insights have not been widely implemented by employers.

One of the dangers that stem from exclusively extrinsic motivation of employees is that employee morale suffers. Peter F. Drucker made the following comparison: "And so just as an orchestra can sabotage the most capable and self-assured conductor, the employees of a knowledge-based organization can most certainly sabotage a capable but arrogant leader" (Drucker 1999, p. 37). Motivation is often used as the magic word. Motivation gurus are notorious for saying things like "anything is possible!"; "think positively!" or total nonsense like "Tschaka – you can do it!" The result can be a sense of increased depression when the guru is gone and employees realize that all they received was a verbal placebo – and strangely enough, that the company that just encouraged them to think positively and move forward still has the same old managers, policies, and ways of doing things.

The father of modern management research, Peter F. Drucker, encouraged intrinsic motivation through the sensible assigning of employees, good information exchange, and extensive empowerment of employees, allowing them to be part of decision-making processes. He did not believe that leaders need to drive people, but felt they should instead release their employees' internal drive through favorable conditions. "Only someone who has achieved something can have a sense of achievement. Only someone whose work has valuable can have a sense of their own value. The only true basis for real pride, a real sense of value and achievement is the active and responsible co-determination of ones work and organization" (Drucker 1956, p. 370).

2.3.2.3 Understanding Those You Lead

With Drucker's words in mind, the *path-goal theory* calls for managers to put themselves in the shoes of those being managed. Management must know the immediate and long-term goals of the employees in order to reconcile them with leadership and business goals. The employees' goals therefore determine the method of leadership. Additionally, managers have to have empathy. The path-goal theory illustrates the factors influencing readiness to perform, factors that can be used as the basis for suggestions on how to promote results-oriented leadership, or "management by objectives."

In *attribution theory*, which enjoyed its heyday in the social psychology of the 1970s and 1980s, the focus is also on monitoring and grasping the behavior of others. In this context, "attribution" refers to the motivations people assign to specific types of conduct. For example, on the job people tend to congratulate themselves on their achievements but blame uncontrollable external factors for mistakes and failures. In the long run, attribution theories do little to answer our initial question of what constitutes good leadership.

In contrast, *social learning theories* can help us. Such theories are based on the assumption that management, leadership behavior and the leadership situation are mutually influential. This means that managers learn not only from their own actions, but from those of their employees, and employees learn from the behavior of management. This process is designated as "learning by example," and is an important prerequisite for development and change. If everyone had to primarily learn through trial and error, learning would be an embarrassing and lengthy process. For example a child learns by observing its mother that the stove is hot without having to put its hand on it. The situation is similar in business, where we learn by observing others – every mistake is only made once, at least in theory. Social learning theories provide a basis for the delegating leadership style, emphasizes the need for self-management (as everyone serves as an example – and possibly as a role model – for others), and offers valuable approaches to working in teams.

2.3.2.4 Beneath the Surface

All these approaches and findings are always jeopardized by irrationality, because human behavior is not only determined by logical, conscious factors and decisions: "A person with management responsibilities should be sensitized to the fact that his or her employees are not only rational and proactive, but that irrational processes are a part of them that they themselves often cannot justify and leave them almost speechless" (von Rosenstiel/Regnet/Domsch 2003, p. 23), warns Munich-based organizational psychologist Lutz von Rosenstiel.

Irrational and subconscious factors that shape the behavior on both sides can have consequences within organizations, such as conflicts when various defense mechanisms (displacement, compensation, transference, identification), are triggered and lead to projection, feelings of resignation, aggression, self-incrimination or fixation. If the management understands these mechanisms, it can more accurately perceive its own role and the behavior of employees and respond more appropriately (Rosenstiel/Regnet/Domsch 2003, pp. 27–40).

My "artificial" division between approaches focusing on managers and those mainly dealing with employees should not serve to diminish the interrelation and interplay between the two. A relationship always has two sides, which influence each other through their actions, perceptions and communications. The exchange processes between leaders and employees have been studied in interaction theories, role theory, and group-dynamic approaches, two important names in this regard being Peter R. Hofstatter and Klaus Macharzina. The limit of these theories lies in the enormous complexity of interactions. Therefore, they are of limited value in practice, and also far too complicated – despite the fact that models and theories are intended to explain and simplify reality. The relationship-oriented, systemic leadership approach put forward in this book represents a practical alternative to these schematic, lumbering and limited theories, which have little practical value for daily management work.

2.3.2.5 What Employees Want

The employees' *expectations* of the leadership play an important role in the work of managers, and depend on the degree of maturity and value orientation of the employees. An international study of more than 60 countries found that nearly 70% of participants put "building trust" at the top of the list, followed by the ability to appreciate and cultivate employee potential (46%). 42% listed "communicating a vision," while 38% cited "developing networked thinking" (Personnel Economy 10/2002, p. 43).

Employees want authentic and trustworthy managers, not someone just living up to a role. In the mid 1960s, Peter F. Drucker wrote, "A superior is indebted to an organization to use the power output of employees as productively as possible. Yet he is even more indebted to the employees placed under his authority, whom he must assist in attaining the highest level of performance possible" (Drucker 1995, p. 154).

In the age of employees as associates, leaders would be well served to accept the advice of Dieter Frey, professor of Economic Psychology at the Ludwig-Maximilian University of Munich. Frey has put forth the following principles: leadership must convey meaning and vision, must be based on autonomy, participation, transparency and fairness, must allow constructive feedback and personal growth, and must offer stable social integration. According to Frey modern leadership is always situational leadership (Frey 2003, p. 20).

A study conducted by the Academy in 2004 lends statistical support to this view. With regard to what characteristics managers should have in order to motivate employees, 92% of the participants endorsed truthfulness and authenticity, 86% cited the ability to competently deal with conflicts, 84% called for the ability to inspire enthusiasm, and 61% put their focus on empathy (Academy Study 2004).

2.3.2.6 Career Instead of Wages?

Business consultant Towers Perrin (Frankfurter Zeitung, January 19, 2004) examined the reasons why employees join companies, remain there, or choose to leave. Simply stated, employees primarily join based on the reputation of the business and stay because of the salary. Employees leave due to lack of upward mobility and career opportunity, and/or due to poor relationships with the managers. More specifically:

Reasons why employees join:

> Reputation of the company
> Competitive salary
> Challenging work
> Promotion
> Corporate culture

Reasons why employees stay:

> Challenging work
> Competitive salary
> High level of independence
> Opportunities for promotion
> Corporate culture

Reasons why employees leave:

> Lack of opportunities for promotion
> Relationship with managers
> Poor work-life balance
> Work-related accidents
> Non-competitive salary

In order to retain qualified employees, other measures are necessary as well. The management must align individual goals and organizational goals on a certain level. At the same time, the management should invest in developing the employees' skills and abilities and should delegate demanding assignments. In this way, both parties profit and motivation remains high.

2.3.2.7   Motivation – A Myth?

While both Maslow's hierarchy of needs and Herzberg's theory of motivators and hygiene factors assume that the meaning and purpose of leadership is to influence people and offer them an incentive to display a specific type of behavior, Reinhard K. Sprenger, a best-selling management author and PhD of Philosophy, considers this form of motivation to be a dead end.

To him, it is obvious that "motivation" means nothing more than the following five factors: rewards, praise, bribes, threats and punishment. Leading with mechanical stimulus systems, Sprenger claims, creates the opposite of motivation, "demotivation." I consider this conclusion to be correct and of central importance. For this reason I would like to cover the central thesis and observations in the following section, and provide commentary on each.

2.3.2.8   The "Wonder Weapon" Motivation

Sprenger asserts that "motivating" has become quite synonymous with leadership, and is a top demand placed on managers. In general, it is understood that "producing, increasing, and receiving the behavior (motivation) results from incentives by management" (Sprenger 1999, p. 22). Therefore, motivating means moving employees to action, and managers are called upon to get the best out of their employees.

Most managers understand the task of motivating based on the old perception that employees do not voluntarily give their best, are inherently idle and unwilling to perform, that they save their energy for their leisure time and keep good ideas to themselves. Therefore, they must be motivated by pushing and pulling. To me, this very much smacks of the X theory. For Sprenger, "motivating" is essentially a form of external control, a more or less secret form of manipulation designed to influence behavior systematically. He differentiates between motivating and (true) "motivation," which involves the internal drive of the individual, controllable by the individual (Sprenger 1999, p. 24).

Optimal motivation is intended to combat the specter of inner resignation that haunts our companies, e.g. in the form of early retirement, which can even spread to the top management. Staggering figures on employees who have fully or partially internally "quit" have prompted companies to search frantically for increasingly sophisticated incentive systems.

Thus, in 2004 the market research firm Gallup examined the "internal commitment" of employees in Germany. The figures had not improved over those of the previous year: 87% claimed they felt no real commitment to their work. Sixty-nine percent of the employees simply followed company policy (and gave nothing more), and 18 claimed to have given up caring once and for all. The overall economic damage resulting from this low level of commitment in Germany amounts to roughly 245 billion Euros due to high absence rates and low productivity. Gallup accurately sees the cause of this problem less in the employees and more in the bad leadership in German companies, where, the firm also noted, praise and recognition were in short supply (see Frankfurter Allgemeine Zeitung, November 14, 2004. Read more at www.gallup.de).

The only response most companies have to these figures is the individualization of the reward mechanism – a contradiction in terms. But no one comes up with the idea to seek the causes for the leisure orientation of so many employees precisely in company's efforts to motivate them, even though, according to Sprenger, this is where they are to be found. We now know with sufficient certainty that motivation itself has not diminished, and that only the opportunities companies provide to implement values have failed to keep pace with employees' changed understanding of values in the modern working world. Money and status do not necessarily attract the new generation; work that is fun is just as important as a high income for employees in today's world, and tasks that are meaningful are more important than career status. These days, individuals expect the opportunity to invest their entire potential in their job, and find this rewarding. Yet businesses either fail to react, or react too slowly to the changing expectations of goal-oriented employees, as a result of which the latter's free energy, interests and creativity are channeled into leisure time rather than being used on the job.

2.3.2.9   Motivating Demotivates

Sprenger has claimed that: "motivation is the abundant seduction to inner resignation" (Sprenger 1999, p. 32). Motivation (the inner drive and not the outer effect) does not consist merely of ethical, psychosocial or economic factors, but depends on a multitude of circumstances and influences. It is therefore simply utopian to believe that universal stimulus systems will work for everyone.

External efforts to motivate them can hinder employees' inner drive, as they signal mistrust and a lack of respect. Bonus systems or provision systems may imply that employees are not capable of delivering full performance without pressure. The suspicion from the top remains, as managers highly appreciate their own readiness to perform while de-valuing that of their employees. In many organizations, a culture of suspicion reigns. In such a climate, responsibility and information represent status, and the development of ideas and initiatives is hampered.

Employees lose motivation when the motivating system is based solely on provoking a response to an attraction. It presumes that the incentive just has to be big enough. All the management has to do is to determine which section of Maslow's hierarchy of needs the individual occupies in order to select a suitable "carrot" (i.e. money, advanced training, leisure time, etc.). Unfortunately this negative view of human beings has the character of a "self-fulfilling prophecy." "When managers consider their employees to be stupid, lacking in drive, and dependent, that is exactly how the employees conduct themselves – or at least that is all the eyes of the managers see" (Sprenger 1999, p. 44).

The motivator's repertoire includes compulsion, baiting, seduction and vision. With compulsion, threats and punishment become acceptable motivation methods. According to Sprenger, the consequences of compulsion are a lack of effort and a desire to escape if given the chance. Baiting includes indirect rewards and punishments in the form of variable salary shares and bonuses. The consequence of utilizing baiting in motivation processes is that employees focus on the rewards and perform only to the level necessary to gain them, and bonuses must eventually be increased in order to keep the employees' interest. Employees receiving fewer rewards than others tend to disengage themselves due to feelings of resentment and being treated unfairly.

The strategy of seduction combines bribes, rewards and praise. Here – unlike the first two strategies – the attitude of the employee is crucial, and identification with the company is crucial. "Often the cover-all term of 'corporate identity' is understood as if the employees, like teenagers, should tattoo the company's logo on their biceps," Sprenger says cynically. In his opinion efforts to stimulate identity resemble a pubescent fan culture.

The strategy of vision ultimately also depends on the attitude of the employee and his or her identification with the company: "Continuously threatened by inner resignation and external distractions, the people swallow higher corporate values against their will and are willing to reject not only critics, but even those who do not want to share them." (Sprenger 1999, p. 59). Sprenger goes even further, claiming that the quest for a common vision shows a "paramilitary basic pattern" and a "totalitarian tendency."

With all due respect to Sprenger's flowery language and its polarizing approach, the question remains: what's wrong with identification? Why are all those who identify with their job and their company automatically immature teenagers? After all, there is such a thing as voluntary commitment. And where does this suspicion of values and visions come from? Despite all individuality there have to be common values creating a sense of community within the company; otherwise the result is nothing more than a loose bunch of egoists without any clear direction or orientation.

At this point, Sprenger does exactly what he demonizes companies and managers for. He lumps them all together and assumes all have the same predictable, unreasonable reactions: if you offer an employee more money, he or she will always want more and therefore work less. Employees are weak adolescents who can easily be brainwashed. And the manager is the old enemy, driven by cold and inhuman capitalism and with only one goal in mind, namely to manipulate and exploit their employees and in a cowardly, lazy manner to delegate leadership responsibilities to incentive systems. Regardless of how leaders behave, whether they act in an authoritarian or democratic style, and what they do – for Sprenger they are all under general suspicion; his faith in the goodness of human beings does not seem to include executives.

2.3.2.10 Challenging Instead of Seducing

A new kind of leadership that is not based on seduction and demotivating pushing or pulling begins with a change in attitude and a shift away from the negative view of human beings. Research has shown again and again that people are motivated. Basically everyone has creative energy that yearns to be developed and high potential for action. People are curious by nature, like to discover new things and like to have fun doing what they do. In Sprenger's eyes, the presumed motivation gap that needs to be artificially bridged does not exist.

Sprenger reminds us about something very important that has almost become lost in the entire debate about motivation, and which I want to stress here as well because it is an essential component of leadership: every manager has the right to make clear demands on the staff, to make arrangements and monitor their compliance. He or she has the right to demand performance on the basis of defined objectives, and the duty to openly confront and criticize employees when they fail to uphold agreements. A manager has to find out why the service is not provided – and analyze his or her own contribution to that failure.

"In light of the big picture it seems to me that a clear relationship of demands between manager and employee is significantly more beneficial and consistent than any punish/reward system" (Sprenger 2003, p. 187). In this scenario performance is always relative and a matter of expectations that the leader has to define in advance together with the employee. Viable agreements are achieved only through communication and negotiation processes. If employees approve the agreements which meet their performance needs, efforts to motivate them may become unnecessary. Thus Sprenger re-establishes the concept of "management by objectives." He feels that management is justified only if it is confined to a predetermined function and clear agreements. Anything beyond these minimum leadership standards violates human dignity and is therefore inadmissible. Sprenger rejects mechanistic and motivation-oriented goal agreements.

The only factors that can truly motivate employees to long-term performance and commitment are freedom, trust and esteem, which plant the seeds for real commitment. "Only if we begin to see the meaning of our work again, will we feel truly motivated" (Sprenger 2003a, p. 111). What companies need are success-oriented and not failure-avoiding employees. To achieve this it is not enough to make the business goals more attractive to them with a 14th monthly salary or a larger company car; motivation calls for a deeper understanding and genuine empathy.

The question is: what drives people to commit themselves enthusiastically to their company? And this question quickly leads us to the demotivating factors, which are actually more meaningful and important than motivators, such as: unequal treatment of employees by the management, lack of fairness, lack of tolerance, caprice and incompetence on the part of the management.

2.3.2.11 Avoiding Demoralization

Motivation cannot be boosted from the outside without long-term consequences and costs for all parties. If an employee fails to provide the agreed-upon service, it is caused by something that discouraged him or her. There is only one thing a manager can do now: take the incident seriously and find the reason for the lack of motivation and, if possible, correct it. Sprenger has defined demotivation as blocked, sluggish energy. Accordingly, leading is controlling the energy flow within the company, which primarily means detecting where that energy is blocked. Although this metaphor may sound a bit like feng shui, Sprenger's use of it is fundamentally correct.

But how can this be achieved? There are several ways to meet this objective: by observing and asking what is going on within the company or the department; by identifying patterns and structures; by sensing moods, conflicts and problems rather than covering them up, and by having personal conversations with the staff. Discouragement can be caused by relations or by work structures. The number one in the former category is the employee's relationship with their immediate supervisor, according to Sprenger: "The relationship with the immediate supervisor is the Achilles heel of satisfaction at work" (Sprenger 2003, p. 204). But managers, he claims, only rarely seriously look for flaws in their own behavior. Nor do most focus on their employees, but instead on their own image as a brilliant leader who has everything under control.

Here, again, Sprenger tends to make all managers into villains, a view I can't subscribe to. However, what Sprenger says about relationships and about self-reflection is interesting: "Managers are often completely blind to the consequences of their behavior – they do not listen, they do not ask for any feedback, they are not interested in their 'blind spots'; they are quite reserved and try to maintain distance, and they are in love with their own self-image of being big and tough." This is a flaw I myself have found countless times in my practice as a consultant and trainer. It is the point of departure for the relational, systemic management approach I will explain in Chap. 3.

Therefore for Sprenger leading primarily means avoiding demoralization. The following behaviors of the executive are considered to be particularly discouraging to employees:

The supervisor can do and always knows more than his or her employees.
Decisions are made top-down.
The boss badmouths staff behind their backs.
His or her criticism is loud, arrogant and personal rather than objective.
The boss shows a dynamic of dominant behavior, constantly interrupts the staff, only allowing them to utter keywords before he or she takes over the talking.
The employees are overlooked, ignored, and quickly "handled."
They receive insufficient, partial and delayed information, dealing only with the bare essentials of their work.
The boss is horribly pedantic.
The boss does not trust his or her employees and lets them feel it through verbal and nonverbal messages.
The employees have neither individual freedom nor choice.

According to Sprenger the question that every manager must face when they notice that their employees are unmotivated or have even resigned internally is not "What should I do?" but "What should I not do?" This is hard for many executives, who see themselves as "doers" that are paid for their actions. But: "Sooner or later we cannot avoid the insight that our current hyperactivity, the constant intervening and manipulating, is just a bizarre variant of our paralyzed acceptance of many employees' inner resignation. I do not propose doing *more*, but less" (Sprenger 2003, p. 218).

The manager should stop doing those things that hamper the motivation of their employees and prevent the growth of natural relationships in their business life. In other words: in the long run, each leader has the staff that he or she deserves.

Yet another aspect plays a major role for Sprenger when it comes to good leadership: self-respect and human dignity should be at the center of attention.

Leadership must take people seriously and respect them – but at the same time, managers should not lose respect for themselves and their work; otherwise they will fall prey to the cynicism of disappointment and disillusionment, and will distance themselves from others in order to avoid injury. But this is exactly how a good leader should be: vulnerable and human. Every manager must then decide for himself or herself whether they choose "the straight approach of making demands, negotiating and arriving at agreements, or continue to play games of psychological seduction. You must choose between the spirit of fostering self-esteem and the specter of motivating from without," as Sprenger concludes (Sprenger 2003, p. 259).

Sprenger's book closes with these thoughts on the "I" of the executive. Here he touches on a very important issue, which I feel to be the core of successful leadership, as I will show in Chap. 3 of this book. Whether a manager has the courage and the strength to refrain from motivating and thus from demotivating and relies on the employees' will to perform and intrinsic motivation, depends essentially on the "self-awareness" of the manager and their role.

2.3.3   Trust

One of the most important prerequisites for successful relationship management and an expression of high emotional intelligence is the ability to trust and to gain the trust of others, claims Reinhard K. Sprenger. If the manager does not trust their employees and vice versa, leadership will not succeed – even if the right tools and techniques are used. Lack of trust paralyzes collaboration and the productivity, creativity and flexibility of employees and the entire organization, something Sprenger shows quite impressively in his book "Trust: The Best Way to Manage." His approach should serve as an example for all those dealing with this subject and who have made the demand for more trust a leading topic in the past few years.

2.3.3.1   Trust – A Scarce Commodity

But how do German companies really approach the issue of trust? Sprenger's bottom line is devastating: "We talk about trust when it is lacking. (...) The more we talk about trust, the worse the situation is" (Sprenger 2002b, p. 16). While all managers claim to trust in their subordinates, the former themselves want to receive more trust from their superiors – and the same is true a level higher up in the hierarchy. Mistrust dominates the relation of managers to their employees and vice versa. The employees suspect that "up there" nobody adheres to the agreements anyway, that everyone has only their own interests in mind and that managers are generally untrustworthy. At the same time, the superiors suspect their employees are generally reluctant to do their jobs and need to be stimulated into working at all. Quite a few executives are obsessed with the idea that their employees want to betray them. According to Sprenger, there is also a form of "horizontal" distrust that makes competitors out of colleagues and the daily work a constant battle.

The reason for this distorted image is a widespread shortcoming of German bosses: their penchant for perfection. If one assumes that others do not work or do not work well enough, it is the worst possible basis for trust. Indeed, many executives would prefer to do everything themselves, but this is impossible. Therefore, they must delegate – but it is best to always keep an eye on the staff, because trusting in their ability and determination is not enough. Although tasks are delegated, responsibility is not. In these economically difficult times trust and letting go requires considerable effort and courage. Instead of taking this leap, often everything is declared an "executive priority" or is "escalated" into a managerial decision so that nothing can go wrong.

Many companies are dominated by an early industrial labor organization in a modern guise, which focuses on the duty to show presence, on systems of control, and on meeting rituals. Some companies practically have their own "distrust departments" that are just busy figuring out if others are doing what they are supposed to be doing. Overwhelming their victims with forms and regulations to the point of neurotic stress and fatigue, they succeed only in keeping them from doing what they are really supposed to be doing. Many people have had enough of their employer's bureaucracy and excessive control and are tired of the perpetual distrust. Internally, they "resign" and no longer identify themselves with their work, let alone with their company. Only a person who is responsible and has the freedom to act independently will fully commit to a task, show initiative and do more than just working by the book.

There is supervision at every step: in production, the employees are supervised by punch-in clocks and with video cameras. On the upper floors, it is a bit more subtle: the distrust manifests itself in the rampant "meeting mania," in piles of reports, notes and memos (since it is better to have everything in writing), in completely over-the-top monitoring activities, waves of reports (with constant updates on the intranet), the ever-increasing flood of emails (because the boss wants to receive a copy of each of his employees' emails), and in the hypertrophy of measurement (if it can't be measured, it can't be managed).

Sprenger's analysis paints a devastating picture of German corporate culture: "Many companies are mere 'suspicion organizations.' Distrusting managers put out manuals of biblical thickness, defining even the smallest roles in the company. They do not believe that people want to do a good job. A deep insecurity transforms ostensibly rational executives into police forces, police managers who monitor 'control margins.' They have no faith in the self-imposed quality standards of their employees and are extremely cautious when it comes to employees finding their own ways of achieving the goal" (Sprenger 2002b, p. 22). Distrust is the rule, confidence the exception.

Many companies have locked themselves into an invisible high-security wing, where bureaucratic, rigid governance and an excess of policy guidelines preclude any entrepreneurship or innovation. The bars of this prison are false, outdated assumptions about business and human behavior.

2.3.3.2 Why Trust?

The old means of control, power and money, are no longer sufficient to coordinate the actions of knowledge workers in modern organizations and rapidly changing markets, continues Sprenger. Because everything depends on the cooperation of employees it cannot be controlled by the old measure of inspection. Here trust has to be added as a new means of control. "Trust is the key factor in successful management" (Sprenger 2002b, p. 25).

In today's world, trust has become the key basis of organizations. Globalization and information technology have produced serious changes in the economic system and the labor market: strategic alliances, outsourcing, agency agreements, new public management, internationalization, franchising, telecommuting, mobile working, network organizations and virtual enterprises have sparked a change from closed systems clearly isolated from their environment to open and flowing systems, systems that call for physical and mental mobility. "Blind" trust across thousands of miles, and extended towards people whom we've never met in our life makes this system work. "Trust allows coordinated action between partners who do not know each other. It is a substitute for knowledge of others and their motives" (Sprenger 2002b, p. 28).

The need for trust is steadily growing, while the traditional sources of trust fall by the wayside, as it can now develop on the basis of less and less familiarity. In the modern business world trust is no longer based on reputation, experience, and familiarity. This is the reason why trust is indispensable as an organizing principle. In today's markets, organizations have to be highly flexible and willing to change. In the process of transformation from rigid hierarchies towards flexible, customer-focused approaches, trust is essential. Empowerment, business process optimization, flat hierarchies, teamwork and learning organizations only work on a foundation of trust, according to Sprenger.

In most cases the employees know that change is necessary if their company wants to survive. However, they support the change process only if they trust that the changes take place not only to their disadvantage. The management has to convince them that it also has their interests in mind. But among employees there is encrusted black and white thinking that prevents them from having the necessary trust: socialist slogans of "the exploited down here" against "the capitalists at the top" do not help. The picture of executives that Sprenger presents in his books even exacerbates this, in my opinion.

Trust also facilitates the necessary reorganization of enterprises, since changes lead to uncertainty, fear and resistance in most people, according to Sprenger. But every organization needs to transform itself and adapt to the changing environmental conditions in order to survive. Only in a climate of trust and security can old routines and structures be dismantled in a short time frame. Only in such a climate can managers initiate a process of change that is supported by the employees on all levels from the start.

A leader who understands how to establish trusting relationships – not only internally but also externally – is of great advantage for an enterprise, as trust creates customer loyalty. "Confidence is the beginning of everything," as a bank advertisement claims, and customer loyalty is invaluable. Customer satisfaction increases when a company responds quickly to its customers' demands. This is only possible if there is a relationship of trust within the company itself and employees can decide spontaneously and independently without having to consult with three managers on whether the customer gets a discount. The costumer might already have turned to the competition before the manager has ever taken the time to read the request of the employee responsible for customer service. So trust can also give us a decisive lead.

Only in an environment of trust can information and knowledge flow freely. People who distrust their colleagues, superiors or subordinates, hide know-how in their desk drawer or in their own minds and do not share it with the organization. But innovation requires an unobstructed horizontal and vertical knowledge transfer, as well as taking risks and being able to accept mistakes. Ideas have to be openly expressed, have to be tried, to be accepted or rejected in an atmosphere of trust. "If you want creativity, you have to reduce the pressure of justification. Uncertainties must be accepted. Let go. Give up control" (Sprenger 2002b, p. 42). Therefore, in Sprenger's view there is no entrepreneurship without trust.

Distrust increases costs immensely and destroys values. The costs arising due to distrust are immeasurable in the truest sense of the word, such as the loss of missed opportunities, unmotivated staff, etc. Half of the total costs of most companies is caused by distrust, estimates Sprenger. An infallible indicator of this unfortunate development is if administrative costs increase faster than revenues.

Many of these expenses never arise if organizations do without all of those resources that they invest only as a safeguard against the dreaded "worst-case scenario":

The cost of the losses due to constant arrangements, negotiations and new agreements.
The cost of explicit contractual safeguards and monitoring activities.
The cost of the development, implementation and monitoring of monetary incentive strategies, with all of their disastrous side-effects.

2.3.3.3   Trust Motivates

Psychological and sociological studies show that human beings flourish under conditions of trust. One of these conditions is that the people – i.e., the employees – have degrees of latitude without supervision. These spaces generate interest and responsibility to support the commitment to the cause and to the company as well as the so-called "intrinsic motivation." And these spaces create individuality and originality. Without trust, Sprenger feels, there is no durable and resilient motivation. A business climate that is characterized by trust is a real competitive advantage in times of difficult employment situations for high-potential staff. Incidentally, I can confirm that from my own experiences.

There is no other choice for the executives than to trust these highly skilled and specialized knowledge workers, because they can no longer monitor them.

They lack the necessary technical and detailed knowledge, and often also the direct access, if the employees work in virtual teams several hundred or thousand kilometers away.

Again and again Sprenger has observed that managers, even though they violate classical textbook knowledge or make management mistakes, get good results and lead their company successfully, the reason being that their employees are willing to follow them because they trust them. This means that these managers are considered to be credible, predictable, straightforward and honest. Employees listen to the manager and believe him or her. "The substantive message is preceded by the trust message. As a filter, it decides whether the substantive message is heard at all, and even more so whether it is also believed" (Sprenger 2002b, p. 50).

If trust has been established, people are willing to follow a person and to believe in them, even if they do not always share their views. They forgive mistakes and accept inconvenient measures. Trust creates a robust position for the manager, because it requires the voluntary consent of the employees. If it is lacking, the entire relationship between boss and employees will be missing something: each well-intentioned act and positive intention will be suspected of being mere manipulation and therefore become ineffective, strategies and policies fail.

2.3.3.4   What Is Trust?

According to Sprenger, people depend on one another at an existential level. Thus, trust is a fundamental human experience beginning with the trust between children and parents. Our working lives involve another kind of trust: as a social convention of the society and as a choice. This kind of trust does not grow slowly on the basis of many positive experiences. It is given consciously and in awareness of the risk connected to doing so, and it must compensate for the impossibility of monitoring everything and counterbalance our lack of knowledge about the other person or the project. Sprenger defines trust as follows: "I am willing to refrain from monitoring someone else because I expect that the other person is competent, upright and has good intentions" (Sprenger 2002b, p. 66). Therefore trust enables us to act under the conditions involving cooperation and uncertainty.

Trust – just like knowledge – is a resource that is not reduced by frequent use but increases. The more trust is used, the more of it is created. This can be seen in companies with well-honed official procedures, the constant exchange of benefits, with expectations of the leaders that they make decisions, of the employees that they implement decisions, and of colleagues that they be cooperative. According to Sprenger, trust is an effective and indispensable means tool for organizations.

Sprenger feels that trust in itself is neither good nor bad; it is not a moral factor believing in the good in the individual. It arises from rational consideration and serves the reasonable principle of maximizing benefit: "We do not need to climb up on the high chair of morality. Trust as selfishness is a more effective and powerful strategy. (. . .) The smart egoist will always cooperate." Investing in trust pays off for the entire organization: companies that succeed in creating a culture of trust maximize their cooperation profits and reduce the costs of transactions. "Especially modern forms of organizations such as virtual companies and networks depend on the boosting of their own resources by cooperation across distances and time in order to be successful. Thus trust as principle of organization continues to gain importance" (Sprenger 2002b, p. 182).

2.3.3.5   Creating Trust

Creating a climate of trust is not only a question of controlled and conscious behavior. It is based more on the subconscious sending and receiving of signals that express "I trust you." These signals arise naturally from an emotional connection and affection and cannot be forced. Therefore, trust is never a question of mission statements or guidelines according to Sprenger. It cannot be created by propaganda. Advertising for trust usually results in the opposite – distrust. The request "Trust me!" is a manipulative communication technique and leaves behind feelings of guilt and shame when it fails.

Traits such as reliability, directness, fairness, loyalty, sincerity, honesty and credibility can only maintain trust, but cannot make it arise. Managers who constantly have to manage paradoxes cannot always be straightforward. The demand for "authenticity" is often used as an excuse for disrespectful behavior among the rougher executives.

There is only one way to establish a real culture of trust: as Sprenger rather abstractly puts it, it comes down to the actual behavior of the person setting values in cases of conflict. Or more simply put: "Actions speak louder than words." This active, direct approach creates a strong momentum that draws others in. Executives should place trust in their employees, because it is only in their actions that you can determine whether someone is truly ready for a trusting relationship.

2.3.3.6   The Implicit Contract

The first step towards greater trust is to conclude a "contract" between the giver and the receiver of trust. The trusting manager expects that employees use their discretion in the interest of cooperation and not in ways that will harm the leader. According to Sprenger leadership is therefore described as the "management of exchange relationships." Mutual expectations are exchanged: the organization offers learning opportunities, prestige and a good climate. In return, the employee offers his or her commitment, flexibility, willingness to learn and resilience.

Trust is therefore an implicit (because it is not written down) contract. The implicit contract between managers and employees is framed by explicit contracts. The explicit part of the employment is for example "money for working power," while an implicit aspect is "security for loyalty."

The manager starts the trust mechanism by actively making himself or herself vulnerable, for example by extending the contract, by letting go of explicit safeguards, doing away with progress reports and abolishing regulations: "Vulner-ability is the means to begin a trusting relationship. It is the amount you wager that you have to fear when giving trust. The bigger the potential loss, the greater your faith" (Sprenger 2002b, p. 100). This risk is accepted by those in your environment and accurately perceived and interpreted as a signal of trust.

The trust that the leader gives commits the partner, e.g. the employees. Trust creates a kind of claim. Niklas Luhmann has stated: "As with gifts, trust can be captivating." Trust is addictive and disarming until the person who receives it can give something back. Trust is a deposit on a relationship's account, an amount the other has to compensate for in order to get rid of the obligation, as Sprenger describes this psychological mechanism. I find this comparison extremely good. However, employees often try to escape the pressure of the commitment by favoring schematic exchange ratios such as "vacation against overtime."

Since 1954 McDonald's and Coca-Cola renew their cooperation every year with only a handshake and without long contract negotiations. The agreement that the Star Alliance cooperation is founded on consists of just four pages, regulating only the bare necessities. The partners make themselves vulnerable, and thus commit to each other to get repaid equally with trust.

In daily leadership there are many opportunities to actively make ourselves vulnerable, trusting that we will not to be taken advantage of by others:

Delegating a task to an employee without checking on them constantly

Refraining from declaring everything an executive matter in difficult situations

Not reserving the key market and customers for yourself, but letting others work on them

Sharing information that could be used against you

Holding an "election" and giving the employees the opportunity to choose another boss

In times when the growth of a company greatly depends on finding and keeping the right people and the competition for the best minds is heated, the employer is not automatically the donor of trust and employees are not necessarily the benefi-ciaries. Rather, the two sides of the relationship alternate. Nevertheless, it is upon the leader to take the first step and not to wait for others to do it. Being vulnerable is too difficult for many managers because they fear nothing as much as the supposed weakness and vulnerability. The way the leader approaches the organization deter-mines how the employees will react. This first step, this pre-investment without any guarantee of a return requires courage, self-esteem and empathy. But trust is a safe investment and pays off.

Trust is always based on responsibility. According to Drucker: "Trust does not mean that everyone likes each other. It only means that it is possible to trust each other, and this requires an understanding of each other. Therefore it is essential to take the complete responsibility for the relationship. This is an absolute must" (Drucker 1999, p. 260).

In order to move towards a culture of trust, mainly "trust in trust" is needed, i.e., the trust in the willingness of others to trust. Each stakeholder, no matter where they work in the corporate hierarchy, is at the same time a giver and receiver of trust. The willingness to trust also depends on the institutional framework, according to Sprenger. Managers should therefore ask: "Is trust a social norm in our company? What are the trust issues in our company/our department? What are the biggest obstacles to trust? Which of our rules are hindering trust? Are there too many rules?"

Another prerequisite for mutual trust is "self-trust" (self-confidence), as Sprenger describes it. In order to be successful, the leader must dare to go out on the open sea and lose sight of the safe shore for a moment. They must have inner serenity and the strength to endure the tension between expectation and the possible betrayal of trust. Timid managers try to control their environment; managers who consider themselves "enablers," however, know that people are cannot be controlled but can be influenced. Self-confidence is not a "Look out, here I come!" attitude, but instead calls for respect for other people and the calm and sovereign certainty to deal even with the unexpected, to survive even a breach of trust.

The courage needed to trust stems from this self-confidence, because trusting means daring. Leaders need courage to make themselves vulnerable, and they need courage to attend to conflicts in a timely manner rather than delaying dealing with them.

2.3.3.7   Trust's Greatest Enemy

To Sprenger the principle of competition, which is especially prevalent among men, is the greatest enemy of trust. Competition and struggles over rank prevent cooperation. Hierarchies and pecking orders can turn all the members of an organization into opponents in the struggle for higher positions, but competition is a zero-sum game: one person's gain is the other's loss. Each employee becomes his or her own profit center. So far this is understandable and logical. Yet Sprenger has also claimed that in flat hierarchies competition is even tougher, because the prospects are lower. In a flat hierarchy there are usually other symbols of success that are less concerned with status, power, etc., such as the recognition of a job well done.

In any case, the question remains: What can a manager do in order to promote cooperation and trust? It may be an awareness of common problems. What welds people together is the understanding of common problems and working together to solve them. This can be achieved only through cooperation. Here the problems that people are working on together have to be important and self-explanatory. "They must therefore succeed in making the company into a problem-solving community with the focus on shaping a common future" (Sprenger 2002b, p. 152).

2.3.3.8   When Trust Is Breached

Trust is fragile. You have to invest considerable time, effort and openness in order to create a trusting relationship with employees, superiors, customers and partners, but in an instant it can be destroyed by a deliberate or inconsiderate word or action. But here Sprenger calls for caution and for accurate differentiation: did the other party truly break the implicit contract of trust, or did they just fail to meet our (too high) expectations? Trust will also be broken if the other fails to comply with agreements without having made the attempt to renegotiate them.

Once it is too late and an employee has abused the trust of the leader, the latter must reflect on his or her own share of responsibility and on what the consequences could be. Sprenger emphasizes that, above all, managers shouldn't allow themselves to become frustrated, insecure, suspicious, and vindictive, starting a spiral of distrust.

When the supervisor for any reason starts monitoring all employees more closely, they feel the withdrawal of trust (for the most of them this is totally inexplicable) and no longer feel bound by the implicit contract. They reduce their commitment, motivation declines and the balance of trust is lost. This only confirms the suspicions of their superior, who responds by further tightening the controls. Not infrequently this spiral leads to a complete collapse of the relationship.

Distrust in relation to an individual might be legitimate and indeed protect you from harm; however, the reflexive generalization of mistrust is both unintelligent and counterproductive. In general, you should both trust and distrust only on an individual basis. Otherwise distrust will become a self-fulfilling prophecy. And: "With trust you can win or lose. With distrust you always lose" (Sprenger 2002b, p. 173).

But why do isolated breaches of trust lead so quickly to the rejection of the entire concept of trust? The reason, says Sprenger, lies in our skewed perceptions: the enormous gains made by well-placed trust in many successful collaborations are recorded without comment and taken for granted. Yet the loss created by the abuse of trust is felt immediately and intensely. After a theft nobody counts the things not stolen, but only the stolen ones. Therefore, it is extremely dangerous to introduce policies to prevent 5% of the people from doing something that the remaining 95% would never dream of doing. You won't succeed in catching the 5%, but you will succeed in hindering and demotivating all of your staff.

In the event of a breach of trust the leader must not simply look away because of some misguided tolerance or vain magnanimity. Anyone who does not act sends the message: it is perfectly fine to abuse my trust and has no consequences. Doing so destroys trust, as it must be clear: trust has its price. In keeping with the "ethics of the second chance," Reinhard Sprenger offers concrete advice on how to respond when the implicit contract of trust is broken. The rules are:

Cooperate! First always offer cooperation.
If cooperation is accepted, work to establish lasting trust. Otherwise punish immediately and without mercy!
After a certain time, make another offer of trust. But do not make a third.
Open confrontation creates trust and makes our behavior predictable. It is precisely how conflicts are handled that is the "glue" that keeps a company together, as Sprenger correctly observes (Fig. 2.8).

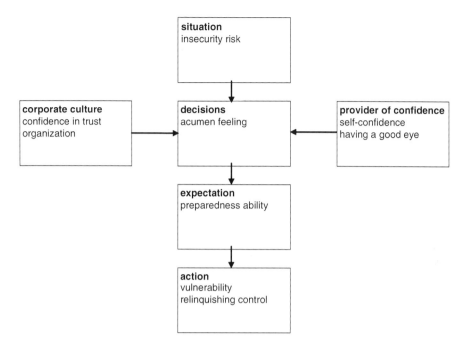

Fig. 2.8 How trust is created (*Source*: Sprenger 2002b)

2.3.3.9 Unlimited Trust?

The trust between managers and employees, between colleagues or between the company and the customer is a form of trust extended in advance, for a limited time, to one or more specific individuals and in relation to a particular task or action but not for life and not for all areas of life. Trust in Sprenger's sense is neither unlimited nor blind. "Trust is always better when it is limited" (Sprenger 2002b, p. 67).

Just as there is no freedom without boundaries, trust is also subject to conditions. These conditions are not automatically an expression of distrust, for Sprenger sees no contradiction between trust and distrust; it is more a continuum of more and less trust. Also trust and supervision are not opposites. Trust is not conceivable without supervision, which is essential to ensure that trust works. The greater the trust, the more supervision has an informative and supporting character, he says.

The emphasis on trust must not go so far that all barriers disappear and all control mechanisms, inquiries, and checks become taboo. It must not come to managers blindly handing over their decision-making power and losing their sense of responsibility – trusting blindly that everything is going well and the others know what they are doing.

Nor should it allow defensive leaders to rest on their trust or hide behind it in order to neither have to supervise nor act. Trust does not mean passivity and retreat.

"A modern trust involves choosing a mix between trust and distrust, between control and the surrender of control" (Sprenger 2002b, p. 77). Here Sprenger largely reverses his initial crusade against control – and with a somewhat succinct statement he gets to his point, namely that in reality trust is all a question of the right balance.

2.3.4 Personal Responsibility

In addition to overly controlling superiors who keep their employees on a short leash in order to motivate them, achieving just the opposite, there are managers who let go of responsibility and want to empower their employees. They ask the following questions: What can I do to make people take responsibility? How do I best use the potential of my staff? And how do I manage a company where the employees love to come to work in the morning? Reinhard K. Sprenger has also dealt with this issue and sought answers to these questions. I would like to include the core of his responses in this book, as they show how very good leadership depends on the relationship between the leader and the led.

"We are not a country rich in resources. Our main commodity is the willingness to join" (Sprenger 2002a, p. 11). We try to utilize machines to the fullest, but we do not use the same approach with people's capabilities. In addition to high labor costs and structural problems, it is the systematic under-challenging of employees that puts the German economy at risk, laments Sprenger.

Through decades of disenfranchisement, many people have lost the sense of responsibility for themselves, their motivation and their performance. If something is expected of them that does not match the exact wording of their job description, they respond as Pontius Pilate did, washing their hands of it. Who has not heard the words "I am not responsible" when they asked at the ticket counter why the Inter City Express train was delayed an hour? Or in a clothes store complaining about the poor quality of a piece of garment that after the first washing looked like it came from a second-hand shop? But this mentality is not limited to commerce or public service.

Games are won in the head. The harder the competition and the faster economic change, the more important employee attitudes and leadership behavior count. "There is no more important economic role than shaping the reestablishment of personal responsibility in a company" (Sprenger 2002a, p. 12).

2.3.4.1 Organized Irresponsibility

There are companies where the staff whines all day long. They are veritable victims' clubs. And nobody can do anything about it, no matter what. It is always the others who are to blame. Hardly anyone accepts full responsibility for their actions and performance. Each person sits in their limited workspace, in their "area" and performs only a clearly defined and demarcated set of activities, according to Sprenger. The reasons for this are easy to identify: division of labor, organizational fragmentation, hierarchical structures, large organizations and internationalization.

There is also a general confusion about what responsibility actually is. And this uncertainty is manifested in the behavior of all parties, ranging from accusation to compassion, indignation and guilty consciences. Responsibilities are confused, everybody has an opinion on everything and even the top management gets involved in the minor details. In the age of job rotation, no one feels responsible for the long-term consequences of decisions.

The standard case: the employees try to do everything right for their boss (and not the customers) or at least to behave in a way that does not get them in trouble. Fearing for their careers, they repeat what they hear and do not say what matters. And the bosses do not trust their employees and monitor them because after all it is their job to do so. Problems are systematically shifted from one level to the next, to "up there." Personal responsibility is lost in the wake of countless orders, directives and service regulations, and the internal entrepreneurship needed degenerates into a fight against regulations and policies.

But why is organized irresponsibility such an epidemic, as Sprenger has diagnosed? Because responsibility has two meanings: one is the responsibility of accountability, which is experienced as a burden and sounds like indictment if something goes wrong. The other is the positive interpretation of responsibility, which is accepted actively and provides employees opportunities to develop and to prove themselves. Unfortunately, in most companies the secondary responsibility of accountability overshadows the primary responsibility based on duties. As such, responsibility is something that nobody wants to have (see Sprenger 2002a, pp. 18–35).

2.3.4.2   Everyone Has a Choice

Nevertheless, everyone working at a company still has responsibility at different levels in different areas and in different functions. In practice the acceptance of a task is an irrevocable commitment to act and to be held accountable in case of negligence. This allows us to make the following definition of personal responsibility: "The everyday practical importance of personal responsibility simply means the willingness to exercise jurisdiction, even without an *a priori* clearly defined task responsibility" (Sprenger 2002a, p. 37). For Sprenger, personal responsibility means:

1. Autonomous and voluntary action, or *choosing*
2. Committed action based on personal initiative, or *wanting*, and
3. Creative action, or *responding*

Anyone who is aware that their work, their boss, the company they work for and their attitude towards their work is their own decision, no longer regards himself or herself as a victim or their work as a service. But there is a problem if people do not want to choose because they do not want to bear the consequences. They do not want to trade one option for another, because they want to have everything but pay for nothing. That is dissatisfactory and the employee does not feel free. And, as we all know, suffering is easier than acting. According to Sprenger, "True personal responsibility arises from a conscious choice. (...) Commitment means being aware of your freedom of choice and being aware that you are the one who has selected everything" (Sprenger 2002a, p. 63).

At this point, someone might argue that this is not only true for creative, challenging and varying activities. Also in jobs that seem to be boring and unimportant to most, there are always people who see the opportunities for action and development, for themselves to grow and enjoy their work – because they have chosen their work and internally say "yes" to it every day. That does not mean remaining at the status quo. The opposite is true: whoever chooses can also choose again, can decide otherwise, can change because they feel responsible for what bothers them, or what is not going well.

Anyone who deliberately chooses it has a different attitude towards their job, identifies with it and performs it with all their heart and full devotion. Even if the external circumstances cannot be changed, the attitude towards them can be, according to Sprenger. Each person decides for himself or herself whether or not to be angry and frustrated, whether they consider their colleagues annoying competitors or partners, whether a complaint is a mere annoyance or helpful feedback. Every situation is open to a variety of interpretations and defines the space for self-sufficiency of thoughts and actions.

There is no better motivation than passion, because work that we do not enjoy can make us sick. In this Sprenger – just as I do – contradicts Fredmund Malik, for whom the demand for fun at work is psychologizing nonsense. Sprenger asks: "Do you love what you do?" (Sprenger 2002a, p. 70). It is also crucial to realize that you do not work for the boss, not for the company and not for the family, but only for yourself. And Sprenger feels this is perfectly acceptable. He takes up the cudgels for ego and individualism, which must not be confused with social coldness. In fact, the moment you think you are doing something only for someone else, you deny your own responsibility.

2.3.4.3 The Responsibility of the Leader

The fewer leaders there are and the bigger the departments led the more it is necessary that the employees act responsibly. But unfortunately, many managers believe that it is their duty to tell their people what to do and not to do. What these managers call "duty" or "responsibilities" is for Sprenger nothing but a holdover from an outdated convention of superiority. This misconception of leadership results in docile and obedient employees who are never responsible, regardless of the subject.

Commitment cannot be created by structures, instructions or guidelines. It can only be made possible through leadership. And this requires a healthy, vibrant, open and trusting relationship with the employees because according to Sprenger "leadership is a relationship." Well put, but what does that really mean? How do you do it? Sprenger only offers one practical hint: "Maintain a warm social-emotional climate" (Sprenger 2002b, p. 164). Nothing could be easier, many might now be sardonically thinking to themselves. And: "Only someone who can smile should become a manager." Well, that sounds reasonable, but this surely can't be the only trait in the field of emotional intelligence that a good leader must have in order to manage relationships, can it? Of course not! In Chaps. 3 and 4, I will cover this topic in more detail.

For Sprenger a relationship, personal responsibility, creativity and motivation are only possible if the pyramid of the traditional corporate hierarchy is turned upside down and the leadership is behind or below the staff and supports it, rather than vice versa. This is an amusing idea, I think. According to Sprenger it is not only emotionally unintelligent but also economically misguided to keep employees on a short leash and to take all responsibility from them. Managers that make vassals of their employees prevent the company from benefiting from the latter's full potential and block the entrepreneurial thinking and action that companies desperately need today. They are wasting precious human capital.

Sprenger's call to the leaders is: "What we need is a framework of awareness that focuses on personal initiative. Does the employee develop his or her own ideas? Do they pick up on suggestions? Do they finish the tasks they start? Do they work independently? Do they wait in vain for tasks to be delegated to them or do they constantly look for tasks and goals themselves? Do they think about changes concerning their tasks? To what extent do they voluntarily gather necessary information? Do they remain on-task even in unusually stressful situations? (. . .) With staff who are always waiting for the bell signal like doormen, we will never master the competition of the future. So the key questions are: do you encourage initiative and courage? Or do you give instead communicate that just going by the book is rewarded?" (Sprenger 2002a, p. 83). If the latter is the case, the manager has done something wrong.

According to Sprenger, managers must not force their employees to adapt to universal standards, because the latter know best what high performance means in their specific job. Yet I find this recommendation problematic. And here Sprenger also contradicts himself. Concerning trust, he said that it is the task of leaders to agree upon goals, to monitor their achievement and to punish if they are not met (see Sect. 2.3.3.9). How can employees who are young, are new to the company or who do not know the international competitors and the market set their own performance standards? How can performance be appropriately rewarded this way? One of Sprenger's fundamental assumptions is that everyone has their own individual view of things, including their own performance. Therefore I think it is absolutely necessary that, in dialogue with their staff, leaders set mandatory guidelines and standards, which are of course in keeping with the performance capabilities and goals of the employees.

2.3.4.4 Enabling Personal Responsibility

It may occur that employees reject the freedom of choice and responsibility and avoid decision-making situations because they are not ready to pay the price of the possibility of failure. Rather they run to their boss and let them make the decision. Then it is upon the leader to refuse to make the decision and return it to the employees because otherwise he or she would be doing their job. The leader can and should support the employee in choosing by considering options and consequences together and by giving them courage to risk something, by taking away their fear of making mistakes and making it clear that they are capable of solving the problem. But he or she does not give advice (or only in exceptional cases), directions or protect the employee – this is personal responsibility.

Even if malevolent employees, colleagues or the manager's superiors accuse him or her of not providing forceful leadership in this situation: letting go is not faltering but a reliance on the personal responsibility of the employee. They alone are responsible for the job they took over. They must decide how it is done and what they need in order to do so. They must make decisions and bear the consequences. The manager must learn to resist the temptation to always play the heroic savior for his or her subordinates. To use Sprenger's metaphor, the manager can show them where the tongs and the gloves hang, but it is up to the employee to pull the coals out of the fire.

A manager must ask their employees to abandon their dependence. It is not the responsibility of the leader to know more than the staff or to have the answer to every problem. The superior's core duty is to invite employees to (re-) activate their independent abilities. Errors may and will happen. Without errors there can be no growth, and some of the greatest inventions have been "errors" or waste products. Executives must create a mistake-friendly climate and must not punish defeats but sympathetically consider them learning opportunities. The fear of making mistakes hampers problem-solving skills. Not the mistake is the problem, but the hiding of mistakes – which is also and especially true for leaders.

Motivation and commitment stem from the harmony between people who are doing something together, who are moving together towards a goal, and who see each other as cooperation partners. This relationship is destroyed by criticism. Criticism is destructive and harmful because it suggests that one knows the truth while the other is wrong. Criticism condemns and degrades others because it requires change from them, and because the way the person is, is considered wrong. Therefore, the person criticized will totally reject the criticism and by all means (at least inwardly) rebuild their own self-esteem by degrading the person who criticized them, shoving away their own responsibility in the process. With criticism, leaders only reinforce the behavior criticized.

Feedback on the other hand leaves the other person the choice of accepting what they hear. It provides them with information they previously did not have; it opens a different perspective that makes no claims to being perfectly correct. It thus reduces the "blind spot" in the self-image of the recipient and is an opportunity to learn.

If an employee's performance is permanently lacking, it may be due to one of the following reasons, in which case the leader should be held responsible (see Sprenger 2002a, pp. 180–208):

The manager has failed to establish a culture of feedback, so that problems are not openly discussed together, but instead are ignored until they can hardly be resolved.

The expectations and standards have not been discussed and agreed upon, as a result of which everyone only thinks they know what the other one wants, can and should do.

The employee is not sufficiently educated or trained for the job.

The employee is a notorious "slacker." The manager was mistaken to hire them, did not intervene early enough, or lacks the courage to lay them off.

Making personal responsibility the basis of the relationship between leader and led is an option that can be pursued at any time. The leader need only decide to do it – they must choose personal responsibility, concludes Sprenger.

By discussing the subjects of trust and responsibility we have now come close to the content of the fourth and last category of leadership approaches, which answer the question of what good leadership depends on by applying the question to the concrete leadership situation.

2.4   The Leadership Situation

Good leadership is always determined by the specific situation.

The *situationists*, as Kets de Vries calls them, do not consider leadership to be the product of certain traits of the leader, specific needs of the subordinates, or the right methods and tools, but of the relationships and patterns of activity of a group. This means that the leadership will change with the current situation. The person with the best solution to a problem or for the task at hand takes the leading position. Or, from a different perspective: a successful manager may adapt to the current situation and select the appropriate leadership style from their repertoire.

In combination with the persons involved, the situation is decisive in determining leadership behavior and the success or failure of the leader. This can also mean that a manager with optimal conditions and personality still might fail in a very specific culture or in a particular market. In brief: "Nobody is always and under all circumstances a good leader" (Sprenger 2004b).

2.4.1   The Parties

"The situation and the individual must fit" in order for leadership to work, writes Sprenger, a good introduction to this chapter. And further: "A good manager is a correctly deployed manager" (Sprenger 2004b). If they want to succeed, the leader must be accepted by their employees; otherwise it does not matter how many university degrees, certificates and references they have. Leadership must always happen in specific situations and relationships and must prove itself in a concrete company and a specific market.

2.4.1.1   Contingency Theory

According to Fred E. Fiedler's *contingency theory*, the distinction between task-oriented and person-oriented leadership according to the grid model by Blake and Mouton does not present a clear statement on the effectiveness of leadership. The interaction between leadership behavior and the leadership situation needs to be given much more weight. The current situation is characterized by three variables: the leader-led relationship, the task structure, and the positional power of the leader (cf. Fiedler 1967).

The leader-led relationship is dominated by the personality of the leader, their relationship to the group and by the trust and acceptance of the group, according to Fiedler. The structure of the task depends on the clarity of objectives, the number of possible solutions, the precision and verifiability of the solution. The positional power of the leader is characterized by the extent of exercised power that the organization allows. So the better the relationship of leader and led, the better structured the task and the stronger the formal power of the leader, the more effective the leadership situation is, i.e., the more likely it is that the manager is in a position to influence the behavior of the group.

The contingency model has greatly influenced the research of the past 20 years, especially in the field of executive development and training. However, I feel that its three variables do not suffice to meet the multitude of different leadership situations. Thus, for example, Fiedler neglects the relationships between the employees. In addition, in practice the variables are very closely linked and cannot be considered separately. Fiedler's contribution chiefly consists in the simple observation that there is no correct style of leadership. Rather, depending on the situation different styles of leadership will succeed, a view that has gained credence in recent leadership debates.

Looking slightly more into the detail of the leadership situation, leadership also depends on the task situation, i.e. the nature of the task, the required speed for problem-solving and the degree of certainty security of the task situation. For example, production is a certain situation: all the conditions are known; the risks are calculable and controllable. On the other hand, greater uncertainty prevails in sales, where the variables of customer behavior and demand are only partially predictable. Managers face the greatest uncertainty in the field of research and development, where neither the costs nor the benefits are truly predictable and risks lurk around every corner.

Paul Hersey, Kenneth H. Blanchard and Dewey E. Johnson (see Hersey et al. 1996) have noted a further influence of the leadership situation: the maturity of the employees. An employee's degree of maturity is characterized by their work-related maturity, that is, by their experience, expertise, knowledge of job requirements, etc. On the other hand, the employee is also shaped by their psychological maturity, e.g. their sense of responsibility, motivation, assertiveness, commitment, etc. Depending on the maturity of the employee, the leader chooses a more or less participative style of leadership.

2.4.1.2   Will or Skill?

A leader has to deal with different types of people. If a set of employees is segmented by the criteria will (their readiness to perform or will to perform) and skill (their capabilities and abilities), four types can be distinguished: the stars (high aims, high skill), the workhorses (high will, low skill), the unmotivated specialists – similar to the fairytale with the frogs that you must kiss to turn them into princes (low will, high skill), and the problem cases (low will, low skill) (Fig. 2.9).

This matrix provides basic criteria to get an idea of your own staff or team. However, such classifications should not be exaggerated or used as absolutes, as they are somewhat generalizing and at times a bit cynical. The matrix can be a "crutch" for the leader to start assessing employees: "Every employee is an individual and wants to be seen as such."

Managers have to deal with the four types of employees in different ways: the stars need to be motivated and retained. You should give them freedom and prospects and offer them many challenging tasks to delegate. The workhorses can grow based on a clear evaluation of their potential. Here delegation should be done

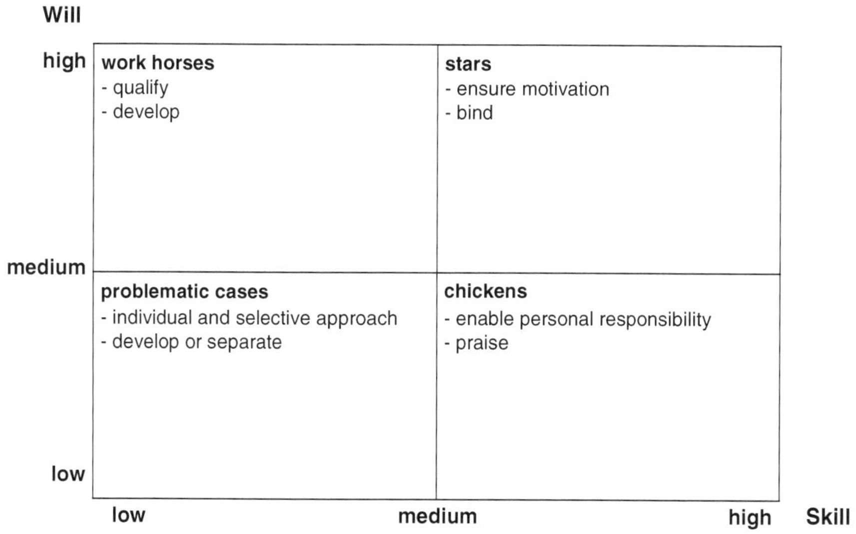

Will

high	**work horses** - qualify - develop	**stars** - ensure motivation - bind
medium		
	problematic cases - individual and selective approach - develop or separate	**chickens** - enable personal responsibility - praise
low	low medium high	**Skill**

Fig. 2.9 Will-skill matrix (*Source*: The author, on the basis of various management approaches)

cautiously, following the principle "a little more every day." Through feedback and coaching they can evolve constantly. The frogs should be considered by the leader in more detail: what are the causes for the lack of will? Do I correctly assess them? Are there differences between their self-image and external image? At the end a conflict, talk cannot be avoided. It has to result in a clear agreement on the need for change. The problem cases should not be ignored by a leader – which is unfortunately what happens time and again. Either the employee can still develop or a parting of ways is inevitable. The leader should engage in focused change discussions with these inefficient employees.

A further distinction can be illustrated by the experience and seniority of employees: am I dealing with an old pro or with a beginner? The old pro needs e. g. to be treated with respect, while the young employee wants someone to look up to and learn from. Moreover, we know that in a group of analysts, implementers, team players and other types there are complementary expectations, interests and roles. Thus the analyst prefers facts and figures and a factual, concise discussion of leadership. The implementer does not want to just talk but act, and feels most talking about results. And the team player mainly wants to cooperate in harmony with others. Here, the executive must make people the heart of the talks.

Our journey has now led us to the point at which we need to examine some representatives of leadership teaching, to define the factors of good leadership that are outside of the leadership process but affect it – the organization and the environment. Leadership is thus a response to conditions inside and outside the company.

2.4.2 The Organizational Structure

Organizational structures provide the framework in which leadership takes place. They are therefore a crucial variable in the leadership process. The dilemma is that the manager must remain within the formal and legitimated framework of the company's structures: their duties, powers and responsibilities are defined and limited. However, they must also change existing structures (and the dominant culture) in order to enable and encourage change processes. The first principle for any organization is "structure follows strategy"; the company's structure is both a means of achieving and product of its strategy.

The organizational structure consists of division of labor, including the distribution of duties, the communication structure and the power structure, including the formal management hierarchy. The communication and the power structure are determined by the structure of the division of labor, but also have an effect on it. The distribution of duties relies on hierarchical relationships and subordination, and influences the ability of individuals to lead or be led.

The division of labor also leads to the development of certain role expectations of managers and subordinates concerning their own function and the function of other members of the organization. The more complex and more specialized an organization is, the greater the potential for tensions and conflicts. Here good leadership is called for.

The communication structure is reflected in both planned and unplanned information relations. The information of each individual and their ability to get information and to share it depends on their position within the communication structure. Due to the great importance of information for the leadership, this structure has a particularly strong influence on the management processes in a company.

The formal power structure clearly defines the subordination relationships between the individual and other members of the organization and therefore determines who has legitimate claims to manage. Yet there is also informal power that is beyond the visible hierarchy in every company. We all know the multipliers and influences of power. Whether it is the personal assistant or veteran project manager – they are all listened to by the truly influential people. Even though they have no formal power, they wield considerable influence and usually have high social intelligence even without leadership positions.

In short this means: the type of leadership also depends on the shape and complexity of the present or desired organizational structure. This structure can be used with the help of five dimensions, which are: specialization, standardization, formalization, centralization, and configuration (see Heinen 1998, p. 171 ff.). In addition, a distinction is often made between the operational and organizational structure, i.e., between the organizational chart of reporting lines on the one hand and the numerous processes of the company on the other.

The observable developmental trends from employee to co-entrepreneurs, and from steered authoritarian and hierarchically organized companies towards participatory firms in a rapidly and radically changing environment have forced a softening of rigid structures. There is no perfect organization, but instead many organizational forms are ideal for their specific purposes (see Drucker 2000).

There are already several prototypes of new organizational forms that take into account this paradigm shift in the economy and employment: the project organization, which is staffed by steering committees, project managers and multi-departmental working groups and is shaped by the principles of project management; the "network" organization, in which autonomous possessors of know-how are connected only by common objectives, a high degree of trust and modern communication technologies; and the "virtual" company, the components of which are loosely connected together, coming closer if required. There is also the concept of the "primordial soup," in which spontaneous new combinations and structures are established, or the "amoeba organization," which is constantly dividing. Virgin, Goldman Sachs and Southwest Airlines are American examples of these new forms of structuring. Their survival principle is "be quick or be dead," and they are characterized by flat hierarchies and organic structures, making them extremely flexible and action-oriented (see de Vries 2002, p. 51).

Christopher A. Bartlett and Sumantra Ghoshal do not consider the present or future central task of leadership to be forcing people into the corset of organizational structures, but creating a flexible organization that promotes the staff's resources, puts them to the best possible use, and values the person as a whole: "We must no longer consider a company a hierarchical pyramid with the value-creating process divided into leadership and organization, but as a house with a horizontal value creation processes and a roof, which gives strategic direction and objectives with a flat hierarchy and a central nervous system, information system and communication system" (Bartlett and Ghoshal 2000, p. 112).

For example, Hans-Jörg Bullinger, President of the Fraunhofer Society, sees a cause for the continuing decline of the German economy in companies being the way they are: "I believe that many companies are still depending on organizational leadership structures from the industrial age. At that time, work was divided in small steps and then put together. For the creative service society of today, but also in the innovative product area, we have to work with much freer working methods in order to develop innovative technologies. For example in the development department of BMW there are no defined working hours; only the result counts" (Forum, 02/2004, p. 13).

In his book "Management Challenges for the Twenty-First Century" Peter F. Drucker claimed: "Forms of organization must be equipment in the tool box of the leader" (Drucker 1999, p. 28). Various forms of organization must be analyzed for their strengths and weaknesses in dealing with a given situation. "It is not about finding a unique form of organization, but about finding, developing and verifying a form of organization that is designed to fit the task to be achieved" (Drucker 1999, p. 32).

The objectives of an organization – whether a company or public administration – decides the strategy and the strategy decides the structure (see Drucker 2004, p. 97). It is also Drucker's opinion that the ideal form of organization does not exist. Organization is merely a "tool, which enables people to cooperate in a productive way" (Drucker 2004, p. 98). The task of leadership is not to find the proper organizational structure, but to find the "appropriate organization for the given task" and to constantly optimize it. Sometimes it takes a strictly functional organization with a clear specialization, sometimes decentralization is useful and sometimes teamwork is required.

Drucker also cited more universal organizational principles: first, the organization itself has to be transparent. People have to know and understand the structures in which they work. In addition, the authority has to take responsibility. The captain must be authorized to decide on behalf of all. Drucker also considered it important that all members of an organization have only one supervisor. No one should experience conflicts of loyalty and no one should serve more than one "master." Drucker was quite skeptical about modern cross-departmental teams that have to report to multiple managers; he would most likely have felt similarly about matrix organizations.

According to Drucker the role of companies is dominated by four aspects: firstly, a company creates resources, which means it transforms costs into energy. Secondly, it represents a link in an economic chain, which has to be considered to be a unit. Thirdly, it is a social institution designed to produce wealth. And fourthly, it both forms a physical environment and is at the same time a product of that environment.

2.4.2.1   Flexible, But Not Chaotic

The opposite of rigid structures is not creative chaos. This point is very important to me. My work as a manager and as a management trainer have showed me time and again the importance and benefits of structures and generally recognized rules, especially in situations of change. They enable a manager to delegate tasks and responsibilities, to give the employees more freedom and to maintain at the same time the company's effectiveness and productivity.

Drucker too saw the need for this: in a dangerous situation the survival of everyone involved depends on "a clear chain of command." There must be a "boss" making the final decisions. If a ship is in danger of sinking the captain does not call a meeting but gives a command. Of course, we as modern managers tend to respond negatively to the term "command," but Drucker showed that there may be situations in which participation and empowerment of employees is (and has to be) subject to clear limits (see Drucker 2004, p. 98 ff.). But Drucker also maintained that a flat hierarchy, where the number of decision-making levels is limited to a minimum, is a good structural principle.

Structures and rules ensure that quality standards and good practices are used regularly, without their having to be reinvented them each time and by each individual. Structures are not inherently contrary to change and innovation. The opposite is the case: they can ensure that information is conveyed more quickly, that processes are set in motion sooner, and that ideas are better implemented.

But structures – and this is the minimum requirement – have to be reflected upon and above all they have to be "lived out": federalized structures and principles have to replace hierarchies. A structure of related departments has to be transformed to an alliance of independent power bases, with decentralized communication and coordination institutions and their own governing bodies. The culture and structure have to support creativity and innovation. Companies need flexible structures that promote cooperation, that connect people and help them to see and act beyond the boundaries of their tasks. There has to be an emotional climate that embraces creativity, innovation and change (see Kanter 1998, pp. 74–119). People are no longer perceived as "organizational people," as small cogs in the huge gear works, but instead flexible organizations that utilize the knowledge and resources of the staff must be created (cf. Bartlett and Ghoshal 2000, p. 19). The organization needs to be (re-) created around the people. Admittedly, this is easier said than done – but I mention this point because it still has not been sufficiently embraced by managers in my own experience.

In addition, organizations must be designed in order to not only best achieve their designated objectives best, but such that bad, incompetent managers can do only minimal damage and are quickly discovered and replaced (see Malik 2001, p. 45). Each organization must have mechanisms and structures that monitor the people in power and constantly check their performance. Management floors cannot be ivory towers, because managers need feedback in order to continually improve themselves. Power must not be isolated and must always remain in the service of the organization – not in the service of the leader.

2.4.3 The Corporate Culture

Leadership does not take place in a vacuum. Rather it should always depend on the values, the attitudes and the mindsets of the organization's members. These are formed by individual socialization and experiences, the culture of our environment and by the spirit or culture of the organization itself. Management is always anchored deeply in the culture. If a leader requests something from their employees that they are not used to as part of their culture, that leader will fail. Similarly, economic changes in a society will only be successful if the corresponding change in culture has taken place beforehand (see Drucker 2002).

A leader has to be sensitive to the cultural reality of the organization and the society. They have to be aware of the perhaps implicit rules of the system, which values are lived out, and what social context the system is implemented in. This is especially important for working abroad. The leader has to acknowledge the culture at hand and its opportunities, even and especially if he or she wants to change it.

Two approaches of leadership theory deal with the cultural factor: corporate management and the theory of open systems. Corporate management investigates structures and processes of leadership in different cultures of the world and examines the differences and similarities. The theory of open systems deals with the question of how influences develop in organizations that determine the perceptions and actions of the organizations' members.

Also research results of neighboring disciplines show the effects of the cultural environment, organizational environment and possible subcultures within the organization on leadership behavior and the success of leadership. Different cultures determine different roles for the individual in a social system. They rely on different elements of motivation. They lead to different structures of power and control. And they produce different control systems shaping behavior. Conversely, the style of leadership influences the culture of the organization. Therefore a strong interaction exists between the philosophy of leadership and the culture of the organization, where each can be both cause and effect (see Heinen 1998, p. 174).

As mentioned in Sect. 1.1.5, the environment plays an important part in the certainty or uncertainty of completing a task, and is an important factor shaping the leadership situation. "Just as people uphold certain values, organizations also have values of their own. The values of the individual must harmonize with those of the organization – otherwise they cannot work efficiently" (Drucker 1999a, p. 14).

Thus, corporate culture and leadership culture are closely connected and mutually dependent. The good leader is part of the corporate culture but also shapes it with his or her values, conduct, communication and the rules he or she establishes.

At the same time, the personality of the leader should personify the corporate culture and live it out every day. All of their actions should follow the basic rules of the organization and provide benchmarks for everyone else – but without becoming rigid laws.

A good culture of leadership can be established through good networks of relationship, the development of existing potentials of leadership, by offering values, goals and challenges, but also through decentralization. Successful corporations such as 3M, Hewlett Packard and General Electric have succeeded in establishing unmistakable, respected, productive and innovative cultures of leadership as part of their organizational cultures. "The solid foundation of corporate culture in alignment with true leadership is the highest the art of leadership can achieve" (Kotter 1999b, p. 66). If the power is in one set of hands, there is a strong connection between the leader's personality, the style of leadership and the corporate culture – all three of them shaped by the social environment.

Let us now move from the micro-level to the macro-level. Not only the corporate culture plays a part, but also the culture of the society and the nation. It shapes the personalities of (future) leaders and the expectations of the subordinates. For example, a leader in the US is a successful man or woman of action who is admired by others. Yet such a cult of personality is frowned upon in the Netherlands. There the manager is seen as more of a martyr sacrificing himself or herself for the company. French leaders lead differently than for example German leaders; the former are more network-oriented and person-oriented. "Factors such as power, status and hierarchy play different roles, also control and authority are considered differently by leaders of different cultures" (de Vries 2004, p. 65).

Especially upon the backdrop of globalization, the organizational culture receives a connecting, border-crossing function. Or, as Rosabeth Moss Kanter has put it: "Common procedures and a common language help people of a different background or from different countries to work together efficiently" (Kanter 1998, p. 25). At the same time the management has to integrate its concepts and methods into the context of the given national culture (see Drucker 2000).

I would like to only briefly mention the theories of substitution. They shift the focus away from the direct, interactive influence of the leader towards the indirect and structural effects of guidelines, structures, systems and strategies on the leadership process. The practical benefit of these theories is rather limited (Heinen 1998, p. 171 ff.).

A good overview of the most important organizational influences (including corporate culture) can be obtained by using the 7-S model developed in the early 1980s. (see Peters/Waterman 1982). This model identifies seven factors of success for an enterprise: firstly the strategy, secondly the structure of the organization, thirdly the systems of management, fourthly the style of leadership, fifthly the staff, sixthly the technical and social skills and finally the shared values.

This model makes it clear that all factors of success need to be considered simultaneously. No single factor must be stressed, because they all interact. The 7-S model can be an effective tool for understanding a given organization. It is important to consider that each organization has to find its own way, both with

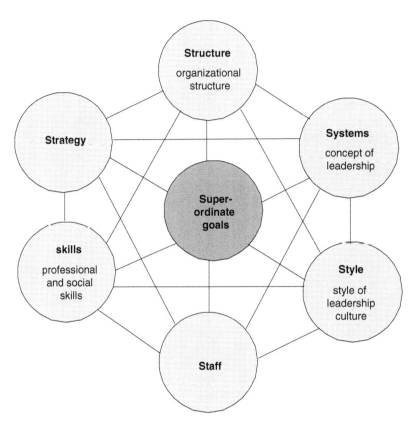

Fig. 2.10 The 7-S model (*Source*: Peters and Robert 1982)

regard to the interaction of the forces at work in it and especially with regard to leadership (Fig. 2.10).

2.5   Conclusion: The Power of Soft Factors

The different approaches presented above all have their value, as most of them provide practical benefits for leadership. However, they are mostly limited to a single aspect and neglect other important factors. Leadership is neither only a question of the leader's personality nor of his or her skills; likewise, it does not solely consist in the leadership situation or focus on the subordinates. Leadership takes place in the intersection of all these factors. The truth is – as always – in between.

In the next step, the four factors – though their number can be increased or decreased arbitrarily – can be combined into two categories: "hard" and "soft" factors. The "hard" factors are tangible and can be measured. These are structures, market and environment conditions, leadership situations and processes. The "soft" factors are relationships, emotions, motivations and expectations, none of which can be easily calculated or determined.

The attention paid by most companies to the "hard" and "soft" factors of good leadership by no means reflects their real meaning. Comparing the influences to an iceberg, the visible hard factors make up the 15% above the surface. The remaining 85% of soft factors are hidden below it. (More about the iceberg model in Chap. 3.) Money, time and energy are mostly invested in order to adjust the visible and measurable factors of success. Such diffuse dimensions as emotions, ethics, motivations and relationships are not easily calculated. However, today's leaders have skillfully manage precisely this kind of capital. They have to recognize the resource potentials of their employees, cultivate and foster them if they want to thrive in the face of competition and want to do more than just "a good job."

Chapter 3
Systemic Leadership or: Designing a World That Others Want to Be Part Of

One must love what he does, then every kind of work, even the roughest, turns into a creation

Voltaire

3.1 Considering the Whole

The answer to the challenges of the developments in the twenty-first century is systemic leadership. Systemic leadership based on person-related development and change is an approach in the conflict field between the requirements of globalization, networking, speed, knowledge management and the individuality or – put a bit more dramatically – the egomania of the individual leader.

The systemic perspective is open to relationships, communication, change and the environment. It leaves room for personal growth, entrepreneurship, responsibility and trust. Systemic leadership allows decisions to be made by networking as needed under the complex, dynamic and critical conditions of today's world. Systemic leadership means individual leadership, having a flexible, personal style and being able to always adapt that style to the organization and the people of the current leadership situation rather than working with schematic standard tools.

The term "systemic" is open to interpretation. Everything and everyone claims to be working in a systematic or systemic way. However, no one can really explain what systemic means. Apart from the systems theory in social sciences, in terms of leadership "systemic" simply means thinking in contexts. Moreover it means considering without judging. Working systemically means asking questions instead of having ready answers. What is this good for? What lies behind it? What is its purpose? What depends on it? On which levels do specific processes and actions take place? Which connections are there?

The systemic view expands the focus from the person or the problem to the complete web of contexts. It does not focus on single parameters but more on what happens between them and the actors. By posing focused and systemic questions

D.F. Pinnow, *Leadership - What Really Matters*, Management for Professionals, DOI 10.1007/978-3-642-20247-6_3, © Springer-Verlag Berlin Heidelberg 2011 and listening carefully to the answers, the inner "map" of a person or an entire organization can be "read." In addition to asking and listening, observing is also a prerequisite for any systemic behavior. It is crucial to observe how others see things – and what they fail to see.

3.1.1   The Titanic Problem

Systemic leadership sees the whole issue, including aspects that are not immediately apparent. Other approaches consider only the obvious, measurable processes, problems and results following the simplified principle of cause and effect. They assume that human behavior and decisions are mainly conscious and rational and can be controlled. In these approaches the success of business and leadership depends on facts, structures, job descriptions, mastering the management tools, goals, strategies and corporate policy (Fig. 3.1).

By doing so they see only a small part of reality. An organization is more like an iceberg. What you see above the surface is only the smaller part of the whole; the majority lies under the surface. There mighty forces are working which must not be underestimated. They determine the direction of the iceberg. They are unconscious, irrational and informal and include structures of power and influence, as well as group dynamics, emotions, relationships, individual needs, convictions,

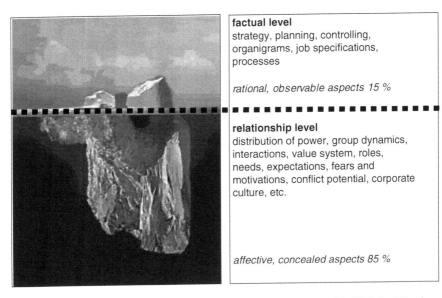

factual level
strategy, planning, controlling, organigrams, job specifications, processes

rational, observable aspects 15 %

relationship level
distribution of power, group dynamics, interactions, value system, roles, needs, expectations, fears and motivations, conflict potential, corporate culture, etc.

affective, concealed aspects 85 %

Fig. 3.1   The iceberg model (*Source*: Pinnow Daniel F., Management Guide 2001, *Bad Harzburg* 9/2000)

values and cultures. Failing to see this hidden part and underestimating its size and shape can cause leaders to fail, despite all of their technical skills.

3.1.2   The Leader as Part of the System

According to systems theory, leaders are observers. They construct their reality from what they see. An "objective," measurable and invariable reality does not exist according to systems theory (see Neuberger 2002, pp. 593–641). There are only individual concepts and perceptions of reality. Thus, leaders observe – ideally themselves first and then the system that they are part of. Leaders have to realize that they not only work "within the system" but also "on the system." That means they must leave their comfort zone in order to be able consider the system with all of its advantages and disadvantages from the outside and to change it if need be.

According to Niklas Luhmann, former professor of Sociology in Bielefeld, Germany a business organization is a closed system of individual parts that is distinguished from its environment by its borders. These borders are at the same time the basis for the system's identity. The fundamental cornerstone of the system is communication. Relationships between the parts of the system are formed and sustained by communication. A system is not directly controllable from the outside. Instead it processes inputs using its own laws, it is self-organizing (autopoietic) and adapts independently to changes in the external environment by processing the corresponding signals from the outside:

> A social system comes into existence if an autopoietic communication connection develops and delimits itself from the environment by constraints of communication. Social systems therefore do not consist of individuals nor of actions but of communication. (Luhmann 1984, p. 269)

This last sentence is only of theoretical value and does not help us with practical leadership, because there we indeed deal with both individuals and actions. The point I want to make here is instead the importance of communication for the system and for systemic leadership. In my work with leaders, especially in this point I repeatedly find major shortcomings regarding structures and forms of communication within the organization as well as the individual readiness and ability to communicate. Communication is more than distributing information in memos or company magazines. Communication is also more than giving orders. Communication is interaction, is listening and speaking and comprehending – in exactly this order.

Concerning this problem the communication researcher Friedmann Schulz von Thun talks of the four sides of a message (see Schwarz 2005). Besides the already known aspects of contents and relationship, Schulz von Thun added the points of self-revelation and appeal. What is his point? That every communicating individual reveals a part of himself or herself. And moreover every statement contains an appeal to the receiver. In order to decode this information, leaders have to be able to read between the lines.

Thus, if a leader talks about a situation or an employee he is at the same time also talking about himself and to himself, because he, being a part of the system, is limited by the individual perspective as an observer with his own scheme of perception and his own mechanisms of selection. He is never an uninvolved outsider and therefore his perception always has a blind spot. What a leader sees and how he reacts reveals how he organizes his own reality. Instruments such as feedback, coaching, supervision and interviews help to make this blind spot visible.

Often leaders perceive the exact opposite of what their employees see. The US management consultancy Clarke and Crossland presented a drastic example: 90% of all leaders think that they are quite capable of communicating visions and contents, while only 30% of all employees share that view (see Clarke and Crossland 2003).

Applied to a business organization, the principle of autopoiesis (the self-creation and self-conservation of systems) means that the long-term success of that organization does not depend on a single leader but on the systemic forces that influence the survival of the organization, enable decisions and convey knowledge, independently of individuals.

In short: the best boss is the one who makes himself or herself superfluous.

The systemic point of view does not claim to be the only one in the world that sees the "true nature" of things and to be able to determine what the "whole" looks like. Instead, it establishes relations between the individual parts forming the entire picture. It questions the factual relations: which decisions and effects stand in relation to one another? What can be delimited from each other? Moreover it deals with social connections: in which network is the social actor embedded? How does another person see the situation? And finally it deals with the relation in time: What is the history of an event and what will be the consequences? Instead of simple causes, the systemic thinker looks for patterns and processes.

These three dimensions of relationships give the leader opportunities for indirect control. Systemic leadership does not come from above but starts from below – or, better said, from the inside. That leads us to another important feature of the systemic approach – namely the attitude towards change: change is the norm. Circumstances or events are only snapshots of processes. Order and stability constantly re-emerge from variations and fluctuations. Structures and relationships, too, change constantly, and not in causal, linear and evolutionary but in grid-like, circular and complex patterns.

Therefore it is necessary to establish some stability by organizing through structures, loose coupling, programs and rules, in order to avoid every action resulting in a flood of unmanageable reactions throughout the entire system. Systemic leadership does not mean that we just let happen what cannot be controlled anyway, but that we control what can be controlled. Systemic leadership also means giving the system rules and limits, and initiating changes, indirectly but purposefully.

3.1.3 Stimulating Instead of Giving Orders

The goal is to not interfere with existing systems but to stimulate them in order to improve them and therefore initiate sustained and lasting change. According to the theory of self-sustained systems (autopoiesis), which is the basis for systems theory, it is impossible to change the systemic patterns of interaction and the laws behind from the outside, because these patterns and laws were developed by the system in order to sustain itself. A system exists only in a floating balance; halt and paralysis will cause it to collapse.

Systemic leaders utilize and strengthen the potential for self-development within an organization. This potential is relevant for survival in a permanently changing environment. The knowledge needed for change exists in any company; it has only to be activated by networking with the relevant people, introducing new points of view, maintaining communication and providing the information the system does not have yet. Only in this way can the knowledge distributed to many people be united and made utilizable for the entire company.

The system, which is to say the group, the department or the company will decide for itself how to respond to this stimulation. Nothing is forced or ordered. A person truly working systemically does not whip out their toolbox, turn a few screws and the problem is solved. The harmful side-effects of such procedures – such as employees sabotaging the measures or managers implementing them far too quickly – are considerable, and the benefit is small. The existing system needs to be appreciated and integrated into the change process.

It is characteristic of systemic leadership that the leader thinks strategically, goal-oriented, in broader contexts and in long-term patterns. In a constructive mind problems and disturbances are welcomed because they initiate change and progress. They force the system to stay flexible and to keep learning. Systemic managers think in both ways, analytically and synthetically. Analysis provides the knowledge of the parts of the system, while synthesis provides the knowledge of their roles in the system.

Systemic organizational development does not happen in the ivory tower of the executive level and behind closed doors. Instead it takes place in the daily routine with the active participation of key personnel at all levels of the company. It is always oriented on the people and the culture of the organization. It takes into account the uniqueness and complexity of the company and is understood as a continuous process.

The basis for systemic leadership is networked thinking that moves in cycles, as in complex systems there is never only *one* cause for a specific type of behavior or a specific situation. Everything is connected and needs to be considered. Changes starting in one part of the system will lead to changes in other parts and therefore often end up affecting themselves. This also means that the leader has to give the change process time to show effects and does not expect that after pressing a button everything and everyone reacts as expected or, if not, will be "brought in line."

The points of departure are "dynamics," which, as the sociologist Niklas Luhmann determined, arise from interactions, actions, decisions and communications. These determine the essence of the organization. Organizations function and sustain themselves by connecting decisions to previous decisions. The people are quasi coupled to these dynamics. The "hands-on" type of leader, who thinks they have access to their subordinates and can dictate what they have to do, is outdated. The systemic leader leads by communication and by means of a densely interwoven information network. To change the behavior of their employees, the systemic leader changes his or her own behavior first.

3.1.4 Learning Instead of Steering

Moreover, systemic leadership assumes vagueness and uncertainty as inherent to complex systems. Complex systems organize and develop themselves, making 100% reliable predictions impossible. In addition to the desired effect, every influence has uncountable and unpredictable side-effects because all parts of the system are connected.

Therefore, good intuition and a certain willingness to take risks are important qualities of the systemic leader. He or she develops solutions based on the inherent dynamics and properties of the system rather than using ready-made standard solutions. Leadership and system autonomy are in harmony if the leader merely establishes and monitors the conditions for action and provides the information and authority for self-control to the people he or she leads.

This includes the leader supports the capability of the system, i.e., the company and its employees, to learn and develop, just as it involves the leader continuing to learn himself or herself and always critically questioning their own style of structuring and steering. The ability to learn also includes the ability to unlearn, to give up outdated patterns of behavior and to leave known structures behind. In this regard, flexibility is essential (see Probst and Gomez 1991).

In this context, development does not mean revolution but learning. All members of an organization have to constantly learn. Lifelong learning is one of the central success strategies in the knowledge society. A systemic thinking leader stimulates others to learn and gives them opportunities to acquire new knowledge. At the same time he or she is in a constant process of learning, always asks for feedback and is open to other perspectives and ideas.

3.2 Leading with Your Head and Heart

The late strategy guru Sumantra Ghoshal forecasted the end of the capital-oriented philosophy of management. In the last 50 years the scarce resource of capital was considered the flywheel of the economy, and money was the lever to be used to the advantage of the company. This traditional conception is about to vanish.

Today financial capital is no longer in short supply. The actual bottleneck is related to ideas, knowledge, entrepreneurship and human capital. And this strategic resource will become even scarcer in the next 50 years. It is the people that provide the biggest gain in value for the company, which means employees, who have primarily been considered cost factors, now become investors.

In addition to intellectual capital people contribute two more key factors that will be crucial in the competition between companies in the future: social capital, i.e., the ability to form long-term relationships with others based on trust and reciprocity, and what Ghoshal referred to as emotional capital, the power to turn ideas into actions. Intelligence and knowledge, the building and maintaining of relationships and true drive to act – these are the new important elements that leaders need to understand and master according to Ghoshal (see Ghoshal 2004).

The market value of a company depends on its employees: in German management theory and practice it is commonly accepted that companies can only be as good as their employees. In the year 2005 leadership was defined as the ability to find, to guide, to motivate, and to keep employees. The basis of successful leadership is sensitivity to and for people, situations and processes between the lines. "Leading by giving orders – even if they are given politely – and monitoring procedures and result has become a thing of the past" (Rosential 2003). Emotions are not only allowed, but are necessary for effective leadership. Apodictic management tools following the "is X, then Y" approach are less important and often do more harm than good.

The term "internal relationship management" describes the effort of a leader to use the interpersonal structures of an organization to achieve its goals and optimize its structures. Hence, interpersonal matters are discussed: communication, team leading, project management, moderation, feedback, and coaching. That covers the theory. But what does this look liken in practice?

A survey conducted by the Academy in 2001 underlines the change of paradigms in the self-understanding of managers but at the same time indicates the gap between requirements and reality: only one third of the managers interviewed were happy with the management of relationships within their companies. Nearly half claimed they spent less than 3 h a week on building relationships with their employees. Many spent most of their time travelling. But leaders need to use every minute they can to be close to costumers, products, and markets. Accordingly less time is left for leading teams, training new employees and giving feedback.

Despite these constraints it can also be assumed that many of the respondents simply wanted to meet social expectations by claiming they simply had "no time." Lack of time is still seen as a status symbol of successful people, as an expression of vigor and creativity – and not as proof of poor time management. This is especially true for male leaders. Women in leading positions rely much more on teamwork than men in order to meet the company's goals. They also count much more on the positive transformation of conflict energy than do males.

The more people who work at an organization and who have responsibility for each other, the more important interpersonal communication becomes. Cooperative relations between all levels, connecting cultures and interests are needed. Beyond all sentimentalism and all superficial claims that "we all love each other," emotions, expectations, fears and taboos need to be communicated clearly. As such, I feel relationship management is the highest art in cooperative leadership.

This makes it all the more a pity that this strategic discipline in companies of all sizes too often devolves into "management by firefighters." It is often only after finding an important employee's written resignation on their desk that managers appreciate (too late) the value of management and marketing of human resources. In a certain respect the best employees are identical to the company's best customers: the loyalty of both groups is driven by their personal ambitions and standards. Only the honest and consistent management of relationships and values enables leaders to make full use of employees' potential.

Abroad German managers are considered emotionally cool and disrespectful by foreign colleagues – despite the fact that Germany is one of the top-ranked countries in terms of "technical human orientation," i.e., participation, job security and social systems. For Sprenger this is not a contradiction; after all Germany handed over dealing with the human element of work to systems and instruments (see *Handelsblatt*, November 12, 2004).

The Academy has addressed this issue in training for many years. Leadership work is to a great extent the ability to make and main contact and appreciate others. It cannot be replaced by the best incentive systems. However, as the goal is always to achieve effective leadership under the given circumstances, leaders should also receive instrumental help in the form of training, coaching and guidelines. This reduces inhibitions in order to make the leaders actually deal with relationship-related subjects. My experience has been that these inhibitions truly exist, because communication and appreciation still tend to be associated with images of the esoteric, psychology and sentimentalism.

3.2.1   *Hard and Soft Factors – The Mix Makes the Difference*

Good relationship management is an important basis for successful companies. However, this is not enough for success. The challenge consists in connecting soft and hard success factors and balancing emotions with the company's goals. The right mixture mobilizes these energy reserves in employees and leaders alike, and is decisive in determining whether a company is successful or not. Here again we are indebted to the late Sumantra Ghoshal for his crucial insights into what makes companies grow:

It is not enough to make everybody feel good or for the executives to make their employees happy. A vision and a strategy need to be created that appeal to the employees, that "sweep them up, awaken and maintain their zeal for action and give them opportunities to develop" (Bruch and Ghoshal 2004, pp. 62–65). Leadership means creating optimal conditions and incentives in order to make the individual perform better than he or she would otherwise.

The energy level of a company is determined by the intensity and quality of its energy. Activity, interaction, the ability to react and to fascinate are indicators for the intensity of energy. The quality of the energy can be positive – creating excitement, joy and satisfaction – or negative, creating fear, frustration and sadness.

Weak emotions, whether positive or negative, do not encourage people to act. If a weak positive energy prevails in a company it is in its "comfort zone" and the employees are satisfied and relaxed. However, the energy intensity necessary for strategic advances or changes is lacking. Companies in the "resignation zone" are characterized by weak negative emotions. The employees are lethargic and feel left out of the whole. Without attention and activity, they grow idle.

High-energy organizations are characterized by a strong feeling of urgency and an enormous "drive" that makes them more productive: strong negative emotions in combination with a high energy intensity can land a company in the "aggression zone," which is characterized by intense competition, a high level of activity and a tooth-and-nail battle to achieve the company's goals. Finally, in the "passion zone" companies flourish because of strong positive emotions such as enjoying working and being proud of what they achieve. The fascination of the people in the company means that attention and activities are oriented on shared priorities.

Various dangerous factors can rob companies of energy, such as the acceleration trap, the lethargy trap and the corrosion trap. Constant pressure to accelerate or to change can lead to the burnout of the entire company. If the company loses the ability to access and utilize resources it is caught in the lethargy trap and the company is no longer able to react to environmental changes. A company is caught in the corrosion trap if it simultaneously has to deal with threats (or opportunities) from the outside and internal conflicts and is hampered in doing so because its employees expend all of their energy on these internal disputes.

3.2.2 No Fairy Tale: Of Princesses and Dragons

So far we have seen that the issue of the energy level is essential, especially in change situations, and can come down to a company's life or death. Companies that successfully make changes usually select one of two approaches to free and channel organizational energy: The "slaying the dragon" or the "winning the princess" strategy.

With the "slaying the dragon" strategy the management intentionally leads the employees into the aggression zone in order to spark attention, emotion and action. A very good (if also drastic) example was provided by Jan Timmer – CEO of Philips Electronics – in 1990. In a meeting he presented the company's executives a pre-dated fake newspaper with the headline "Philips files for bankruptcy"; this represented the threat of the "dragon." He succeeded in channeling the anger and fear this prophecy set off in his employees into energy and commitment in order to turn the company around.

By pursuing the "winning the princess" strategy, the leadership drives the company into the passion zone by creating fascination for a (new) vision. In this case, too, it is essential to illustrate the "object of desire" graphically. For example the Sony CEO Nobuyuki Idei created the virtual Vaio world in order to make the "princess" something his employees could see. At the beginning of the twenty-first century Sony was facing the major challenge of changing from a TV manufacturer to a multimedia group (see Bruch and Ghoshal 2004).

Ideally the leadership is able to both kill the dragon and win the princess, combining the immediacy, discipline and decisiveness of the aggression zone with the joy and pride of the passion zone. However, this ideal case is rare.

Whether they opt for the dragon or the princess, the management has to be able to emotionally and relationally adapt to the situation in order to bring out the right emotions in their employees and in themselves: "If the dragon is to be slain tremendous energy, brave and assertive leadership are called for; to win the heart of the princess, a company needs calm, gentle, charismatic and sensitive leaders" (Bruch and Ghoshal 2004, p. 64).

3.2.2.1 The Magic Triangle: "Self" – Employees – Organization

The heart of good leadership is the management of relationships. Leadership always takes place between three poles: the personality of the leader, hence the "self", the employees and the organization. These three poles provide a frame for the work of art that is successful leadership. Thus, leadership is an art, not just a handcraft. It calls for power, technique and skill, but also inspiration, emotions, ideas, passion, courage and individuality.

Leadership has changed massively in the last 15 years I have been working as a leader: in the past I made basic decisions and left their execution up to the employees. Today employees want to decide and contribute. Leading has become more demanding but the results for all involved and for the company are better and more satisfying. As a leader of today I have to be able to step back and let go. Still it is important that the leader sets the frame, provides security and orientation. If these conditions are not met, letting go is very dangerous and can end in chaos. "More structure, more guidelines" – this is often heard in German companies. At the same time we hear "more shared responsibility, more room for personal development." Both are correct and important; leadership is always a balancing act between the two.

Thus, perfect leadership guidelines do not and will never exist. Even Fredmund Malik, who in a sense has argued the opposite, cannot offer universal guidelines for leaders. Too varied is the life at the companies, too manifold the personalities of the leaders, and too great is the variety of situations and constraints on cooperation.

That does not mean, however, that leadership cannot be learned and that there are no true and less true practices, fundamentals and benchmarks. There is no doubt that some leaders do a better job than others. Hence, in my opinion it is not valid to draw a black and white picture in practice. Not only is there a gray zone, but it possesses many different shades. Dark gray for example might be permissible in one situation but lead to failure in another.

Successful leadership is not the product of recipes or checklists; instead, it intensively concerns itself with the potentials and resources of the employees of the company and develops them. It works best if employees sense that they are appreciated at the workplace and if their individual interests can best be harmonized with those of the company. Creating values cannot be done without appreciating employees' work. If authority is combined with clarity, assertiveness, and employee orientation then it is moving in the right direction. Thus, cooperative and authoritarian leadership complement one another.

3.2.2.2 Leading People – Leading Humanely

Emotions always play a role when people work together. There are six basic emotions that everyone carries, even to the workplace: anger, fear, sadness, joy, disgust and surprise. In companies, often the emotions get on the wrong track. The very same emotions meant to inspire loyalty and help employees enjoy their work lead to secret alliances, intrigues and false kindness. Leading employees means not only allowing for emotions, but also being able to manage them.

The Academy's systemic approach to leadership describes four important features of personal, relationship-oriented leadership skills: inner conviction, ability to make contact, appreciation, and an orientation on resources.

1. Inner conviction
   Only the person who believes in something – and in himself or herself – is able to convince and motivate others. Inner conviction is the credo of a corporate world that others want to belong to, even in hard times. But inner conviction is more than a set goal, it also means trusting in your own employees. Without the people who implement goals, they remain nothing but plans.
2. Ability to make contact
   Contact in the form of genuine interest and intensive, open dealings with employees is truly what keeps an organization together. That does not mean, however, spreading a warm, soft blanket of harmony over everything until the smoldering conflicts underneath have poisoned the climate in the company and smothered productivity. Ideally this is a little bit like a long-married couple: they argue extensively, but ultimately love each other again.
3. Appreciation
   Appreciation needs to come from the heart and must be experienced as such by the employee. It makes a big difference if somebody has to perform under substantial doubts from above or if they are told: "You are welcome here, we believe in you and your potential." That is also true if the leader and employee do not always share the same opinion.

4. Orientation on resources

It should be the first maxim of a good leader to truly make use of existing opportunities. They should ask the employee: "What do you need in order to perform?" This kind of leadership increases loyalty and the employees' willingness to contribute significantly.

The decisive difference between the classical and the modern understanding of leadership is that modern leaders not only consider the desired goal – such as turnover, sales and profit – but on the way to achieving it keep in mind their own and the employees' emotions. And again, this is not about "buying harmony"; it is about sensing and accepting people's actual emotions.

3.2.2.3 The Supreme Discipline

Leading staff is not a part-time job. However, almost no leader can afford to devote their time entirely to the "supreme discipline" of leadership. Many good approaches fail in practice due to a (perceived) lack of time, increasing job stress and the insecurity of the leader. Hence, insecurity is an emotion that can also be used constructively. Only leaders who are able to analyze their own position and performance can lead teams to give their best.

Leading managers need to keep observing not only their own employees but also stay close to costumers, markets and products. Thus, there is a great danger that in times of crisis the leaders save time at the wrong end. Instead of taking their time to weld together their team, they try to run everything themselves and make themselves even more indispensable than before.

This is a slip in judgment that can backfire badly: teams and departments can only cooperate optimally if they are dedicated to common goals and visions. Therefore they need room and opportunities for personal exchange, talks and orientation. If in difficult times fewer and fewer people want to be part of the (corporate) world that a leader has created, because that world is dominated by the spirit of "every man for himself," fear and pressure, then the manager has failed in their job as a true "leader."

In addition to technical know-how, each company and each team has its own "group wisdom" and its own "grammar." It is essential that the different characters in a team (strategist, controller, heavy hitter, etc.) can actually live out and feel their positions. Only in this way can they develop their individual potentials and transform a group of people into a team. This cannot be achieved with formal instructions. Team development, feedback conversations, coaching and above all open communications are indispensable.

Due to alliances and fusions, today organizations can change their face and their structure overnight and old connections can become meaningless within hours. Then a leader has to rely completely on his or her personal authority, integrity and acceptance. However, this only works within a corporate culture that supports trust, openness and appreciation.

Peter M. Senge has shown in his management classic "The Fifth Discipline" (see Senge 1996) that leaders and companies alike can only implement their visions if they are able to withstand emotional stress. This requires skill as well as time and work spent on internal relationship management. And this seems to be lacking in German companies. In 2002 the Academy conducted a survey of 242 leaders from all over Germany: most of them claimed to recognize the importance of relationship management, but only one third were satisfied with the relationship management in their company.

It is the leaders who sow the seeds of growth in a company – or crush them. Their leadership behavior, especially their integrity in dealings with their employees, costumers and investors makes the difference. It is not surprising that, after being all but lost in the euphoria of the New Economy, the honorable merchant's virtues are now becoming popular again. Slowly the insight is dawning that economic success is based on ethics and morality.

The trick with this insight is that these value principles cannot simply be barked out in orders. The constant demand for the Academy's "Systemic Leadership" seminar shows that there is an acute need among decision makers to create a new climate in their companies. Yet one thing should not be forgotten: competence and knowledge of the industry are more necessary than ever. Of course leaders still need to have learned their skills and be able to use them, from controlling the company up to conversation techniques and the definition of goal agreements.

Moreover it holds true that not only the technical competence is important but also literally putting yourself to the test: reflect on your own values, goals and effects, because leading means learning, over and over again. Leadership is most successful when it combines both: mastering the tasks and instruments and developing the leader's personality in order to truly move and inspire the people in their company.

In Chap. 2 of this book I presented many correct and important answers to the pressing question of what effective, successful and relationship-oriented leadership depends on. Now I would like to "distil" ten statements from all these partly contradictory, partly redundant approaches, theories and models. Here I do not intend to paint an ideal (and unattainable) portrait of how leaders should be. All leaders are still only human and that is exactly what they should be. In my opinion, leading depends strongly on human qualities and capabilities and not primarily on management tools. Leaders have to be brave enough to face their own emotions and constructively use them for their tasks.

The following basic rules are not dogma. They are goals worth aspiring to – for the people lead as well as for the company. Leading does not start with the employee or the goal of the company – it starts with the leader. One of the most important tasks of a leader is to reevaluate their own understanding of leadership regularly and to ask if their own behavior in a given situation is helpful, effective and adequate.

To me, good leadership means designing a world that other people want to be part of. This world cannot be measured – at least not using figures, balances and forecasts. But it can be felt if people want to join this world because they are convinced of its worth, or just because they do not see a chance to change jobs or are too well paid to quit. In this way one can gauge whether the employees are really involved or are simply doing their jobs; and, especially because these factors can hardly be measured by instruments, for leaders evaluating success starts with evaluating themselves.

3.2.3   Leading Means Knowing Yourself

The systemic approach of the Academy considers leadership as an integral phenomenon, but focuses on a dimension that remains a blind spot of other systemic approaches: the leader itself.

Leadership requires self-knowledge. If I want to establish and maintain a relationship then I cannot perform the calculation with completely unknown variables; at least one variable needs to be known – myself.

Everybody thinks: "But I know who I am, what I want and what my goal is," especially confident, strong leaders, which is why especially leaders balk at introspection. The reason is that they do not trust their perception of themselves nor their emotions. As an example: A leader does not feel sufficiently informed by his employees. But he does not dare to express his anger clearly. Instead he starts his own internal (mental) blacklist, which finally leads to a hard step. And when that happens the employees cannot understand why the boss reacts so harshly. The leader did not want to share anything – and has to bear the consequences.

We like to fool ourselves concerning our self-perception. Our emotions, thinking, acting and our relationships are not controlled by rational, obvious and known motivations only. It is much more the case that we are the product of irrational, partly unconscious principles, images, messages and role expectations. The thought of being controlled by something beyond their own control is hard to accept – especially for leaders.

A great number of managers simply "function." They do not know what they feel and certainly not what others feel. In many cases – and that is worse – they have stopped feeling anything. In psychology this deficit is called "alexithymia." The list of typical symptoms reads like a brief description of the average German manager: lack of imagination, limited emotional life, lack of joy, lack of spontaneity, little empathy, extremely factual expression, and a total concentration on facts. At the same time these people think they are socially competent and pleasant-natured, in short that they are good bosses (see de Vries 2002, p. 113 ff.).

Reinhard K. Sprenger analyzed another dimension of this problem: "Most leaders are not aware that not the "matters as such," but their perceptions of them, their frame of coordinates become visible through these matters. Therefore, they are not interested in themselves and certainly not in the uniqueness of their experience. They are interested in everything that is taking place at the periphery of their existence without acknowledging that something is taking place within themselves" (Sprenger 2002a, p. 107).

3.2.3.1 The Inner Mirror

Leading requires us to know the determinants of our own personality, our individual shaping, our images of roles and our (limited) point of view: What is my inner script? What are my beliefs concerning good leadership, right and wrong, and other people? What motivates me? What makes me vulnerable? What do I refuse to see? Only the person who knows the answers to these questions can distance himself or herself from these issues, can decide for or against them instead of reacting by reflex only.

Thus, a leader has to be able to step back from their conscious self-definition in order to realize who they really are – not who they want to be. Self-awareness includes recognizing our effects on others, because these effects determine relationships. How a person is, how they affect others and how they see themselves – these are three completely different things.

Consequently gaining a self-perception is one of the most important building blocks of modern management. Leading yourself and others begins with reflecting on your inner beliefs. How do I as a leader deal with power, influence, competition, performance, stress, weaknesses and emotions and how does my behavior affect teamwork and the corporate culture? These are questions a leader should confront himself or herself with.

Only those who trust themselves will be trusted by others. In order to build this trust you have to know yourself very well. This includes accepting your own emotions, especially if they seem to be negative and not in keeping with the culture and rules of the company. Moreover, the leader has to be able to express his or her emotions appropriately and to share their inner life with others.

It is essential that leaders constantly work on their own self-awareness. That does not mean, however, that they are not able to act due to all the pondering and questioning. But self-reflection is the foundation of successful action. However, self-reflection is not being taught to junior managers, although it should be the basic education for leaders. The subject of self-reflection is surrounded by a suspicious aura of the esoteric and psychoanalytical and is therefore avoided – even though the consequences for leaders, employees and companies can be fatal.

A leader may have the best education in management skills, they may be trained in delegating and motivating – they will still fail if they do not see or understand that they react to certain people in certain situations extremely aggressively or defensively and unintentionally sends out the wrong signals to the environment, just because they do not have an inner (or by using feedback an outer) mirror.

Our self-perception crucially shapes the personal style of leadership and the company, because there is no complete objectivity, no unbreakable reality and no absolute truth, but always only an individual understanding of it. In the experience of a leader the company is a projection of his or her inner world. Each manager will see something different in one and the same company, because each is designing his or her own map of it (see Sprenger 2002a, pp. 24–98).

3.2.3.2   One Individual – Many Faces

Virginia Satir is one of the most influential figures in the family therapy-oriented approach to psychotherapy. Her work centers on the notions of "self," "growth" and "communication," and the starting point is the person's own personality and how intra-mental processes and communication are connected. This link is of great importance for the work of managers.

We as a whole consist of many parts that reinforce and support, but can also hamper and weaken one another, depending on the situation and our health. Most people are afraid to "lift the lid" and look into their own interior, or they do not even know that there is this "lid," which the unknown parts of their personality are hidden under (see Satir 1988, p. 14 ff.).

What are these internal parts? These can for example be driving factors such as "You've got to be perfect," "You have to be fast," "You have to be strong," "You have to work hard" or "You have to fulfill the wishes of others." These may also be positive forms of permission, like "You are allowed to be happy" or "You are allowed to enjoy receiving support." Our inner parts also include factors that slow us down, like "This can wait until tomorrow," "If you're in a rush, go slow," "Don't be a baby," "Don't lose your temper" or "I can't stand up for myself."

Everyone should accept their different faces and facial expressions without evaluating and judging them, or those of their fellow human beings. Each individual should seek wholeness, and not just fulfill some strange expectations or seek to fill niches assigned by others. "Our outer faces fit to our inner faces and are mainly influenced by them" (Satir 1988, p. 78). Once you know how the various parts interact with each other, you get an idea of how you treat yourself and others. This especially applies to leaders.

Our actions, thoughts and emotions are always a stimulus response to the inner or outer world, but mostly we don't recognize this relationship: "Strictly speaking, we live in an emotional prison without knowing it" (Satir 1988, p. 40). The walls of this prison only get stronger if we never question our beliefs. Breaking free means change, and change creates fear. Changes always consist of three phases: fear and anxiety, confusion about the new, and the integration of the new into the old.

If, instead of following our old beliefs and experiences, which limit our options before we even start, we were to consider all of the opportunities present in a situation, we would make our choices more consciously and not just react to internal constraints like a puppet.

Each step out of the prison is a step farther into uncharted territory for which there is no guide, claims Satir. Each person must use their experiences and insights to create their own map to lead them through life. Over time this map becomes more and more accurate, and the more of our own parts we know, the more empty spots are filled in: "If we are truly the master of our own house, we have the power to overcome external difficulties, and we can design our own map for our own lives. Viewing our life as an ongoing process is an encouraging thought" (Satir 1988, p. 66).

Virginia Satir compares the different faces of a man with a vibrant mobile, the parts of which form a whole in harmony and balance. Stages of change bring the mobile temporarily out of balance, because they are naturally accompanied by fear and uncertainty. When this occurs, it is important to recognize this imbalance and re-balance the mobile. Many people recognize their inner lack of balance only in extreme situations, e.g. if they become seriously ill or lose a loved one.

Therefore, she formulated a type of life task or motto: "Each of us can – regardless of age – still discover something new about ourselves. This makes our life interesting for us and for others. To the extent to which we accept ourselves with all our parts, we become a rounded personality, we are loving to ourselves and others and approach others in an open and loving way" (Satir 1988, p. 109).

3.2.3.3 The Inner Script

Our lives can be compared with a stage: we determine what is on the stage, we perform our own internal drama and we play a part in it. We are scriptwriter, director and the leading actor all in one. And consciously or unconsciously we are constantly looking for events that fit in our life script. We interpret the world so that it corresponds to our script. But we do not play just one role in our one-man screenplay; we are a team of protagonists. At the drop of a hat we slip into another role. Depending on the scene, we are a dominant leader, compassionate friend or a small child, afraid of their parents' anger.

In each role, we show another of our many faces. And in each role, we are speaking a text consisting of life statements. We know them by heart and recite them automatically, without thinking about it. Everyone has their own life statements; together they represent the inner script. They consist of phrases, idioms, demands or opinions that we heard from others and have saved. These are permanently saved on our internal hard drive.

We learn our life statements very early in our childhood. We learn them quickly, because we realize that they help us to reduce the complexity of the environment and also provide security. We can hold on to them if we are afraid, if we feel uncertain, if we feel weak, if everything collapses around us. Then, the phrase "You can do it" we once heard from our mother or father, teacher, grandparents or older siblings becomes a mantra.

The downside of these mental supports is that they can quickly become bars that imprison us and inhibit our development. They give us, for example, the feeling that we must do everything on our own – a typical mental trap executives are prone to fall into. Life statements cannot be erased, but by recognizing them again and again, you can greatly lessen their negative impact. For this you have to go back to childhood, where the most statements, and the most powerful ones, have shaped you. You can track them down by asking questions: What have I learned, heard in my family, at school, from friends? What impulses did I have as a child? What role did I slip into in certain situations, for example, in confrontations with my father?

The inner script, also called the "inner drama," has a decisive influence on individual leadership style and thus, on the way you behave in conflicts, the way you communicate, the way you deal with power, responsibility and change, and how you approach others. If you know your beliefs and you know their origin, you can take a step back in situations in which they come into play, and you can analyze your behavior and your learned responses to similar situations. Thus, you are no longer at risk of becoming a puppet for your life statements. We have to listen to our life statements and look at our inner images; we have to accept our parts – and not just the desirable ones – in order to really know ourselves and to be able to lead. Here the greatest challenge lies in integrating all of the roles into our current adult selves.

As a personality model, transactional analysis distinguishes between three sub-personalities or ego-states: the parent, the child and the adult. Each of the different types represents different kinds and qualities of messages being "expressed" inside every person – whether employees or boss. If you can listen carefully, you will note that there are repeated dialogues between these inner personalities. These dialogues can be constructive or derogatory, can release energy or drain it.

The "parent" sub-personality stands for the values, norms and rules that influence a person. A distinction is made between the critical (moralistic, schoolmaster-like, punitive) and the caring parent (pampering, helping, saving). The "child" ego-state represents the feelings and impulses of the child in us, in short: our emotional experience. It can manifest as the well-adjusted (polite, hesitant, defiant) or free-rebellious child (boundless, spontaneous, playful), either consciously or unconsciously. Lastly, the "adult" ego-state (analyzing, unfeeling, observing) processes the information and is goal-oriented and solution-oriented, in short: reasonable. This ego-state can choose to consciously integrate the "child" and "parent" – or not to.

Starting from their own "ego-states," in the next step the leader is able to better understand their employees and adequately respond to them because he or she knows that the employees' behavior is also based on their respective life statements, that they also play a role on their own stage and follow their own inner scripts. And the manager then recognizes that the reaction of an employee is a partly unconscious and learned response to the behavior of their superior, which somehow triggered it. The leader can learn – at least to some extent – to decipher the behavior demonstrated by employees, customers, superiors and partners and to translate the messages behind that behavior.

In this way leadership can take place on another level, beyond personal sensitivities, over-the-top "striking back," wounded pride, unnecessary power plays and mutual demoralization. Employee behavior that at first glance only looks like confrontation, rejection or withdrawal can allow you to draw conclusions about your own leadership behavior and be used synergistically for the work process.

3.2.3.4 Leading Yourself

Thus, a modern developmental concept starts with the personality of the leader, with their inner drive, their disposition, their inner images and their life script, and it supports them to recognize themselves and to develop into an authentic personality. Peter F. Drucker meant exactly that by his famous phrase that a leader can basically only lead one person – himself or herself. Only then can he or she lead the way forward, "direct" (not in the sense of manipulation, but in the sense of promoting) and take responsibility for others.

"Successful careers are not planned. They develop when people take chances because they know their strengths, their ways of working and their own values" (Drucker 1999), as Drucker aptly put it. The answers to the three questions "What are my strengths?", "How do I achieve performance?" and "What values do I pursue?" are for him the basis of effective self-management. What is important is the question of your own performance. Just like individual strengths, it is also the way that performance is achieved. This is part of your personality. How results are achieved also depends on how knowledge is absorbed – that is, whether one is more of a reader or a listener – and on what learning method one uses (see Drucker 1999).

Leading yourself is not as easy as it sounds, because it has nothing to do with the arbitrariness, self-complacency and ego trips at the company's expense. It has much more to do with self-criticism, the courage to make and recognize your own mistakes and shortcomings, to overcome your own limits, and the proverbial look into the mirror, which reveals not only the exterior but also the interior. And you have to be able to take a good, long look without flinching.

Leaders of German companies tend to underestimate the mistakes that they make themselves and prefer to ignore the symptoms of crisis until, when they finally do admit a personal failure, it is far too late. Eight out of ten managers principally do not feel the causes of a crisis could be found in either themselves or their company. It is always the others who are to blame. The discrepancy between self-perception and exterior perception are striking: in the event of a company crisis, only 37% of entrepreneurs see the reasons for the crisis in their own errors and behavior, while for 60% of the external observers the leaders are to blame for the crisis.

Shifting guilt from ourselves to external factors or other people is only human, and perhaps understandable. In addition, in most cases it is not the reflecting and doubting people that make it to the top, but those who are (excessively) self-confident. But from an economic and entrepreneurial point of view this behavior is disastrous, because it prevents a timely intervention before everything gets out of hand. Recognizing the limits of their own self-awareness is of absolutely critical importance for managers, as well as being unflinchingly honest with themselves and with others (see *Handelsblatt*, August 22, 2003).

Leading yourself also means regularly questioning your own actions, requesting and accepting feedback. It means facing your own doubts and fears, expressing your views, even when they conflict with other opinions, and sensing and pursuing your own impulses. A leader should ask himself or herself the following questions and answer them honestly: "Do I really want to lead?" "Do I have enough inner commitment to put aside my own ego in favor of the talents of others?" "Does it truly make me happy to encourage others and to do all I can to develop their potential?" "Do I love my work?" "Am I doing my job well?" And last but not least: "Do I see myself the same way others see me?"

Today, in dealings with customers, employees and supervisors, leaders have to define their role and, above all, rewrite it time and again. The more leaders try to provide "clarity" with detailed orders, precise objectives and rigid control mechanisms, the more they paralyze the organization: Why should the employees think and pay attention for themselves, when their boss does it for them?

The systemic leadership style that I support is not easy to live up to and calls for several prerequisites: trust in others and certainty about your own strengths. Then, leaders can also allow themselves to have weaknesses, can acknowledge them, and can conduct themselves authentically based on this feeling. This kind of leadership has nothing to do with laissez-faire or any incentive events in the Canary Islands.

Working on your own leadership style can only succeed through unconditionally working on yourself: How do I come across to others? What is the basis of legitimacy and expertise for my leadership position? What drives me to be a leader? How do I show genuine appreciation for my staff? How do I make true contact? How can I transform self-doubt and defeats in order to gain self-confidence? How do I get back up after a failure and face a situation that I can no longer control? These are questions managers must ask themselves over and over again.

It is also these questions and tasks that contribute more to establishing a sustainable leadership style than mere knowledge of control mechanisms and principles of delegation, however important these factors may also be. And if in terms of management tools German managers primarily use personal talks, they would do well to also start a dialogue with themselves on a regular basis in order to check and adjust their own perceptions. Only then is it possible to actually get and stay in contact with their employees.

This is important because self-management, as defined by Peter F. Drucker, does not end with the individual person of the leader. It also requires taking responsibility for relationships and their upkeep, and accepting people as they are. Whoever wants to be effective must first know the strengths, working methods and values of their staff and stay in constant communication with them.

3.2.3.5   Being Authentic

People are very astute when it comes to sensing when someone else shows his or her true self and when not. From CEO to technician, from senior partner to trainee, people react like a seismograph to the openness of others and can very quickly sense whether appreciation is real or just for show. Only when we know ourselves, and know why we act, how we act, what drives us and what is important to us, are we authentic. And authenticity is a prerequisite for successful leadership. Only those who face up to their own feelings, interests and views, only those who respect themselves, can respect others.

If a manager is not "real" and does not practice what they preach in the company, they sow the seeds of a highly toxic plant called cynicism. John P. Kotter sees in this a great danger for any social community: "Outstanding leaders have always understood how to use the power of positive emotions: optimism, trust, hope. And they also recognized the cancer that arises from poisoned emotions. Unfortunately, many companies systematically create a climate of cynicism that can be called the most insidious cancer of a society. Charismatic leaders prevent this disease from growing. Thus, they can help others to achieve the extraordinary" (Kotter 2004).

It cannot be the goal of the leader to be liked by everyone, to satisfy everyone, or to always "go with the flow." More than a few managers, however, have internalized their function as role models to such an overblown and misguided extent that they come across as amateur actors, reduced to a stereotypical role others force them to play, a role that makes them look almost dehumanized. They act out the martyrdom of the self-sacrificing hero, giving up their own "self" in the truest sense, as Reinhard K. Sprenger pointedly described it (see Sprenger 2002a, pp. 142–143).

Good managers have an "internal moral compass" (Warren Bennis), which they can rely on regardless of which direction the wind is blowing. They have principles, a belief system, and solid convictions. This does not mean that they are not flexible, that they are not able to learn and adapt. Successful leaders are neither always in a good mood nor perfect supermen or superwomen. But they are real personalities, and they stand behind what they say.

Being authentic does not mean always being in the spotlight and the center of attention. In fact those leaders who work quietly and clear the stage for others are often the best. Another advantage: those who are not in the public eye are also less vulnerable, and small mistakes do not automatically make them the target of general criticism, which in most cases freezes processes and cuts productivity. Or restated: let the PR department worry about PR. The leader has to do just one thing: lead.

3.2.4 Leading Means Communicating

Relationships are based on communication. No relationship can exist without some form of communication. In order for people with different skills and different knowledge bases to be able to work together; a well-designed, growing communication structure and a culture of individual and mutual reliability are needed.

This is especially true in times of crisis and change. Unfortunately it is in precisely such times that many managers tend to "shut down" and cut off communications. Thus, what is really behind the commonly heard call for automatic motivation techniques is often a desire to avoid open communication and openly working out conflicts, as Sprenger knows from experience. I agree completely.

The leader can and should use his or her network to share and exchange ideas with employees, and to show them the necessity and benefits of his or her plans for change.

But there is also a lack of communication in the opposite direction, i.e. from employees to managers, as Drucker observed: "Most conflicts stem from the fact that people do not know what the others are doing, how they work, what priorities they have or what results they expect. And they don't know this because they didn't ask and therefore nobody told them" (Drucker 1999a, p. 16). Successful managers ask their employees: "What should I know about your strong suits; about your way of working; your values; and what you want to contribute?" According to Drucker, in order to work together in a good and trusting way, people do not have to like each other, but they do need to understand each other.

It is especially important to conduct the regular employee interview more often than just once a year (in which executives often "give away" much) and instead have a dialogue, free of hierarchy, in the context of everyday work in order to optimize processes; to have a continuous, open, largely unregulated and non-bureaucratic exchange of experience and information.

Drucker claimed that communication is at the same time perception, expectation and demand. Moreover he noted that information and communication can be clearly distinguished from one another: "The more we succeed in liberating information from its human component, that is, from emotions and values, expectations and perceptions, the more accurate and reliable it is" (Drucker 2004, p. 309 ff.). Information does, however, depend on communication. Conversely, communication is not necessarily dependent on information, according to Drucker. In fact, the best communication can consist solely of shared experiences, without any logical information. In this respect, perception always takes precedence over information – especially in businesses.

I feel Drucker's call for the separation of the factual and the emotional levels (information and emotion) of communication is unrealistic. Interpersonal communication is never free of feelings, interpretations and connotations. It is the task of the leader to sense this relationship and the constant "ping-pong game" between the two levels and to adjust their own communication – verbal or nonverbal – accordingly.

The question arises: How can executives get messages "across" and establish real contact in the communication situation? Firstly, it is important that they inform their employees in a timely manner. And if they do, they should not only present the results or the bare facts of the decision, but also explain how and why it was made. Employees do not just want to be informed, but to be taken seriously and be involved. They want to understand part of the process and not just the last link in the chain. If they are granted this sense of inclusion, they are also more willing to accept painful or unpleasant decisions.

That's why good leaders are also gifted storytellers. That does not mean that they like to hear themselves talk or to embellish the truth. It means that they can make their visions vivid using words, images and symbols in the minds and hearts of their listeners; that the enthusiasm of their words is infectious. The stories they tell contain an important message that others can orient their actions on, and they captivate the listener. Throughout the evolution of humankind, knowledge has primarily been passed on in stories – and only recently by PowerPoint. And even children understand the world in terms of stories (see Kotter 2004).

3.2.4.1 Communicating on All Levels

Communication is the heart of every organization and fulfils numerous functions: through communication, knowledge, opinions, ideas and expectations are exchanged, reviewed and modified. Relationships are established and maintained, and the capital of the modern enterprise – namely, knowledge – is increased in the process. Communication supports both rational and emotional understanding. It is, according to Paul Watzlawick, impossible not to communicate, because even silence is a message (see Watzlawick et al. 2000, p. 72 ff.).

The iceberg model (see Sect. 3.1.1) not only explains how communication works in an organization, but how interpersonal communication works in general. It can be applied to different communication types and situations, whether face-to-face interactions in conversations and discussions, or full-scale change and restructuring processes in organizations.

While the visible part of the iceberg above the water indicates the "what," the content level of the negotiated issue or matter, there is often the "how" of communication, such as issues of the climate of conversation or relationship issues between the communication partners, which lurk invisible beneath the water's surface.

Just as in the case of the iceberg the invisible main body determines the position of the visible tip of the iceberg, often the character and quality of the relationship level, or the nature of the "invisible-unconscious" communication aspects determine the success of the communication on the "visible-conscious" surface of each topic. A rule of thumb says that up to 80% of all decisions are made at the relationship the level. This also shows how important it is to understand the body language of the person we are talking with in order to bring a conversation or a negotiation to a successful conclusion. It is also essential to be sensitive to the importance of the relationship without neglecting the substantive issue of communication (Fig. 3.2).

The relationship level of communication always dominates the content level. If the "line" between the manager and the employees is missing, the relationship-based disorders will distort so many signals from the daily work that the content can be completely lost. Without a concrete context or reference at the relationship level, the message doesn't get through. If, for example, appreciation of the organizational members is missing, even if the board has a very good concept for a substantive change, it will fail due to underlying problems of acceptance and motivation.

Most communications in businesses, as I have observed, take place mainly on the content level and rarely (intentionally) on the relationship level. Often feelings are masked by factual statements because no one wants to talk about their own

Factual level (content)	Social level (relationship)

- This is what has happened.
- This is the damage that has occurred.
- These goals are jeopardized.
- What has it been like until now?
- What is necessary to find a solution?
- What effects are to be expected?
- Who is effected?
- What would be ideal?
	- Who is afraid of being regarded as
	  responsible?
	- Who is not interested in finding a solution?
	- Who likes (doesn't like) whom?
	- Who has goals of his or her own?
	- Who plays which role?
	- Who is to be "used" for what?
	- Who has what kind of power?
	- What human effects will the solution to the
	  problem have?
	- How were conflicts dealt with until now?

Fig. 3.2 The two levels of communication (*Source:* Pinnow, Daniel F., Management Guide 2000, *Bad Harzburg* 9/1999)

frustration. And this in turn leads to two things: first, many messages are not understood, and secondly some apparently factual conflicts can simply not be solved, because the solution is being sought at the wrong level. After all, communications also takes place unconsciously.

3.2.4.2   Leading by Dialog

Far too often, when leaders talk about "communication" what they have in mind is pure information, i.e., only half of what makes up communication. True communication requires a "dialogical setting," as Reinhard K. Sprenger put it. This entails attentive, interested listening and an effort to truly understand (and not just to hear) the other person and to share in his or her perceptions. Each perception is subjective, influenced by personal experiences and judgments. Especially supervisors often insist on having a monopoly on truth and objectivity; anyone who sees something else must not really be watching. This narrow-minded attitude is a breeding ground for misunderstandings.

"A dialogic attitude means acknowledging the fundamental differences between two people in terms of their perceptions and judgments and making them the starting point of the conversation. In this approach, the contribution of the other person represents an opportunity, even if – or precisely because – their point of view is quite different from yours. It can contribute to the completeness of the overall picture – a source of enrichment" (Sprenger 1999, pp. 194–195). If a conversation was a real dialogue, you will notice that you leave it feeling differently than when you entered into it.

Acting dialogically means being curious and open to thinking and talking. It means a fundamental openness to alternative possibilities for action. According to Sprenger (see Sprenger 1999, p. 194 ff.), on the behavioral level leading dialogically means:

Inviting the other person to talk and asking the right questions
Visiting the other person and being their guest
Paying attention to the formal symmetry of conversation
Communicating reversibly: "I can tell you what you can also tell me."
Taking into account as many different perspectives as possible
Making decisions based on a broad consensus

Needless to say, leading by dialog costs more time than giving orders. But as Sprenger quite correctly points out, you have to consider the time lost by not engaging in conversations and the resulting confusion, lack of information sharing, non-satisfactory performance, unclear objectives, and disruptions and feelings of ill will in the leader-employee relationship. Quite a simple and straightforward calculation, I would say.

3.2.4.3 Twelve Rules for Clear Communication

Poor communication has serious implications for the organization and its members at all levels, mainly creating information gaps, misunderstandings, rumors, mistakes, conflicts and feelings of ill will. The following simple and effective rules help to avoid misunderstandings and disruptions in daily communication with staff (and colleagues):

1. No "one," "it" or "we": Employees should be addressed directly.
2. No "need," "should" or "could" – instructions are not given in the subjunctive, because this makes their implementation vague.
3. No "maybe," "possibly" or "actually" – instructions need to aim at specific effects and are given in order to mobilize others.
4. Everyone is right – from their own point of view: Instead of preaching to others and insisting on their own position, leaders have to understand and clarify the positions of others.
5. Show absolute loyalty: Leaders must always and necessarily stand behind their statements and actions.
6. Ask specific questions: Unclear questions will be met with unclear answers.
7. Never ask several questions at once: They only confuse people and cost time.
8. Never start questions with "Why?": Managers should make statements instead of asking for justifications. Exception: The personnel review talk, in which backgrounds are to be clarified.
9. Do not answer your own questions: Otherwise you will never learn the position of the other(s).
10. Avoid giving "Yes, but. . ." answers: Seek to complement the statements of the other person rather than refuting or qualifying them.

11. Active listening: Listen patiently, then think, and then respond.
12. Agree on specific appointments: Prevent misunderstandings with clear priorities.

Communications should be free of distractions and harmonious. That does not mean that everyone has to have the same opinion, but that each conversational partner is treated respectfully, attentively, and as n equal. Signal your openness and interest in them and their verbal and nonverbal messages. Harmony means consensus, contact and being on the "same wavelength." It's hardly a coincidence that the word "communication" is derived from Latin – and *communis* means "common" in the sense of "shared." Communication is primarily about arriving at a *common* understanding.

Harmony can on the one hand be achieved by non-verbal means, such as the posture, body language and breathing rhythm, by eye contact, a nod or a smile. On the other hand harmony can be created verbally by repeating or briefly summarizing the messages of your conversational partner or by putting your words in an order that matches your partner's internal processing strategy.

In a good conversation the harmony is mutual. Even in disagreements and conflict conversations, both parties should try to stay in contact and maintain the exchange, instead of resorting to unilateral verbal attacks to simply "silence" the other person.

3.2.4.4   Active Listening

Good managers are also – and especially – good listeners, because effective communication is always a dialog. They are open for the views of their conversational partner and do not always have to lead the conversation. In this way, they show trust and learn decidedly more from their counterparts. Too many executives today communicate through memos and e-mails instead of direct conversation.

Productive communication takes focused and attentive perception. This especially includes listening attentively, which is supported by observing closely. How can we understand our conversational partner if we don't listen to them? Similarly, we cannot grasp their written communications if we don't read them or just skim them. Productive communication requires concentration. This is not easy, because our thoughts constantly tend to wander. Especially when our heads are buzzing with information and questions, it is difficult to completely focus on new situations. Unwinding is a skill that many do not have. In addition, frequent disturbances can distract us and put us under further stress. Especially in longer conversations, our concentration often suffers.

A fundamental and indispensable technique of dialog-oriented discussion is the previously mentioned "active" listening, which goes far beyond mere listening. This technique aims to ensure that:

We understood what the other party really wants to say.
We can recognize whether the other party really means what they say.

The other party feels understood and taken seriously.
The other party gains a sense of trust and security and opens up.

Active listening not only helps us understand our conversational partner better, but also gives them the feeling that they are heard, understood and are accepted as a person. Active listening also especially expresses, at least during the conversation, the other party is the most important person.

As such, active listening is referred to as being "partner-centered." To implement it successfully, the following recommendations should be observed:

Concentrate on the comments and the behavior of your communication partner: What did they say? What did they mean by that? What does their body language tell us?

Show interest in your conversational partner through eye contact, asking questions, agreeing and using an "open" body language (e.g., do not cross your arms, turn away, or nervously play with your fingers). These are ways to indicate interest.

Put yourself in the position of the conversational partner in order to understand him or her better.

Do not make up your mind right away; find out the position of your communication partner first.

Make sure to clear up uncertainties, inquire about the facts in important respects, and gauge the emotional state of your communication partner.

Check whether you have understood the content of your partner's statement correctly by repeating their factual statement ("paraphrasing") as well as their emotional message ("verbalizing").

Keep the conversation going by asking focused questions.

To maintain the "emotional balance," volunteer your own information without waiting to be asked.

Signal your empathy by expressing your own feelings. In this way, leaders show that they are only human.

The basis for active listening lies in astutely sensing what your conversational partner is truly saying. Even more revealing, however, is what has not been said explicitly, but is meant. In this regard, your partner's body language can provide a number of clues. A similar idea holds true for understanding written information. "Reading between the lines" is more important than just noting what is written.

Let me once again point out the aspect of asking questions: They serve to clarify doubts and misunderstandings, and to ascertain whether your conversational partner has been properly understood. In addition, you can signal your interest in or concern for their views, thus winning them over. Inquiries are also very conducive to building trust. For all their positive effects, however, these questions must not be asked too frequently, or your partner may get the impression that you're either not competent or not truly listening.

Lastly I would like to list a number of sample formulations to show how active listening works in practice:

One option is to repeat the content of what your conversational partner has said. This can be done using phrases such as: "Did you say that. . ." or "You're wondering why. . ." Or you can repeat the content in your own words, using: "If I understood you correctly, you think/feel/believe. . ."; "If I might summarize in my own words. . ."; or "Do you mean that. . .?" In addition, you may wish to reflect the feelings of your conversational partner using phrases like: "I know just what you mean. . ." or "I'm really glad that we can talk about this so openly. . ." Lastly, you can also combine both techniques of active listening.

Phrases like: "Unfortunately the last two projects went totally wrong. . ." or "After this difficult time you're now disappointed, but how can the team keep working without you?" are well suited for this purpose.

3.2.4.5 Body Language

I have already touched on the topic of body language. But here I would like to add something: through our body language we show – largely unconsciously and uncontrollably, but also much more clearly and "honestly" – what really moves us, what we think, intend and feel. Our body language includes:

Our voice,
Our gaze,
Our facial expressions,
Our gestures,
Our posture,
The use of both sides of our body (right and left),
Standing,
Walking,
Sitting, and
The distance to our conversational partner.

The progression and the results of a conversation will be greatly influenced by nonverbal communication. This is particularly true for the decision-making process in negotiations. With our body language we affect others, just as we are influenced by their body language. For most people these processes are more or less unconscious. If we do, however, deliberately control our body language we improve the communication in our best interests. But we should not lose our authenticity by acting against our nature.

Through our body language we positively or negatively affect the trust in our person, the credibility of our messages, the persuasiveness of our arguments, the clarity of our observations and the climate of the conversation. Through body language, we express which attitude we have towards our conversational partners on the relationship level. In this respect massive mistakes can be made. We can distinguish between three different main risks:

Risk No. 1: We declare our conversational partner a "non-person."

This can happen because e.g. we talk in a bored tone or intentionally talk too fast ("How can I quickly get rid of this person?"), do other things during the conversation (e.g. writing something) or use a file folder to demonstratively put up a "wall" between ourselves and the other person.

Risk No. 2: We seek to dominate our conversational partner.

To emphasize our dominant status we get very close to the other person, lift our chin, lean forward and speak in a loud voice.

In both cases, the effect is that the interlocutor builds up resistance. At first there is a non-verbal confrontation, which sooner or later may be escalates in a verbal confrontation.

Risk No. 3: We seek to make our conversational partner feel mercy.

Assuming a bent-over posture, speaking in a soft voice, lowering our gaze and making a very modest general appearance signal our willingness to be subjugated. In situations where we are in a weak position, such conduct may evoke the good will of our counterpart. But if we overdo it, we weaken our position. We will not be taken seriously; we encourage the other to be dominant and will be treated accordingly.

3.2.4.6 Shared Knowledge Means Twice the Benefit

As we have seen communication serves two major purposes: conveying knowledge and information on the factual level and creating and maintaining relationships on the emotional level. Therefore, the leader also acts as a knowledge manager.

Like someone operating a floodgate, he or she has to filter the truly important pieces out of the constantly increasing flow of information. He or she has to reduce the complexity because too much information paralyzes the decision-making process and creates uncertainties and communication problems. The leader has to be able to evaluate information, to weigh it, to set priorities and to channel it.

This knowledge management is not censorship, because the leader is not holding back important information consciously in order to increase their influence. Instead, managers work to ensure that all information reaches everybody within the company who might need it, and help to keep worthless information from stealing employees' time and energy. Especially in turbulent times it is the leader's job to distil new, value-generating information.

In the past networks were deemed "gossip factories." Today successful leaders know that networks make specialist knowledge visible and available to the entire organization – knowledge that would otherwise remain locked up in desk drawers, on hard drives and in employees' heads. "Social networks that share knowledge – with or without computer support – are a module of the learning infrastructure that is characteristic of organizations capable of change" (Kanter 1998, p. 29 ff.)

In the age of globalization and virtual networks the difficulty for managers is to dance with completely different partners without stepping on anyone's feet. This metaphor by Rosabeth Moss Kanter aptly describes the problem faced by many leaders and the reason for their aversion to relationship management. Today's forms of cooperation require a sense for human interaction, business and social matters. Globalization forces leaders to recognize and respect national, social and ethnic differences. Today international strategies and alliances are present on all levels. And if the situation of the economy becomes more difficult the balance of interests between the relevant groups (employees, shareholders, customers, sales and distribution, and partners) becomes more difficult as well.

This does not only affect the executive level: "Since the limits of companies are steadily expanding and partnerships beyond the supply chain and at the economic borders are becoming more frequent, more and more people on more and more levels have to take over roles that are new for most of them: as ambassadors and diplomats outside of the walls of the company" (Kanter 1998, p. 35).

The good news: companies that constantly re-innovate based on internal and external feedback do not need radical changes. "The environment created by managers determines whether changes are a shock – a leap into the unknown – or a next positive step in a long row of measures" (Kanter 1998, p. 37). The best way to initiate change is to create favorable conditions for a natural and systemic change.

Creating Nets

"Networking" is a buzzword of the modern business world. The Internet is also called the "network of networks." Yet I maintain that interpersonal relationships are the "network of networks." Ultimately, the Internet too is just another medium. The biggest benefit I can gain from the technical revolution as a leader is if the new possibilities help me to maintain my real relationships, privately and in business.

After all, interpersonal relationships are the only real thing in this virtual world. They provide support and orientation; they help the employees and the leaders to position themselves. Relationships are a safety net in times of change. Data streams alone cannot create emotions, sympathy or trust. Ultimately, there are still real people sitting at the computers of this world.

No matter which medium they are using – Internet, extranet, intranet, telephone or personal conversations – leaders have to be good networkers and have to be able to form new relationships based on appreciation, trust and genuine affection. They must (no longer) play the watchdog and interfere, but should instead support and integrate: "Partnership is based on trust. Since communal enterprises bring together groups with different methods, cultures, symbols and even languages, good cooperation depends heavily on empathy (. . .)" (Kanter 1998, p. 61).

Where the Strands Meet

Rigid hierarchies and control mechanisms will continue to be replaced by networks of people sharing information and experiences on all levels, across department borders and areas of responsibility to make it available to everyone. Ideally older and more experienced colleagues will become mentors for younger employees: networks can smooth workers' career paths, open doors and provide opportunities. They reveal and support expertise. Networks mean membership and an identification with the whole, and fulfill the desire for social integration.

Good leaders are the knots or nodes of the network, collecting and delivering information and bringing together the right people. From the vantage point of these positions they can detect trends in departments, the company and beyond early and react to them. One such example is Jorma Ollila, the head of Nokia, who sees himself as a person who understands how to connect people. "Connecting people" is not only an advertising slogan for his cell phones but also his maxim of leadership.

"Leaders are bridgeheads between the individual areas of an organization and they should ensure that the departments are able to learn from each other. (...) Leaders have the responsibility to distribute knowledge throughout the company and should act accordingly" (de Vries 2002, pp. 68–69). Successful CEOs see themselves as politicians who open up their plans to the representatives of the company for approval. Their offices have open doors and are accessible to the company and to society at large.

Team Players Instead of Lone Warriors

The main tasks of leaders include seeking internal synergy effects, developing strategic alliances, promoting new endeavors and bringing together effective teams. A successful manager has to have supply, information and support chains; he or she has to have the means to create conducive conditions within the company. Raymond Smith, the CEO of Atlantic Bell put it like this: "The efficiency of the innumerable daily interpersonal interactions is the most important determinant for the success of a major company" (Kanter 1998, p. 90).

To a great extent, leading today means dealing with positive dependencies. And this is even more the case in situations of change. Leaders have to master the classical tasks of management such as creating plans and budgets and acting within hierarchies. Hence, at the same time they have to be able to use social networks to pursue the goals of the company and to introduce inspiration and vision to it: "(...) because leaders work in a complex network of interdependent relationships, this work is increasingly coming to mean an interplay of informal dependencies, instead of just exerting formal power over others" (Kotter 1999b, p. 20).

Connections are flexible assets. Thus, some rethinking has to take place among leaders: their duties are now more related to networks, dependencies and leadership, instead of the formal authority, hierarchies and management of the old school. To me these two patterns of management and leadership are not opposites, but should complement one another: management focuses on business-related duties, while leadership focuses on people, visions and emotions. In this regard John P. Kotter has noted that many of today's companies are "overmanaged" and "underled." For Kotter, the leader of the future is a "leader-manager" combining both profiles.

Networks are not one-way streets. To the same extent that (highly qualified) employees are becoming co-entrepreneurs, they are also becoming central parts of the networks that span all levels of the company. Good relationship management also includes the relationship to your superiors – for employees and leaders alike: "Managing your boss well means understanding them and their context, knowing your own skills and needs and developing and maintaining a relationship that fulfills the needs of both (Kotter 1999b, p. 22). The relationship should meet the central needs of both and each partner should add their own strength and compensate for the other's weaknesses.

3.2.5 Leading Means Letting Go

Most leaders see themselves in the "hands-on" role, moving things and people and having everything under control. However, in many cases they go over the top – surpassing their own goals, those of the company and those of their employees. Managers who do everything themselves at breathtaking speed, living in a state of constant motion in order to prove their indispensability to themselves and others often produce unmotivated employees, costs resulting from rashly made decisions, and a ruined private life. Therefore I maintain that leading also means being able to let go. Loosening their grip on the reins is hard for many managers to learn, but absolutely necessary.

3.2.5.1 Delegating Means Having Free Hands and a Free Head

One of the most frequent causes of failed leadership is micromanagement. Some leaders simply refuse to delegate or want to at least supervise every little thing themselves. The stress and overload that more and more leaders are succumbing to and that in the worst cases ends in burnout evolve from the inability to let go and delegate, as well as the inability to separate important and urgent matters from others. Everyone wants everything immediately because we believe that everything urgent needs to be done right away – and by us personally. The Internet and email have contributed greatly to this mania, with mails showing up on the screen in seconds requesting an answer as soon as possible.

Especially leaders must not get lost in the little things, thereby losing sight of and having no time left for the whole. A person who is able to delegate tasks and responsibilities to others – this is the key – has time and energy for the real tasks of a leader and promotes the development of their employees at the same time. This allows employees to grow with their responsibilities, generating a climate of trust and partnership. Delegating is an art and the secret of efficient managers. Yet 80% of German managers still organize their own schedules themselves; only 16% have this done by someone else. These managers use roughly two-thirds of their time for purely operational business – an alarming balance that leaves precious little time for strategy in their daily work. (see *Frankfurter Allgemeine Zeitung*, August 18, 2003.)

Operational work must neither take precedence over visionary planning nor block the view from the ship's bridge. Matters that are really important must be attended to or decided on by the leader himself or herself. Projects, tasks and appointments that are urgent but not important can be easily delegated to employees. The same is true for tasks that are standardized or can be better handled by others. And everything that after a bit of reflection proves to be neither important nor urgent should get thrown in the trash. Those who set clear priorities will find it easier to make these distinctions, saving a great deal of time and energy; they neither waste time on irrelevant matters nor trouble their consciences by worrying about tasks they constantly put off because they lack the time to complete them.

Those who cannot delegate effectively cannot lead effectively. Leaders are not paid to do everything themselves. It is their job to make qualified decisions and to make sure that all tasks are performed by the appropriate level in the hierarchy. Delegating is an instrument of leadership that ensures that tasks are completed on time and in the agreed-upon quality and quantity, efficiently making best use of all resources. However, delegating is not intended to allow leaders to avoid tasks they don't like by treating their employees as lackeys.

The golden rules of delegation can be expressed in five questions:

1. What needs to be done? The reason for the task and the description need to be clear.
2. Who is responsible? The responsibility needs to be precisely defined and include the corresponding authorizations.
3. Why does the task need to be performed? The background and the importance of the task in the broader context should be explained.
4. How should the task be performed? The decision as to how to complete the task should generally be left up to the employee; it should only be defined in advance if absolutely necessary.
5. When should the task be completed? Solid and realistic dates for tasks and sub-tasks, including a buffer, should be provided. The leader also delegates the necessary authorizations/authority, information and responsibility. Leadership and supervision remain the responsibility of the leader.

Delegating has a number of advantages: the leader has free capacities for other tasks. The knowledge, experience, skills and potentials of the employees are put to better use. The employees improve; the number of people solving problems increases; employee satisfaction increases; their willingness to take responsibility, attention to quality, and personal commitment are all supported.

Why do so many leaders delegate so rarely? Mainly because they are afraid of losing control, because they are convinced of their own indispensability, or they lack trust in their employees or fear competition; or it could be out of habit, due to a lack of perspective, or because of their secretiveness.

The courage to let go, courage to differentiate between levels of importance, and the courage to throw things away are virtues of successful leaders. They do not jump on board each passing trend; hence they follow their goals and do not let themselves become distracted from their course. They consistently make the time for their "A" priorities, keeping out of the daily hubbub in order to work on them in a concentrated and disciplined way. If time is left they work on their "B" priorities. "C" priorities are either delegated or can be left untouched until they just go away. In many cases it is not necessary to act immediately after all.

Letting go also means not grimly holding onto a matter out of pure perfectionism. The Pareto principle shows that 20% of decision-making time is sufficient to arrive at 80% of the solution. For the remaining 20% of the solution you will need 80% of the time – a calculation that doesn't pay off. As such, a further leadership strength lies in the recognizing what amount of effort is really necessary instead of wasting valuable time and power to make your own work look perfect (see Seiwert 2002, pp. 32–59) (Fig. 3.3).

Successful leaders have "SMART" formulations for their objectives. That means their goals are Specific, Measurable, Action-oriented (or Affirmative), Realistic and Terminated. This makes objectives concrete and achievable, and allows them to be

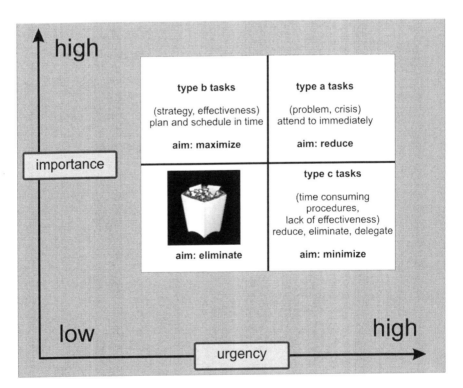

Fig. 3.3 Important versus urgent tasks (*Source*: Seiwert, Lothar J.: Das neue 1x1 des Zeitmanagement, München 2002)

monitored. Goals are also broken down into well defined, challenging but achievable sub-goals. Goals set too high are discouraging, imprecise objectives cannot be reached, and objectives without timelines tend to get put on the back burner.

Time management is important, though it makes little sense to plan every minute of your day. This produces a constant feeling of dissatisfaction if you again have finished only 17 of 35 items on your list or you are 2 h behind your own schedule, which you'll never catch up on anyway. It is better to plan buffer times for unforeseen events such as spontaneous meetings, unannounced visitors, longer phone calls, etc. In planning the day the leader should regard his or her own personal performance biorhythm: some can concentrate best in the morning, while others are night owls. You should schedule the most important projects and strategic decisions for these times if possible.

Good leaders always know when their batteries are empty – and they take the time to recharge them. They keep in mind their work-life balance and also pay attention to maintaining the work energy, motivation and performance of their employees. Modern human resources management provides the instruments needed to create balanced personal time schedules for leaders.

Above all, this includes the focused use of resources and preventive measures in private health management. Both factors have a considerable and growing influence on companies' efficiency and competitiveness. Following the work-life balance principle, human resources departments serve as advisors to and partners of the top management. Stress-related illnesses occur especially in middle management, a trend that must be combated in the interest of both the people and the company. After an analysis of the causes of the problem, individual coaching and seminars on time management and self-management, healthy nutrition, regular medical checkups and corporate sport facilities are recommended.

In many organizations there is no room for feelings of insecurity, weakness and fatigue; the image of the always-dynamic manager is predominant. Many try to live up to this image, denying who and how they really are until at some point they truly believe they fulfill it. However, this is dangerous, not only because it can lead to burnout, mental disorders and depression, but because it also undermines the leader's authenticity and credibility.

One could say that only leaders that are also weak are truly strong. I believe that as a leader it is perfectly permissible for your employees to also witness your being confused, at wit's end or angry at times. Such "human moments" create closeness that helps leaders' credibility. Without allowing ourselves to feel seemingly negative emotions such as fear, anger or sadness, there can be no development.

The phenomenon of burnout is not primarily the result of excessive workloads. Rather, it results from a person's inner attitude towards work, from how they experience that work. People who identify themselves with their work and feel their work to be meaningful and satisfying are experiencing consider higher workloads challenging, but not overwhelming or stressful. The best way to avoid burnout is to let go of our own unrealistically high expectations, perfectionism and self-imposed time pressure, as well as to free ourselves from the feeling of being controlled by others (see Sprenger 1999, p. 114).

3.2.5.2 Conquering Free Space

In many cases the driving force behind the often-heard lament about lack of resources and lack of time is something else: the fear of executives to act according on their own opinions. Instead, all day they are busy doing what they think others expect them to do. According to different estimates, approximately 90% of the managers are thereby wasting their precious time and reducing their productivity – despite well-defined projects and goals, and despite having the necessary know-how for their job.

They are caught in the trap of inefficiency, because they think they don't have enough personal freedom. It is the ability to take the initiative that makes the most important feature of any successful manager. The truly effective managers rely on their own opinion and consider their situation from a long-term, comprehensive and overarching perspective. They break free from given structures and stiff expectations and assume control over their job, instead of being controlled by it.

Good leaders have learned to manage requirements, and in so doing have overcome the feeling of constant strain. They work purposefully instead of just constantly playing the "fire department," because there's always a fire to put out somewhere. They provide resources and develop creative strategies in order to overcome real or perceived limitations, and do not blindly follow any "strict orders from above." In short: effective leaders do not work in the narrow context of individual tasks, but in the broad context of their company and their careers. They have an active and not reactive attitude.

Effectiveness is one of the most important characteristics of successful leaders, and it can be learned. Peter F. Drucker formulated five rules for an effective working style:

An effective leader utilizes good time management to ensure that what little uninterrupted time he or she has is used economically.
He or she is more focused on the results than on the activity.
He or she makes use of positive forces rather than weaknesses.
An effective leader sets clear priorities for a few, central areas and for the completion of his or her primary tasks.
Finally, an effective leader makes only sound and not rash decisions (see Drucker 1967, pp. 44–47).

In order to combat the habit of constant hassle, managers need to liberate themselves from the desire to be irreplaceable and must not bask in the sense of their own importance. It may be easier to put out spontaneous fires than to consistently set priorities and follow through on them. But if managers do not use these options, because they constrain their own room for decision-making from the outset, they needlessly reduce their available options. Many managers make the mistake of constantly having to be reachable for supervisors and employees. Especially young managers feel flattered by the competition for their precious time. And the busier they are, the more important they feel. They want to make everyone happy at any price – a futile attempt that is ultimately unsatisfactory for all parties.

The difference between leaders who take the initiative and the others becomes especially evident in times of major change, when work becomes chaotic and unstructured. Managers who become exhausted by trying to meet all real or anticipated expectations of their environment become confused and paralyzed by the lack of a solid structure. Effective leaders try to expand their latitude; they expand their opportunities and pursue their goals – i.e., the goals of the company – using new and unconventional approaches.

3.2.5.3   Providing Free Space

Each manager has a clear idea of how their employees should be, and they judge them according to their own – very rarely questioned – standards. Letting go means allowing employees to have their own personalities. It means taking them as they are and refraining from shaping them (see Sprenger 1999, p. 218).

Truly good leader make themselves obsolete. They make the greatest impact not through their own knowledge, but through the abilities and skills of their employees, a fact such leaders accept and appreciate. They empower, encourage and urge on their employees; while making decisions, they consider their impact on the development of their people. These leaders make sure that the company can also run without them, and train their successors early on.

Employees today expect more from their work opportunities, in order to get involved with the full potential of their personality. They want to be involved as a person and they want to use their abilities for self-organization and acting autonomously. It is no longer the question: "Live to work, or work to live?" People want to live while working – and not just after. Reinhard K. Sprenger formulated this as follows: "The only organization, which we all work for, is called 'me.' But companies rarely offer opportunities to try out that 'me' and to lead a happy professional life. The opportunity to live a self-determined, self-organized and self-controlled life is the greatest adventure ever. It is about getting to know your own personality and learning to cross your own boundaries" (Sprenger 1999, p. 239).

What people need is freedom. The size of their free space is determined by:

the degree of choice, autonomy and decision-making latitude within their defined scope of work;
the degree of deregulation of labor in the form of eliminating those guidelines, policies and regulations that are not absolutely necessary;
the proportion of time for independent and creative activities;
the quantity of tasks and projects beyond the scope of work that, in light of their talents and inclinations, seem particularly interesting to the employees, and
the necessary learning activities.

According to Sprenger, leading means overcoming limiting "in-the-box" thinking and allowing and encouraging employees to go beyond borders. We can no longer afford to search people who fit narrow job profiles as we did in the past. We must instead create jobs for people in order to use their multiple talents and to implement these people, their multi-faceted personalities and their individual goals into the company. Building organizations around people, not pressing people into existing structures – that is the imperative for today's leaders (see Sprenger 1999, p. 240 ff.).

If executives finally let their staff off the leash, they also liberate themselves from the compulsion to constantly monitor others, from the imagined need to always do everything themselves, and from perfectionism. And they move their company forward.

3.2.5.4 Leading Top Performers

What has just been said applies to all employees – albeit in varying degrees – but especially to the so-called "high potentials." Knowledge work is becoming increasingly important, and more and more activities are now carried out by highly qualified specialists. They need a different type of leadership. Actually, however, this is already a contradiction in terms, because top people are not "led." To collaborate with professionals and get the best out of them, you have to offer them two things: challenges and freedom.

Peak performers will be inspired to give their best solely through challenging, exciting, meaningful and long-term tasks. They work to get something going, to create something new, to help shape the future, to leave something permanent behind. They enjoy activities in which they can contribute all their knowledge and where they can at the same time learn something new, and can continue to develop.

If a company cannot provide them that anymore, or a leader fails to put top performers to good use, they will move on. They normally have no strong attachment to individual companies and are not afraid of change. They are self-aware, flexible and mobile. There is no one-sided dependence of employer and employee, but a symbiotic relationship in which both sides need each other equally.

The old supervisory system is already passé. Leading top people requires common values, standards and priorities, as well as adequate information on how the duties of the employee fit into the company's strategy. Managers have to give professionals the opportunity to choose their own projects and to determine their daily schedules individually. Professionals train themselves constantly in order to improve their performance; the interference of a supervisor would only decrease their personal commitment. Furthermore, the continuous transfer of values and a regular feedback directly to the employees is essential in order to allow them to judge and to monitor themselves. This feedback also includes the systematic transfer of best practices. Strong incentives for high potentials are appreciation and future prospects; such workers do not primarily care about money or working hours (see Kanter 1998, p. 63 ff.).

Even in our neighboring countries, a rethinking in this direction can be observed: while at Fiat the former CEO Giuseppe Morchio still wanted to command his team in every detail like a kind of general, under the leadership of his successor, Sergio Marchionne and the new Fiat president Luca di Montezemolo, the emphasis is on collaboration and delegation. The employees set ambitious goals, but also enjoy considerable freedom and the best working conditions; these are the new management principles that had once been implemented only at Ferrari, but are now also being adopted by Fiat.

By European standards German companies encourage their top people in a much more cost-intensive way than the competition in neighboring countries. A survey of 100 companies in Germany and six other European countries conducted by USP Consulting GmbH shows: German HR departments spend an average of 2,778 Euros annually on the "development" of each manager. In Britain and France the amount is only 332 and 219 Euros respectively. This looks very good at first glance. But, as so often, the second view reveals a different picture: the top German employees spend an average of only 7.5 days a year participating in training – in other countries, however, it is about 12 days (see *Handelsblatt*, May 23, 2003).

The high investments in leadership development in our country are not a sign of their importance and quantity, but the result of higher training costs. Content offered in seminars is often referred to as the "watering can principle," which distributes or more or less randomly: whoever hasn't been at a seminar for a year is simply sent 'somewhere' without regard for their specific development potential or the needs of the enterprise.

Many German companies also lack systematic and individual career plans. Unfortunately, these facts tell a different story than the nice figure on the money spent for management development. It should be on the highest level, in keeping with its actual and in most cases also theoretically recognized status at most companies. But how many staff developers actually work close to the executive and management boards of German companies? What is the position, and hence the influence of an HR manager in Germany?

Conducting Instead of Dictating

The American management expert Henry Mintzberg compares the leadership of highly qualified professionals with the leadership of an orchestra. A symphony orchestra is like many other professional organizations of highly qualified people that, without prescribed procedures or job descriptions, know what they have to do and actually do it. Thus, covert and "silent" leadership plays a larger role than evident and open leadership.

Not the leadership but the activity provides structure and coordination in an orchestra. Everyone is responsible for their own playing, their own preparation and knows when their entrance is. Likewise, most knowledge workers hardly require any direct supervision by superiors – on the contrary, supervision and targets only paralyze and discourage them. First and foremost, conducting means delegating tasks, authorizing decisions, and synchronizing the performance of individual staff members. To do this the conductor is essential, especially for large orchestras.

The conductor leads the orchestra not like an outsider, even if their elevated position would suggest this. They work as part of the orchestra on "project concert." A good symphony orchestra requires both highly trained, talented musicians and an undisputed leader whose authority is recognized by all. With their leadership they inconspicuously create the shared climate that true art needs in order to unfold. Like in modern organizations, the musicians come from different countries and cultures, and only come together for rehearsals – if at all. Orchestra musicians do not need empowerment; what they need from their leader is much more inspiration.

The approach of an outstanding conductor such as Bramwell Tovey from the Winnipeg Symphony Orchestra, who was accompanied in his work by Mintzberg, is characterized by the interpersonal concerns that he constantly has in mind. Professionals hardly have to be trained or supervised, but protected and supported. Therefore, the conductor or the executive in the company manages the relationships outside the organization properly. Working to maintain the relations with important external parties and stakeholders is an essential aspect of leadership. Internal and external relations must be harmonized; otherwise it creates disharmony.

The example of Tovey shows what leading means today: nuances and direction – and not imposed obedience and concord. "Perhaps we should much more exercise this form of covert leadership in management: instead of management actions for their own sake – to motivate, to coach and so on – unobtrusive leadership, in which all the small things that a manager does can be inspiring to others" (Mintzberg 1999, pp. 9–16).

I fully agree with this conclusion, and my own experiences with top performers have shown me the need to rethink our approach. For the executives it's time to step down from their pedestals and to learn to manage in "soft tones" (Fig. 3.4).

Based on decades of practical work with managers, Henry Mintzberg designed an integrated management model. According to this model, leadership takes place on three consecutive levels, within and outside the organizational unit. The first is the information level, at which top managers work closely with other executives; secondly, there is the level of all parties involved and thirdly, the level of action. Leaders can intervene on each of these levels, but must then also become active on the other two.

The behavior of leaders can be based on information, but it is only effective if people are moved to act. Similarly, leadership can be directed at people, but again has to stimulate action in order to be effective. According to Mintzberg, the most important leadership roles result from the action on the three levels, both internally and externally: monitoring and communicating (leading by information); conducting and connecting (leading by individuals); and acting and negotiating (leading by direct influence).

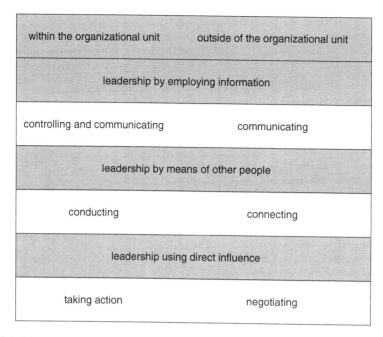

Fig. 3.4 Integrated model of leadership according to Mintzberg (*Source*: Gosling, Jonathan/ Mintzberg, Henry: Die fünf Welten eines Manager, Harvard Business Manager, 4/2002)

3.2.6 Leading Means Coping with Contradictions

Leading is not a linear process, but a constant struggle to find the best solution possible. The everyday life of a leader is characterized by inconsistencies, contradictions, dilemmas and conflicts that he or she must solve. Future leaders do not learn this at the university. In textbooks it all sounds simple, logical and straightforward. But wherever people live or work together detours, conflicts and compromises are inevitable. "In flexible structures, one needs a strong leadership that welcomes change, doubts and the contradictory and does not see them as a threat," Reinhard K. Sprenger has rightly stated. (see Sprenger 2001, pp. 82–83). An important quality that sets good managers apart is clarity. They negotiate and mediate between conflicting positions and groups with clarity, objectivity and consistency, and make sound decisions in difficult situations (see Handy 1993).

Now executives must also increasingly deal with cultural and political differences – between countries, businesses or members of the workforce. Previously, such conflicts were swept under the rug, something companies can no longer afford to do. "Leaders should encourage unease. The feeling of comfort may create a false sense of security" (Kanter 1998, p. 72).

Executives are now not only confronted with the paradoxes of our time described in Chap. 1, but also with the inherent dilemmas of the leadership process itself. They must accept the fact that certain divergent conditions, interests and goals cannot be overcome and that middle ground cannot always be found. This forces them to perform balancing acts and enter into not always easy compromises that they have to justify to others and to themselves.

3.2.6.1 Management Dilemmas

A leader must not only be able to accommodate conflicting positions between employees or between himself/herself and supervisors. He or she must also be able to live in and with factual contradictions where there is no clear way out, the so-called "management dilemmas." The intrinsic ambiguity of leadership requires daily compromises between alternatives that are either essential or feared – the choice between the rock and the hard place, so to speak. At some point, every manager will find himself or herself in one of the following 13 dilemmas (see Neuberger 2002, pp. 342–347):

1. Employees as a means or as an end
   Division of labor, goals, resource constraints, market competition and ensuring cooperation require managers to also consider staff as a means to an end or as a cost factor, regardless of how hard they work to treat them in a fair, cooperative manner.
2. Equal treatment or responding to the individual case
   On the one hand, it is the responsibility of a leader to respect and support the individuality and personal fulfillment and development of each employee, to appreciate him or her as a whole person. On the other, for the organization and work only a part of that person, specifically his or her expertise and work performance, is relevant. Managers must walk a fine line between inhuman egalitarianism and being accused of favoritism.
3. Distance or proximity
   This dichotomy could also be called: objectivity or emotionality. Unapproachable, cool, controlled and neutral supervisors who consider themselves and their entire environment purely rationally and objectively are not well suited to lead others. At the same time, overly soft, emotional and compassionate leaders do not have the necessary perseverance and authority. They can readily be accused of irrationality and indecisiveness.
4. Control or autonomy
   Managers need to ensure order, transparency, predictability and coordination. These limits and targets are needed. But overly narrow rules, regulations and job descriptions strangle creativity, enthusiasm, and self-identification. They produce blind obedience, dependence and immaturity.

5. Specialization versus generalization

 In order to assess the performance of his or her staff properly and in order to put the people and their skills in the right place, a manager needs to have expertise and detailed knowledge. Too much detail orientation can be dangerous because it leads us to lose sight of the big picture and the ability to integrate. Moreover, this can also leave little time for our actual management tasks.

6. Overall responsibility versus individual responsibility

 For the sake of themselves and their staff, managers should and must delegate – not only tasks, but also the associated responsibilities. In practice, however, the boss is blamed for any mistake made by his or her subordinates, because everyone expects them to feel responsible for everything done by those they lead.

7. Preservation or change

 Leadership is a constant balancing act between maintaining the necessary structures, values and rules and the need to adapt to changes in the environment. Constancy, stability and tradition create security and transparency. But deadlock endangers the existence and the development of the company. The manager must at the same time – even in the face of resistance – suggest and implement changes and provide the security and orientation that the employees need for their daily work.

8. Competition versus cooperation

 Competition is an engine of growth. Conflicts lead to new solutions, and competition leads to performance. In our competitive economy, always struggling for scarce resources, especially the Olympic motto of "faster, higher, farther" is what counts. But for the survival and performance of an organization whose main resource is the people who work for it, "soft" factors such as kindness, patience, helpfulness, empathy and modesty are also important. The ideal leader would be a "cooperative tiger."

9. Being active or stepping back

 Leadership means activity. Leaders are "movers"; they keep people and projects in motion. However, leaders should not only supervise but should also be able to let go, because good staff members do not have to be pushed; they gain the necessary motivation from their activity (intrinsic motivation). Executives must be able to withdraw in order to let others become active, intervening only when it is truly necessary.

10. Internal orientation versus external orientation

 Managers have to establish and maintain relationships, both internally and externally: they must be present and available for their people and simultaneously maintain networks outside the company. Networking in the entire system and in the environment is important in order to acquire information and resources; however, it also takes time and energy from maintaining internal relations and weakens the manager's support in his or her own team.

11. Goal orientation or process orientation

 This dilemma involves two other opposed pairs: trust versus mistrust and supervision versus autonomy. Goal orientation means that the manager trusts that the employees are working independently, reliably and loyally and that they achieve the agreed-upon goals through their own motivation. The manager only checks the results and does not supervise the process. However, for many executives this is too utopian and therefore they monitor the process.

12. Reward orientation or value orientation
   Reward orientation means that the employees only show good performance if they are offered external and tangible incentives in return, because they are only focused on the immediate benefit. A value-oriented person on the other hand acts on their own initiative, because they are fascinated by the task, enjoy their work, or gain satisfaction from solving problems. Values, attitudes and norms are the basis for a more stable employment than the pure exchange principle of delivering performance to receive incentives.

13. Self orientation versus group orientation
   The liberal economic thesis of Adam Smith and John Stuart Mill that selfish endeavors simultaneously promote the common good remains controversial. A manager always feels the tension between his or her personal motives and goals (which no one can completely turn off) and the company's objectives. As a third variable there are the objectives of the personnel. What is useful for one person is often at the expense of others. Zero-sum games or win-win situations are desirable but are often difficult to achieve in everyday life.

The personality of the leader develops especially in dealing with these contradictions. Here the individual, unmistakable signature of the leader becomes visible, which is also the "reward" for the stress and having to constantly face these dilemmas. With growing experience managers can better deal with contradictions and easily manage recurring conflicts. To do so they need to create open spaces and corridors for action in which they can move. And they have to reflect on themselves and their decisions, rather than simply and schematically always making the same choice like a reflex. They need a good eye, i.e., they must take a balanced view of their reality in order to successfully come to terms with the paradoxical underlying structures of society and leadership (see Sprenger 2002b, p. 165).

Despite conflicting objectives, competing values, and the opposing interests and needs of all stakeholders the leader must remain able to act. Action means deciding and living with the consequences of your decisions. It is also important that managers acknowledge – to themselves and to others – the difficult position they are in, with all the associated doubts, fears, and inconsistencies, lack of information, missed opportunities and compromises. Finally, once a decision has been made, managers must let go of the options they rejected and look forward again.

But not all dilemmas are real. Some exist only in the eyes of the leader, because they cannot see a different solution to the problem because of their personal "blind spot." Or because it may not be necessary to decide immediately, and it would be better to just wait things out. Or because some contradictions are even better left unresolved; contradictions and conflicts can also be conducive to growth, as change needs the tension between polarities. In such cases, coaching and supervision can help to clarify misperceptions and transform tensions into positive energy.

3.2.6.2 Conflicts as a Motor

In general, we assume leaders are solid and unyielding. But often they do their best to avoid unpleasant conflicts. Leaders – like all people – have a strong desire to be loved and to receive acceptance and praise from their employees, customers and superiors. The fear of isolation and loss of recognition can often lead them to avoid making decisions and exercising their power and authority. But avoiding conflicts is neither successful nor a popular or effective management style. Setting limits may be more important than exchanging niceties – and certainly does more to generate respect and esteem. You cannot please everyone, nor should you try to. Or in other words: leadership actually begins where consensus ends.

A good leader must be able to deal with contradictions and conflicts. More than that: they must ensure that they are openly expressed and resolved. And they must be able to live and work with the fact that their decisions will never be universally approved. Any leader who tries to keep a lid on all conflicts shouldn't be surprised when someday that lid is blown off – and when this happens, he or she may be accused of ignorance and weak leadership.

A survey conducted by the Academy in 2002 has shown that a major reason why teams fail is silent conflicts. 90% of the executives surveyed felt that, when groups do not (or cannot) meet their goals, this issue often plays a part. On the other hand, only 53% of the same managers believed that open conflicts were dangerous for teams (see Akademie-Studie 2002).

According to Sprenger, courage for clarity is needed, courage in order to "actively respond. A leader needs courage to clearly and promptly tell the other that he or she disagrees, or has a different opinion, or a different perspective, without judging or accusing the other and thus not backing them into a corner. Sprenger calls for confrontation rather than criticism. While criticism targets the personality of the other party and tends to unfairly generalize ("You always do that. . .") it is directed at the past and benefits only the person doing the criticizing (namely their right to express their anger), confrontation focuses only on the problem, specifically targeting a common benefit in the future by changing and learning from the mistakes addressed" (see Sprenger 2002a, pp. 209–210). Even if I would replace the word "confrontation" with "debate," I certainly agree with Sprenger.

If all the positions and points are on the table the manager must ensure that an agreement, usually in the form of a compromise, is reached. Here the relationships in companies can be compared with a marriage: Good couples are not so stable because the partners never argue – on the contrary. But after a dispute they always find their way back together again. They have a good conversation culture, a good conflict culture, and they value each other even in conflict situations. They have institutionalized rituals. That means they create spaces that only belong to them and that establish identity and connection for them.

Though in the press and public discourses on conflicts the coverage is limited almost exclusively on the negative side of controversy, these conflicts can also have a positive effect and present new prospects. When working with executives, I see again and again how much they yearn for honest feedback. Apparently, many are unsure as to how they come across. Often the opinions as to how managers see themselves and how they are seen by their employees are reversed. Thus: 80% of executives consider themselves cooperative, while 80% of their employees feel these same executives to be authoritarian.

If a manager demands feedback he or she must be prepared to be confronted with criticism. My impression is that most of the executives have difficulties taking criticism, even though the ability to accept criticism and teamwork skills are mentioned everywhere. But these are often empty words. In a discussion a colleague once expressed the following sentiment: "Many managers think that the ability to handle conflicts means that employees don't break into tears when criticized by their leaders – in other words, a call to accept the executive's criticism uncomplainingly. They hardly expect that an employee might contradict them or that a dispute might ensue."

The ability to handle conflicts has a great deal to do with the ability to make contact. In open conflicts you can get clarity by meeting the other face to face. Germans usually tend to carry out conflicts very seriously. Why is it so difficult to solve a conflict with some lightness and a bit of playful belligerence for once? Whether I as a manager really allow for conflicts depends on whether my attitude is correct and whether I am sure that I can and want to lead people. If so, then I must also be willing to be criticized. If someone, however, has too much self-doubt, then they always feel their whole personality is being called into question.

Conflicts are important catalysts and engines, because they lead to – if they are truly carried out openly and appropriate measures are taken to ensure that arguments are only about the case and not below the belt – clarified fronts, clear positions and the consideration of all alternatives. The parties have to have clear positions whereas diffuse, subtle moods and opinions must be expressed as understandable messages. This is also true for managers, who must not insist on always being right, and should welcome conflicts and opponents.

Well-managed conflicts lead to searching for a solution, for new paths to replace old, blocked ones that get us nowhere. Sometimes in dispute situations, or as self-defense or as an attack, ideas are pulled from the drawer that otherwise would have remained there for all eternity. In the "storm" creative energies can be released and put to good use. One must, however, be able to simultaneously promote the clash and to channel it so that nothing gets out of hand and personal attacks and inappropriate responses are prevented.

The manager must also "balance the conflict," i.e. keep in mind the costs and benefits involved, as constant and intractable conflicts weaken the nerves of all involved. What makes us sick is in most cases not an excess of work but human interaction if it is characterized by envy, injustice and annoying communications. Therefore, conflicts have to be openly resolved, but should never be provoked or celebrated for conflict's sake. A good conflict culture is also visible if the people are not in permanent nervous tension, ready to strike back with equal force when they are attacked. As annoying as employees, colleagues, clients or superiors can be – unfriendly opposition rarely leads us out of problematic situations but guarantees their unrestrained and unproductive escalation (see Volk, *Frankfurter Allgemeine Zeitung*, January 15, 2005).

One common argument is that in their environment leaders "produce" only the type of manager that is similar to them. And this is actually true for mediocre or bad managers. Good managers establish an argument culture and ensure that it is maintained. Where arguments are carried out openly but not offensively, dissenting views are welcome and where the boss can tolerate criticism, there is no fertile ground for intrigue or hypocrisy. Officially the courage to "think out of the box" is often requested. In reality, there is still too little of that today.

Managers must encourage their employees not to sweep conflicts and contradictions under the rug and simply leave tricky decisions to the boss. Employees must also be able to work and live with ambiguities and conflicts and to take responsibility for their decisions. Or, as Reinhard K. Sprenger puts it: "This requires managers with an open view of the values and interests that are both legitimate and, therefore, always need to be balanced" (Sprenger 2002a, pp. 237–238).

3.2.6.3 Between Daily Business and a Vision for the Future

A leader always faces two opposite requirements in practice, which can hinder each other and sometimes even require contradictory thoughts and actions: they must conduct their daily business, and they must prepare the organization for the future. This is a balancing act that requires considerable strength, vision and courage. It involves finding a viable middle course between constant revolution, which comes with great risks and high costs, and stagnation in the current environment, which carries an even greater risk and can cost the leader their head or even ruin the company.

According to Drucker, every company exists in three time zones: in the traditional zone, in the transition and in the transformation zone. These zones represent the past, the present and the future. The traditional area is the status quo, the transition zone refers to what is happening, and the transformation zone refers to preparing the company for the future. In Drucker's view, a successful leader has to manage all three zones at the same time, so that the can already do the planning for tomorrow. As he put it, there are "no future decisions, only the future of present decisions" (Flaherty and Drucker 1990b).

Modern leadership must always connect two dimensions: the structural and the interactive. The structural dimension of leadership includes the culture and the strategy (goals and instruments), the organization (tasks, skills and processes) and the quality of staff (qualifications, identification and motivation). The interactive dimension of leadership is about perception, analysis, reflection, communication, consultation, decisions, cooperation, delegating, motivating, developing, evaluating, etc. (see Wunderer 2002).

For me therefore leadership must always mean being the first to take new and innovative steps, providing an example and giving others courage to do the same. This makes it easier for employees to actively be involved in changes. As a manager I must offer my team a vision that moves our company forward and develops the employees at the same time, each of the two goals benefiting the other.

3.2.7   Leading Means Managing Change

"Change management" is now on the agenda of most managers, whether by choice or not. It is a process in which companies and employees acquire the ability to adapt to both foreseeable and unforeseeable change. Ideally, this process will take place continuously; however, in real life it happens only when stimuli, such as an acute market weakness or a merger come from the outside.

We know now that mergers often do not achieve the desired effect. Very often mergers have failed because the staff did not believe in them. This confirms the results of a survey conducted by the Academy, in which interviewed executives (see Akademie-Studie 1999). Changes often fail because many people feel overwhelmed and are not sufficiently informed about the meaning and purpose of the change. Only if the leader succeeds in providing the employees with a positive attitude towards the new situation can the business develop positively.

A survey by the consulting firm Arthur D. Little among members of the Bavarian Board of German Machinery and Plant Construction shows what change management looks like in practice: according to 88% of the respondents the greatest obstacle to successful change management is the lack of leadership skills, followed closely by the lack of willingness on the part of employees (87%). The main starting points for change were considered to be the organization and its corporate culture (35%), the strategy (31%) and the processes (18%). The main objectives of change management were considered to be saving and strengthening the company's competitive position (88%), permanently higher income (77%) and better customer focus (61%). However, the measurement of the success of change processes is flawed in most cases (see *Frankfurter Allgemeine Zeitung*, July 27, 2004). It's little wonder then that for some companies a more appropriate catchphrase would be: "Change the management."

3.2.7.1 Being the Catalyst

A leader must have a positive attitude towards change in order to accept, initiate and institutionalize it. This has also been understood by Hewlett-Packard, which advertised a new product with the slogan "HP helps companies worldwide to manage and love the process of change."

Peter F. Drucker sees managers as pioneers of change processes: "In the 21st century, each manager must take the central challenge and stand at the forefront of change in his or her organization. The pioneer of change always sees opportunities in changes. A vanguard of change looks for change, finds those changes that look most promising, and knows how to implement them within and outside the organization effectively. Ballast in the form of outdated traditions or outdated processes, products and services should be thrown overboard" (Drucker 1990b, p. 109).

Hand in hand with a positive attitude to change, good leaders often possess confidence and vision, clarity of direction, a touch for finding helpful alliances in a crisis, the ability to accept setbacks, perseverance, the ability to convince others, openness and communication skills, courage and imagination.

The basic assumption of systemic leadership is that a system (companies, but even teams are complex systems) has everything it needs for its existence and self-organization. However, what is needed to ensure that development can take place are the impulses provided by consultants, or by leaders themselves. Before such an impulse is given, there should be a thorough (self-) diagnosis of the system and its environment. A systemic issue is, for example: Who would benefit from our project failing? This question is not asked to snub someone, but to see the relevant influences on the system at any given time. A systemic leader should always ask himself or herself: How can I open new spaces in which development can take place?

Initially, changes need powerful impetuses in order to get the system off-balance and to attract and stimulate reorganization. Companies that rely only on consensus and compensation will not move forward. Limits must be tested, boundaries repositioned and expanded. Only then can a new balance gradually emerge. Changes arise in a mix of irritation, resistance, unflinching openness, sensitivity and tenacity. Only in this way can positive energies be released.

In change processes, the participatory management style (see Sect. 2.1.3.2), stressing convincing rather than commanding, has proven to be the best. Pressure should be a last resort to get the staff on the new track. People need time to carry out changes. The manager should try, wherever possible, to involve all employees in all levels of the process, to let the information flow freely and be open to their suggestions and ideas. Criticism, which is bound to arise, must be taken seriously and accepted, even if it stems from irrational fears.

The transformation of structures and systems is relatively simple; the transformation of cultures, atmospheres and relationships is not. Shaping a corporate culture that sparks acceptance of – or even better, passion for – gradual and sudden changes is the real challenge for managers. No leadership, no culture, no atmosphere for change and no innovation can be implemented overnight. Your daily work will never leave sufficient time for such considerations if you don't make it happen. Everyone has the same time; the question is how you use it. Managing potentials means to me saying goodbye to old principles rather than to good employees.

Reaching milestones on the path of change are everyone's successes – not just the leader's, which all must feel. Here empathy and tact are required of the leader to ensure that recognition and (non-material) "rewards" are distributed generously and that incentives are provided. In order to solve problems or innovate, people need opportunities to do something beyond their daily work. These opportunities can be created by leaders by means of:

multiple reporting relationships,
overlapping areas of responsibility,
unhindered and non-institutionalized flow of information,
not rigidly defined tasks,
multi-functional and above all horizontal rather than vertical relationships as a basis of resources, and
a reward system that invests in people, encourages vision and does not simply reward past performance, as Rosabeth Moss Kanter suggests.

Some managers like to see themselves in the role of the hero, who takes bold steps and sparks revolutionary changes. But precisely in times of change care and special attention must be invested in implementation, in the "push-through and follow-up" process (Kanter 1998, pp. 81–139). Changes bring not only accolades, but also costs, confusion, anxiety and the risk of choosing the wrong path. Great strategies, decisions and brilliant ideas are of little help when it comes to the implementation problem.

3.2.7.2   Caught Between All Stools

The change has to begin with the manager, who has to develop a model and a new style of leadership: the manager as an innovator. Successful innovations are triggered and implemented by people who like to be on uncertain terrain, people who give themselves long-term goals and pursue them with perseverance. And they maintain a participatory and yet situational leadership style. For major changes, however, many small innovations are needed: therefore, mid-level executives and experts can also make a decisive contribution.

Some say that, if things change, then the leadership must have been weak. When old structures are supplanted, there will initially and naturally be uncertainty, confusion and distrust. At this stage the manager has to endure hostility and irritation, and possibly even to live with the situation that the staff thinks he or she was weak. The manager can also expect that the employees will project their fears and worries onto them. The new situation also creates fear and discomfort for the executives: Weren't things fine the way they were? Will I keep my position of power? Will the company really work as I imagine it after the change?

In extreme leadership situations, such as if in the context of a merger, employees have to be dismissed, and the leader has the conflict between humanity and being forced to exercise power. In situations like this they can and should allow themselves to show concern and uncertainty, but only to a limited extent. In such situations a leader must also show determination and the capacity to act. Therefore, they sometimes need a "poker face," as a leader who seems confused can quickly lose their standing.

3.2.7.3 Innovating Step by Step

Unfortunately, transformation processes tend to be characterized by the same cardinal errors. John P. Kotter, an American professor and bestselling author, therefore recommends the following seven steps for successful innovation (see Kotter 1999b, p. 85):

The manager has to create a general awareness of the urgency of change.

He or she has to form a coalition of the most influential staff.

He or she has to formulate a vivid, engaging and concrete vision, and to ensure that this vision is known to others.

Then he or she has to authorize others to act independently in accordance with this vision.

Short-term successes have to be planned, prepared for and achieved.

The achieved improvements have to be developed further.

The executive has to help to firmly anchor the newly found solutions.

Experiments with laboratory rats have demonstrated that, once they have found the way through a maze to find food, they easily get blinded and always choose the same route. For businesses this means that the more perfectly a company optimizes its systems, the more unable it is to cope with unforeseen changes and disturbances. If we always know the solution and solve a task the same way, we barely pay attention to the way we found that solution. Therefore it is advisable to occasionally break with routines in order to once more pay attention to and deal with – at least simulated – changing conditions. The employees should also be included in this "training" process (see *Handelsblatt*, August 13, 2004).

The main reason for the failure of change processes is the resistance of the employees. In three quarters of the companies practical change processes had a significant negative impact on the company's climate. In most cases resistance and unrest resulted from selfishness, misunderstandings and lack of trust, different judgments, or a very low tolerance level. The manager should meet this resistance with open communication, not with monetary rewards, threats or coercion, as Kotter advises. The negative atmosphere can also be due to an imperfect implementation process, or could stem from changes being introduced too quickly. The result: less than half of the managers interviewed were satisfied with the success of their change management projects in the past 3 years.

Serious mistakes are often made early on, while setting the goals for the change process. In most cases the strategy comprises a 150-page document and a 4 m-long wall poster containing a comprehensive list with thousands of points that need to be changed. Often the only results of such planning are a dilution of the objectives and processes, waste of resources and frustration on the part of the employees. When a change process is imminent, the Pareto principle has to take effect must be applied, and accordingly the question is: What 20% of the actions will achieve 80% of the goals?

Therefore Kotter advises leaders who want to implement changes to perform a thorough analysis of their situation and problem. This analysis should take into account the key factors and actors (partners, resistance and those possessing information) and enable leaders to select and monitor the appropriate change strategy. This strategy cannot be "one size fits all" in nature, but should take different types of people, their interests and feelings into account. Attentive, analytical thinking is required rather than mere operational stress and relying on your "gut feeling":

"Good people management is obviously the key to the implementation of this analysis. But even excellent people management cannot compensate for a bad choice of strategy and tactics. In a business world that is more and more characterized by dynamics, the consequences of a too lax choice of methods have to be taken very seriously" (Kotter 1999a, p. 51).

The next, common trap for change projects is fact-free communication, which consists only of marketing slogans and raises more questions than it answers. However, in such situations facts are the only thing that can counter confusion, frustration, and rumors. Change communication should follow four simple maxims: no secrets, no surprises, no hype and no empty promises (see *Frankfurter Allgemeine Zeitung*, August 26, 2003).

3.2.7.4 Mourning and Reorientation

According to Manfred Kets de Vries, just as a person needs time to part with habits, places or other people, organizations also have to "mourn." Such processes are common when companies discontinue old practices and begin new ones. An enterprise goes through various stages, starting with shock and disbelief, through letting go and finally accepting.

In the shock stage – after recognizing the impending changes – the employees feel off-balance and seek security in routine activities. In the subsequent phase of disbelief, vehement rejection and fear can arise. The employees cling to an idealized version of the past and block the change through their passive behavior. No wonder: the change threatens the relationships they have developed, the status they have gained status, their freedom, and the skills they have developed.

At this point the leader should explain to the employees that continuing with the status quo would have had even worse consequences, and what (realistic) benefits the change will bring. To do so it is necessary to force the conflict, so that it is felt collectively and along with it the need for change. There has to be a period of great discomfort in order for people to leave their familiar "comfort zone" and leap into the unknown.

When determining a change of course for their company, responsible leaders should use the existent corporate culture as an "anchor" and point of identification, rather than simply throwing it away. If the corporate vision succeeds in uniting the company's great past with its plans for the future, approval and support for change will be the reward. At the same time, it is the responsibility of the leader to form an alliance with the key people in the company and to create an organizational architecture in order to implement this vision: "The participation and involvement of employees is the key to success. If the organization seeks to change it has to include all employees – and not just those at the top – in the process from the outset. Employees should learn exactly what role they will play as early as the initial diagnostic phase – and not only their role during the efforts to change, but also in the changed organization that follows. They should also be given the necessary opportunities to acquire new skills" (de Vries 2002, p. 169). During the letting go stage, self-reflection begins. The individual employee re-evaluates the situation and no longer denies the problem. Reluctantly, the old ways are left behind and the new ones are tried. Finally, at the stage of acceptance the view of the staff is redirected forward. They can see the initial progress, they can find their place in the newly organized corporate world, and they follow the new course. A human resources director once told me: "Many managers have the misconception that if they leave their employees in the dark as long as possible, they will just continue to do their jobs. But they can always sense when the situation is changing. And of course this also produces the absolute worst level of credibility, because on top of everything else, the employees get the impression that their boss thinks they're stupid."

In crisis situations, what is often ignored is the fact that the staff is in a different emotional phase than the executives. The latter are often informed earlier and therefore at another stage than their employees. The "logic of feelings," as a colleague once put it, is time-delayed. When insecure employees meet leaders who already on sound ground, the situation can become critical.

In German-speaking countries organizational psychologist Klaus Doppler has done intensive work on the topic of "change management": "Changes always happen – not always planned, not always wanted, and not always accepted. They are not simple, rarely go as planned, often take longer than expected, and the difficulties involved are often greater than expected" (Doppler 1999, pp. 25–27). This finding corresponds exactly to the systemic management approach.

For Doppler, there are seven golden rules executives have to obey in change processes:

Firstly, producing restlessness and energy is important, because without these conditions nothing will happen.

Secondly, the people affected have to be involved in a timely manner. Although this sentence has become a dictum in management circles, it is still not always heeded.

Thirdly, in change processes employees and managers should "unlearn" seeming certainties, and this process is often painful.

Fourthly, according to Doppler simple links between problems and their causes can rarely be found in organizations. The location of the symptom is rarely the location of the true problem.

Fifthly, managers should bear in mind that changes are circular, networked, and take place sequentially and iteratively rather than in a straightforward manner.

Sixthly, there can be stability in the change if certain personal values remain constant through all adjustments.

And finally, Doppler calls for taking a deep breath and approaching change processes with a "cheerful sense of obsession" (see Doppler and Lauterburg 2002).

3.2.7.5 A Change of Generations at the Top

A change in company leadership is also a classical change process, which like any development process has typical phases and requires well considered, long-term planning. Beyond the content level and the structure level (guidance and clarification, goal definition, communication and implementation) it has to take the relationship level (involvement of managers, cooperation, conflict culture and feedback culture) into account.

Many changes in leadership are poorly implemented because, though the former leader and their successor clarify their mutual relationship, they only inform their employees and customers without including them. Yet everyone should know what impact changing the name has for a corporate culture. Frequently used statements like: "Actually, nothing will change, because the new boss has been in the business for a long time" are already the first step in undermining the authority of the new leadership; a leader who changes nothing is interchangeable and displays no character. These are not exactly the best conditions for establishing trust and acceptance. Of course, the new leader doesn't have to call for a revolution. But his or her own goals and visions are initially more important than merely concentrating on solid accounting and maintaining the status quo.

3.2.8 Leading Means Creating Meaning

The meaning of life is a life with meaning. And a life with meaning is one that is good for us and for others. A good leader should be concerned about his or her employees, customers, colleagues, partners, and superiors (if any), as well as for himself or herself. A leader will only have lasting success if they support the self-confidence of others and help them to help themselves, in their own interest and in the interest of all (see Hinterhuber et al. 2001).

Expecting performance is based on offering meaning. If the employees do not recognize the meaning of a job, a task or a change project, they will not be ready to support it. But how is meaning created? According to the economic and organizational psychologist Prof. Dr. Dieter Frey, creating meaning consists very specifically of conveying background information, allowing and encouraging "why" and "what" questions and, above all, enabling communication on all channels and at all levels. Conveying meaning has to be anchored in the company's culture as the right to receive as well as the duty to provide (see Rosenstiel 2003).

By "creating meaning," I don't mean postulating an absolute truth that everyone has to believe in. Meaning cannot be commanded or imposed. Meaning has to be found by every individual in what they are doing, where they are doing it and with whom they do it. I agree with Reinhard K. Sprenger's claim that the manager can only create the conditions for the individual determination of meaning (see Sprenger 1999, 201 ff): "What can companies do? Let's imagine a company whose approach is about purpose, people and processes, a company which manages to create meaning, the superstructure of goals, visions and values, a company employees can identify with, whose organization relies on entrepreneurship, integration and ongoing renewal of its own and that does not offer the employees lifetime positions, but at least a reliable contract, sending the message: 'With us you can unfold your professional potential individually.' This is necessary for extraordinary achievements" (Bartlett and Ghoshal 2000, p. 78).

However again and again companies create a communicative crisis of credibility due to conflicting business goals and messages that are mutually exclusive, understandably confusing their employees. Due to "double binds" in the form of open conflicts between management directives and other regulations or less obvious contradictions between guidelines and everyday life, employees and executives find themselves in paradoxical situations and have the feeling that they always do the wrong thing. A typical example is: "Be a team player and cooperative, but rise above competitors if you want to be promoted." Reinhard K. Sprenger calls such "double binds" the "dismantling of credibility," because they are based on an insincere communication strategy that erodes the corporate culture from the within, because it pretends to act productively while at the same time precluding such action.

If the desired culture, i.e. the idealized model, and the actual culture, i.e. the values implemented differ, then dissatisfaction, discouragement, frustration, resignation, lack of motivation and lack of loyalty are inevitable. "If you're going to talk the talk, you have to walk the walk" should be the maxim of every manager. In order to make this possible, the vision and the values of the company have to be realistic. If they are too aloof, no one can envision them and even the most dedicated executive can live up to them. The employees will suffer from the resulting credibility gap, become cynical, passive, resigned and save their energy for their leisure time.

More important than the preached visions and guiding principles published in the company's glossy magazines are the unwritten and unspoken messages, which are visible in specific behaviors, organizational structures and traditions. Actions are the true, clear and unambiguous messages. Credible leaders do not only live out values and principles, they are also able to communicate, to justify, to question, to be questioned by the employees, and to revise those values if necessary (see Sprenger 2002a, pp. 223–241).

For modern knowledge workers at all levels of the hierarchy the purpose of working is no longer (only) monetary. Creating profit and shareholder value are necessary prerequisites for the survival and competitiveness of an organization, but these two goals do not imbue the work with any deeper meaning or represent the true value of a company. Today's managers and employees want to identify with their product or service, and with their company – after investing a large part of their time and energy in their work.

3.2.8.1 Meaningful Work

Sigmund Freud maintained that mental health results from love and work. There is little to add to this, I think. Work should be one of the anchors for our psychological well-being and balance. This anchor can and should help us to find our individual identity, foster personal development, and strengthen self-esteem by providing successful experiences and satisfaction. But if work is to be healthy in this sense, the organizations – and their top executives – have to start investing into meaning. Manfred Kets de Vries confirms this: "It is for the company as a whole extremely important that the individual employees feel good; and therefore efficient, accountable leadership is an essential factor in the health equation at work" (de Vries 2002, p. 245).

Work is a central factor in human beings' search for meaning. A work that satisfies and fulfills a person gives them the feeling of being important, offers guidance and continuity in a discontinuous world, and through financial prosperity provides a form of confirmation. Beyond this individual level, work also has a social meaning and generates value for the public.

For most people today, however, work first and foremost means something else: stress. From interns to CEOs, more and more people are suffering from their normal work. It burdens them and overshadows all other areas of life. The causes are high pressure; lack of recognition, personal responsibility and prospects; the fear of unemployment and a lack of commitment to the company. "Companies refuse to keep playing the (previously acquired, consciously or unconsciously) role of the 'container.' The company's management no longer provides a supportive environment in which people can feel secure, and thus the stress is increasing at the workplace instead of decreasing. And employees' mental health suffers" (de Vries 2002, p. 257).

According to a Fortune ranking, the most successful companies in the U.S. are characterized by an inspiring management, excellent resources and meaningful work. If the employees trust the managers, are proud of their work and their company, and a comradely atmosphere and humanistic culture are dominant, a company is successful.

What does such a climate look like? In order to answer this question we need to go back to Maslow's pyramid of needs (see, Sect. 2.3.2.1). Primarily two of the described five levels are relevant for work: firstly, the need for ties and group affiliation and the urge to be part of a larger context. The yearning for closeness and commonality is universal and cross-cultural. Secondly, the need for knowledge and confirmation is important. This includes the ability to play, to learn, to think and work, and thus forms the basis of efficiency, competence, flexibility, autonomy, initiative and diligence.

Activities, whether private or professional, will be experienced as meaningful and fulfilling if they are compatible and consistent with these two basic needs. The need for community and the emergence of an "us feeling" can be satisfied by companies through the establishment of small units (departments, work groups and teams), decentralized decision-making, and mentoring programs. The need for knowledge and confirmation can be supported at all levels by coaching, seminars, staff meetings and a corporate culture that promotes experimentation and innovation, initiative and ideas and communicates that errors are not strictly penalized, but are accepted as part of the learning process.

According to Reinhard K. Sprenger people will consider their work meaningful and satisfying if planning and implementing go together and if they can creatively shape their environment, if the activity is productive and purposeful, i.e., useful for someone, and if it is interactive and provides a variety of social contacts and exchange opportunities (see Sprenger 1999, p. 231 ff.).

Given the great importance of the meaning of work, it is all the more important for a company to provide a collective value system. Manfred Kets de Vries summarizes how the corporation can provide meaning in five points (see de Vries 2002, pp. 253–254):

The business purpose has to make sense for the employees, and visions and goals must be clearly articulated. By advertising these visions the leadership creates a strong sense of togetherness and important group identity under the slogan "We're all pulling on the same rope and we can move a lot by joining forces."

The management has to provide the employees with a sense of self-determination. They are not small cogs in the gearbox, but major engines.

An employee has to have the opportunity not only to passively do the work others assign him or her, but also to be involved in the company as a personality.

The manager needs to support the skills of employees and ensure that each individual can develop in keeping with their abilities, expanding their strengths and perhaps even discovering new talents. Lifelong learning is the motto. Only this can satisfy human curiosity, preserving creativity.

The company's top must anchor strong common values by embodying them and living accordingly. The fundamental values of each organization should include: teamwork, openness, respect, customer focus, motivation, entrepreneurship, fun, reliability, continuous learning, change, empowerment and trust.

Organizations that meet these basic human needs will shape the future. Kets de Vries refers to them as "authentizotic organizations" (de Vries 2002, p. 245). This term is composed of the Greek adjectives *authentekos* (authentic, credible), and *zoteekos* (vital). In the business context *zoteekos* stands for the energy that a person gains from their work. In the twenty-first century, the demand for enterprise authenticity (a terrible term that nonetheless aptly describes the facts) is becoming increasingly felt.

Authentizotic companies offer their employees work with a sense of wholeness and balance, which meets their needs for knowledge, cognition and learning, but also for social interaction and satisfaction. The employees manage their work and their own time, their interests and ideas, and experience their work as effective and autonomous. They are in essence co-entrepreneurs and "joint owners" who can motivate themselves (see de Vries 2002, pp. 254–257).

Authentizotic organizations also create a supportive and protective environment – although this does not mean employment for life. They look much more carefully at new hires and have extensive training and educational resources. Steep hierarchies are abolished; decision-making and responsibility are widely dispersed. The executives are not just implementers of decisions already made from top to bottom, but are open to suggestions and respond to their employees. They practice "management by walking around," are present and responsive.

Within the corporate structure, there are many mini-enterprises, enabling project teams to take on responsibility. Small, flexible units allow employees to exchange information, get to know and complement each other. "The successful interaction between people and departments is wanted and rewarded, and as a side-effect it shows a high degree of confidence" (de Vries 2002, p. 256).

To Kets de Vries, leading means providing meaning, hope and showing humility – properties that come more from an accurate self-image – and it means never losing your sense of humor. Successful managers can also laugh about themselves and with others, which makes them human and trustworthy and spreads optimism.

3.2.8.2 Celebrating Together

Especially in processes of change good management is based on various criteria such as leadership personalities, formal and informal contexts. The first point, for example, includes the leader's function as role model and inspiration. Here the formal context is strongly influenced by the architecture and project steering committee, milestones, project management tools, etc. And in change processes the informal context includes the social, but also the mental environment of the affected persons, departments and divisions. The mental environment is visible in metaphors, symbols and rituals of corporate culture, not unlike the connecting, creative habits of intimacy in romantic couples, who keep their love alive even after the initial "in love" phase is over, and see themselves as a unit separate from their environment.

In business rituals also provide a feeling of togetherness for teams, departments and employees of a company at different locations and on different continents, or even on a virtual level as a unit. They create a "corporate identity" and strengthen the spirit of the organization. Particularly simple and effective enterprise rituals are celebrations. There are always occasions to celebrate, whether summer or Christmas, big internal or departmental events or just drinks after work. For example: The now-controversial but nonetheless very successful CEO of the Walt Disney Company, Michael Eisner, even personally sold hot dogs at company celebrations as a gesture – and an important symbol to his employees, suppliers and clients.

But unfortunately many companies are currently trying to save money in the wrong places, accuses Reinhard K. Sprenger. Now that for many the profit curve is pointing more reliably upwards and a stable "ongoing crisis" has set in, the feeling is spreading that there is nothing to celebrate anymore. Everyone is waiting for a better tomorrow, and entire businesses are in a nervous permanent mobilization for the future. Or the individual employees are emotionally "already gone" because they feel that they could lose their jobs at any time anyway. The here and now, the "we" doesn't count. But it does – actually, it's the most important thing.

It is at celebrations that the employees feel again that they are all sitting in the same boat and are pulling together. They feel that they are appreciated by the company's management, that they are really the most valuable "capital" of the company, and that the company is ready to go to some expense to ensure they are happy. Celebrations offer communication platforms outside of the copier-room or coffee kitchen and open up (time-) spaces for meetings. "Celebrations create anticipation for what lies ahead of us, allowing us to expect a change for the better" (see *Handelsblatt*, August 13, 2004). This positive team spirit that people can refuel at celebrations motivates them more than anything else. It gives a meaning to overtime and sets a sense of (positive) self-fulfilling prophecy in motion. As Sprenger has put it, "Nobody lives for achievement. We all live for the superfluous, for the surprises, for the little bit of luxury, for the splendor that festivities every now and then lend to our lives. Festivals are part of the identity of a company. For the grand stories, without which cooperation and cohesion are impossible." And he is absolutely right. Even small successes are reason enough to enjoy each other's company and celebrate the performance of others. Celebrations spread a feeling of wellbeing, community and security.

3.2.9   Leading Means Having Power

Today the word "power" has a clearly negative connotation. It suggests fear and sounds like manipulation, abuse, arbitrariness and despotism. For this reason many leaders, however, refuse to see themselves as powerful and to openly exercise power. But even democratic leadership is not without power. Power is a motor, as Peter F. Drucker once put it, and power is the basis of decision-making and responsibility. Especially young leaders often fail to fully use their capacities because they don't yet understood the positive dynamics of power or haven't yet developed the necessary instincts to obtain power and to exercise it, as John P. Kotter notes.

To put it very clearly and unequivocally: even systemic leadership is based on power, because without power you cannot claim leadership or enforce decisions – you can do nothing. If managers on the one hand deliberately sacrifice their own stability in order to give their employees freedom and to spark change, at some point they will have to regain the stability they have lost. In large organizations powerlessness may be a bigger problem than the exercise of power. Consulting and coaching for managers must aim to give them more power or to give them a sense of their power.

Leadership has to be clear and it has to be accepted. Only if the leader no longer has to struggle for his or her appropriate status are they able to redefine their role and act for example as facilitator, mentor or coach for their employees. Successful managers know intuitively what means of acquiring and exercising power are seen as legitimate by other people, and what obligations are associated with their power. They accept that power is a part of leadership (see Kotter 1999b, pp. 94–113).

In order to manage processes of change, a leader also has to have the strength and courage to accept a temporary loss of power in order to gain power in the long term. They may not however infringe on the power of others in order to feel powerful again, or seize everything and seek to defend their territory (see Kanter 1998, p. 157).

Even in stable times – if they still exist – a leader must not neglect his or her real task, namely producing results. Precisely because it is so obvious, they think the least about it and therefore quickly lose sight of this goal. Leadership is not a purpose in itself but a means to an end. A recent study by Droege & Company shows how necessary it is to remind managers to return to the purpose of their work and to stay focused. The results show that 81% of managers do not consider their projects successful. Only 2 of 217 indicated that their project objectives had been fully achieved. The reason for this poor performance is primarily a lack of project supervision. Many projects are on track, and then nobody pays attention to when or whether they arrive at all (see *Frankfurter Allgemeine Zeitung*, July 28, 2003).

A well known exception is the CEO of Porsche, Wendelin Wiedeking. He is a responsible leader, sets clear goals and monitors the results. He does follow-up work and makes good use of his authority and power, considering not only the numbers but also the people involved. And he is very present, not just in his own business but also in the public, by means of which he in turn strengthens the Porsche brand.

3.2.9.1   A New Power

Today, effective leadership is not based on formal power. Formal power is only borrowed and manifests mainly in position titles, status symbols and boxes on the company's organizational chart. The demand for flat hierarchies, teamwork and cooperation could even give the impression that the modern company should be declared a power-free zone. This impression is wrong. Rather, the term "power" should be redefined (see Kotter 1999b, p. 94 ff.).

The traditional sources of power are drying up and the landlord's authority is no longer needed and no longer enforceable. In addition to the formal power, however, there are still other forms of power that are not awarded, but that must be earned or embodied: power through vision, charisma and strength of contact, in other words: power through meaning. This power is person-based and arises from the personality. It is the power of the modern leader (see Pinnow 2003b, p. 7).

This productive power, which is exercised through a network of interest groups, differs fundamentally from the power that executives exercised in traditional bureaucracies. The new power stems from two sources: first, from the access to resources, information and support; and secondly, from the ability to find and mobilize staff and allies. This power requires emotional intelligence and the ability to manage relationships (see Kanter 1998, p. 146).

Today's leadership is no longer about obedience and command, control and punishment, but about the power of relationships. This form of power is obtained by others committing to be led by you, by having a reputation as an expert, or by making others identify themselves with your own goals and values (for a good leader, these are always the goals and values of the company). Another way to gain the power of relationships (that I do not recommend, as it is counter-productive and in my understanding the opposite of good leadership) is to make the employee aware of his or her dependency. The same applies to the method of demonstrating and expanding your own power over individuals or groups by constantly enforcing changes in their immediate surroundings (see Kotter 1999b, p. 94 ff.).

3.2.9.2 The Balance of Power

At this point I do not see any need to go into more detail about power always being a double-edged sword that can also be destructive. There has already been enough written on the subject, and everyone knows negative examples that illustrate how leadership can devolve to arbitrariness, or how corporate objectives and responsibility can transform into megalomania. Jürgen Schrempp, the now retired ex-CEO of Daimler-Chrysler AG, was once a charismatic, visionary leader with an assertive personality. What is left of that image now?

In every organization there are Machiavellians who masterfully play power games for their own advantage. They put their personal goals above those of the organization, they use the performance of their employees to put themselves in the spotlight and use intrigue with cold calculation. They betray others at the drop of a hat if it benefits them, they push their mistakes off on others and poison the corporate climate by sowing fear and distrust. This is how Manfred Kets de Vries characterizes this type of leaders.

His description makes it clear: power always needs a counterweight that ensures the balance. Managers must also be monitored, and in any organization there should be an institutionalized oversight body that the executives have to face regularly. Especially leaders need feedback, because it is lonely up at the executive levels, where they have to decide on the company's future isolated from everything. Even on the 30th floor, executives must work to stay grounded. Power corrupts very quickly, and people can easily lose themselves in reciprocal loops if they get no input from the outside.

A position of power should not lead the person who holds it to burn all the bridges behind them so that no one can follow and perhaps dispute their position – if not today, maybe tomorrow. In the interest of the company there has to be a living development of executives. The old and the young should communicate more and show their mutual appreciation for what the other generation contributes in experience and wisdom on the one hand, and fresh energy and innovation on the other. Both sides stand to learn a great deal, advises Kets de Vries.

Leaders' mistakes must not be swept under a thick, soft rug. And they do not even have to be if there is a corporate culture that considers mistakes opportunities for improvement, rather than something that no one is allowed to make, especially not the boss. It must remain possible to call their choices into question. But they certainly don't have to step down because of minor violations, assuming their overall strategy is right; they also have the right to fail and get back up again.

3.2.10   Leading Means Giving Orientation and Making Decisions

The age we live in does not leave us the choice between change and persistence, between new and old. The change takes place, with or without us. If we do not change, others do it for us. The problem is mainly the speed of the changes, which continues to grow daily. I wonder: are we able to keep pace?

In just two generations, we have progressed from the horse-drawn carriage to the space shuttle and there is more information in the Saturday edition of the Frankfurter Allgemeine Zeitung than a man in the Middle Ages had to process in his entire life. The Internet is becoming such a huge repository of data that neurologists are already worried whether our hunter and collector brains are still able to process this information. Amid the flood of news via e-mail, Internet, telephone, fax, voicemail, videoconferencing, television, press and radio and the option of travelling between Berlin, Hamburg, Tokyo and New York we are already at the limits of our mental, spiritual and physical resilience – employees and managers alike. (see Kets de Vries, p. 81 ff.)

Decisions are becoming increasingly complex, their impacts farther-reaching, and it is impossible to have all the information that should be considered before making a decision. A residual risk always remains. But how does a good manager deal with this? How can he or she offer orientation and security in a world where change is the only constant?

3.2.10.1   Dealing Confidently with Your Own Insecurity

Good managers are honest about their own insecurity and know how to use this feeling. Quite different from the popular opinion: many leaders define uncertainty as a weakness, which they would rather see in opponents than in themselves. Using rhetoric, presentation and media training they seek to get rid of their uncertainty or at least learn how to hide it professionally. This is not only impossible, but absurd. Uncertainty is no weakness. On the contrary: many weak managers fail because they too are certain – too certain to eventually realize how little they really can predict, plan and manage.

In these troubled times how can managers keep a cool head and radiate the necessary level of security that signals to employees, officers, shareholders and customers: here is someone who has the reins in their hand and determines where we go from here"? "In a world full of uncertainty you have to try a lot of things. One can only hope that some of them will work," advises the American economic historian and Nobel prize winner Douglas North quite succinctly. He observed the best performance in executives who try to understand insecurity as a message – to themselves as well as to others.

It is no longer realistic to move from one secure position to the next. Everyone who wants to move forward must therefore plan on insecurity. This is the first step. Courage alone characterizes a daredevil, but not a leader. Successful managers know about their own insecurity, and working from this position they make decisions and communicate not only the outcome of their considerations, but also how they got there. The days are gone when you could hide behind anonymous working instructions, messages and endorsements. Today people do not want to face a *fait accompli*; instead they prefer direct communication with their superiors.

Therefore, communication professionals must be leaders in the best sense and deal with criticism. Here at the latest it becomes clear that "communication skills" means more than just rhetoric and flashy language. They include self-confidence, dialogue and the ability to question yourself. Only those who are aware of their own power of leadership and are self-aware have the courage to admit or reveal their own errors and insecurity to their employees.

Let's not misunderstand this: today, timidity, weakness and fickleness are not part of the good leader's character; they never have been. But the ability to recognize your own feelings of insecurity, fear and doubt, to identify them and to be able to use them, is the edge that distinguishes good managers from the mediocre and certainly from the bad in the twenty-first century. Communication training and rhetoric classes are good things when they help you to talk to employees directly and to clearly express your feelings and thoughts.

This gives employees trust and confidence. Crises are the best test of a personal leadership approach. In good times good leadership is hardly an art form. I have noticed, however, that in bad times many managers feel they can no longer afford employee-oriented management because of financial and time constraints. They seek refuge in being authoritarian, but often then feel they are betraying their principles. A good leader needs to preserve their autonomy and must not be infected by outer confusion. Especially times of crisis show who the true leaders are. They are still standing in front of their people when the going gets tough. For their part, employees can very well sense whether they can trust their leader, or whether they will "fold" with the first stiff breeze.

3.2.10.2 Everyone at Their Own Pace

Opening free space, providing latitude, enabling personal responsibility – these are key tasks of leadership. But that is only one side of the coin. Before calling for universal freedom and absolute self-determination and self-motivation, one should keep in mind that not all employees are equal.

Everyone needs a good balance between security and freedom to feel good, to develop, to grow and to be able to deliver good performance. While some recognize no authority, prefer to work in the middle of the night and find their own projects, others need a stable framework, fixed working hours and requirements for their work in order to orient their goals and arrive at quantifiable success.

People have different speeds. Some live in the fast lane, constantly chasing new challenges, trends and innovations, working on five projects simultaneously and are constantly learning, while the others belong to the "slobbies," the "slower but better working people" who do not rush and reliably and accurately work on one order after the other. This finding is in no way pejorative. Businesses need not only visionary free spirits, but also reliable implementers. The mixture is what leads to success.

Too much space can also mean leading too little. A manager must not only consider those employees who want as much freedom as possible and cannot force everyone else to adopt this style of working, overwhelming them in the process. They must be careful about what type of person is sitting there in front of them and what that person needs. Good management creates the optimal environment for each employee and each is positioned where his or her skills are optimally used.

As a manager you have to switch between and "leading" and "pacing" employees, depending on the situation. Leading means giving impulses, demanding, setting goals, and checking on progress. Pacing means contacting, accompanying, sensing, considering and asking. The executive must be able to see exactly what the employee needs more: someone who leads the way or someone who walks beside them.

3.2.10.3   Islands in the Storm

"For the manager of today, chaos is not merely a scientific theory. It is everyday life," (Kanter 1998, p. 73), states Rosabeth Moss Kanter, and millions of managers around the world every day would agree. Traditional values like flawless, long-term plans, unchanging rules, and strategies that are not quickly taken over by competitors, play a lesser role than in previous years and decades. But chaos does not mean we have to act without guidance or boundaries. Modern leadership grants sufficient support and continuity for employees, but not so much that creative responses to the chaos around us are discarded before they can be explored (see Kanter 1998, p. 74).

Unlike other theorists and practitioners, who are in favor of the end of hierarchies, I am convinced that threatening, chaotic situations require a supreme authority that must be "someone who can make final decisions and who can expect that they are followed," as Peter F. Drucker put it, because: "Hierarchical structures and their full acceptance by all stakeholders in the organization are the only hope in the midst of the crisis" (Drucker 1990b, p. 41). Other situations require joint decision-making and teamwork, and decisions made alone must be communicated to be understood – but in the storm, one must keep their hand on the rudder and determine the course.

Executives must find new sources of security for themselves and their employees in an uncertain environment. These include qualifications, skills and relationships, which create a new, location-independent collective identity. Even mobile people must be given a home, or as Reinhard K. Sprenger puts it: "Leadership can help to compensate for those losses that accompany modernization: against the informal homelessness on the Internet" (Sprenger 2000, p. 24).

Executives must be lighthouses and connect innovation and excellence with dignity and respect, i.e. they must be unequivocal in their decisions, but fair and humane in their tone (see Rosenstiel 2003). They must not break all traditions and values, because old virtues are not necessarily outdated even if new ones are added. The future needs background and experience (see Sprenger 2000, p. 24). Many "dotcoms" learned this lesson painfully during the Internet hype of the late 1990s. Although they had innovation, optimism and creativity, they had no experience how to run a company, how to lead employees, how to operate economically, how to manage efficiently, or how to survive crises.

Successful managers find the right balance between change and continuity, flexibility and stability, and give other people security, even in change processes, as Peter F. Drucker described in his book "Focus on Leadership": "The vanguard of change, however, drive changes forward. And yet this cannot work for them without continuity. People need to know where they stand. They must know the people with whom they work. They must know what awaits them. They have to know the values and rules of the organization. They cannot fulfill their responsibilities if their environment is unpredictable, incomprehensible or unknown. (. . .) And also the company itself needs a "personality" that makes it unmistakable for its customers and the market – and this is again not only valid for businesses" (Drucker 1999, p. 133).

It is absolutely essential that managers serve as role models. "Practice what you preach," as the Americans say. But "role model" is a big title, which many reject because it sounds like big responsibility, idealization and hero worship, even like self-sacrifice. In the end it is especially about your personal credibility and value compass, which always has to give a direction that others can follow. If costs are being cut across the organization, and perhaps even jobs are lost, but the executive board approves a significant raise for itself, then this is an extreme example of untrustworthiness to me. Significant and visible self-restraint on the part of the executives would make them "role models." They should be the first to tighten their belts in such situations, and one hole tighter than everyone else.

This is because being a role model has nothing whatsoever to do with special status – it has to do with fairness, responsibility, reliability and service. Good leaders show that they can make personal sacrifices to achieve corporate objectives, rather than letting others struggle or even lose their jobs. It takes courage to be role model. Ernest Hemingway defined courage as "steadfastness under exterior pressure." People trust those who do not buckle under outside pressure. Peter F. Drucker stressed the role model function of leadership: "The new tasks demand that in all of their actions and all of their decisions the managers of tomorrow be rooted in unshakable principles, and that they lead not only through knowledge, skill and ability, but by imagination, courage, responsibility and character" (see Drucker 1956, p. 452).

3.2.10.4   Substitute Fathers?

In contrast, Reinhard K. Sprenger feels that being a role model contradicts personal responsibility. Executives who see in themselves role models, or who are made into role models by their employees, lose their autonomy, motivation and commitment. I cannot support him in this general rejection and generalization, because I think the role model function of leadership is an important one, as just described. I understand a role model to be something like a mentor. An employee should be able to freely choose their role model and what they like about this person, what they considers valuable about them, not to copy it, but to implement their own version of it, as a consistent part of their personality.

However, management must not transform into "parenthood"; on that point I agree with Sprenger. This happens when being a role model leads to incapacitation, and the employees are educated like little children. Whoever simply copies a role model doesn't have to find out who they themselves really are, what they think and what they're capable of. This might sound very convenient, but it is actually disastrous for all concerned. A company does not need clones of the boss, but individuals with different abilities, characteristics, perceptions and visions. Powerful role models keep the staff small, make them dependent "command receivers" – and then complain (with crocodile tears) about their employees and that they as managers have to do everything themselves (see Sprenger 2002a, pp. 144–154).

Executives who are on a pedestal (voluntarily or involuntarily) appear idealized, remote and inhuman. Thus, no employee should want to become like that, nor any leader. But role model characters can also represent thinking outside the box, authenticity, humanity, fallibility, self-criticism, humility, passion, tolerance and personal responsibility, an aspect Sprenger seems to have ignored in his argument.

3.2.10.5   Between Disruption and Security

"Leaders are there to disrupt the staff at work. Their mission: to brand the 'but we always did it that way!' thinking as the harbinger of a downfall. Leaders spread the will to change throughout the corporate culture." This compact and provocative statement is from Reinhard K. Sprenger's "Leadership in the 21st Century." Leaders are there to use irritation to initiate the system (the team, the department, the company, the society) to reorganize, to change, adapt and remain flexible. Where there is no movement, there is stagnation – and this is the death of any company (see Sprenger 2000, p. 24).

But that is only half the truth and covers only half the duties of leaders. In addition to ideas, new perspectives and alternatives, people also need fixed points of orientation, and a feeling of safety and security. They follow the path of change willingly only if they can roughly estimate where they are going and what their company will stand for in the long term.

An unpredictable boss is in my opinion as bad as a drunken captain on the bridge who suddenly jerks the wheel without having set the sails for the new course. A boss who – as Sprenger postulates – disrupts for the sake of disrupting will lose their credibility and their standing. They confuse their employees and create a climate of fear and uncertainty, not one of innovation. Even Machiavelli claimed that all a leader accomplishes with constant changes is nothing more than to hide their inability to make the right decision.

Especially in times of change – and the future will be a time of perpetual change – leaders will be confronted with the resistance of employees, colleagues, clients or their own superiors, but they have to counter this resistance and convert it into positive energy. They have to redirect the wind that blows against them into their sails so that it advances the company and does not deviate it from the new course. This resistance may take the form of strong gusts, i.e., open resistance, but also as a diffuse crosswind, i.e., emotional insecurity. This case is much more difficult and malicious, as the manager does not know which way the wind is blowing and no fight can truly be openly fought. The company then hums like a hive of rumors, fears, hunches and opinions that are difficult to locate and to invalidate.

In a chaotic, confusing environment that changes every day, the staff has to use all of its power to organize and to re-orient itself. This energy is lost for the operational business and for the maintenance of relationships. What happens to the learning curve if the experiences of yesterday are no longer valid today because the executive jerked the wheel and changed course yet again? Who can finish an idea or plan a project if their work is constantly disrupted by a (superior) trouble-maker? Who can appear trustworthy to costumers if they no longer know what they're actually selling or what their brand stands for?

To avoid misunderstandings: I am not calling for leaders to shelter their employees from the shocks and evils of the world. They must always keep the future in mind, be the first to recognize trends and to prepare the company and the people for them. But not alone! People must learn to deal with uncertainty – and that won't happen overnight. We were socialized in a system that stood for constancy, safety and collective welfare. This system no longer works as it was intended to, but values and attitudes are changing only slowly.

It is important to get the people out of the ruts of their established ways, but not to overwhelm them. That goes for managers as well as for their employees. Finally, even managers can grow afraid when their environment starts to shift and falter. These fears and uncertainties have to be communicated openly, because doing so creates trust between managers and employees, as the latter feel that their boss knows about their concerns and perhaps even shares them. Reinforcing the "we" feeling in an environment of change and risk can be crucial for the success of a company.

Sprenger considers the constant "disruption" of employees' work a tribute to their self-determination. The manager owes them as much change as reasonably possible, because they are adults (see Sprenger 2000, p. 24). But is this really what the people want? Isn't it quite authoritarian to believe that you know exactly what is good for the people – namely, constant change? Creativity and performance require freedom, but also limits, even if only to be able to consciously exceed them. Excessive care coupled with distrusting control kills any motivation, "under-challenges" employees and removes their onus of responsibility – fear and disorientation paralyze people and organizations.

Leadership means traveling the road ahead. This is not about direct control, but rather giving impulses for the development of the individual and the entire organization. It is about creating conditions in which employees have the freedom to develop their own potential, and want to do their best. It is about creating a simple, understandable and clearly formulated mission based on their vision. The leader has to provide a clear business philosophy that the employees can follow. It is his or her task to bundle the performance of the people and to direct them into a collaborative direction so that their strengths are most effective and their weaknesses are negligible (see Drucker 2000). And it is also about taking responsibility for what has changed and what remains, because responsibility is crucial in every management process.

What is important? Creating free space in order to dare new things, to make mistakes, to try to create innovations without having to fear for your job, and without having to fear being ridiculed by your colleagues or leaders. Promoting individualism, providing security: We need you just as you are. Nobody is perfect, but you're the best person we have – these should the messages of the leader. Learning requires security, confidence, and trust.

Change is well and good, not for change's sake, but as a necessary adaptation to a changing environment. Uncertainty must not become a permanent part of corporate culture. Abrupt turning maneuvers, the much-debated "turnarounds," are not necessary in companies that are consistently well managed, because the leaders recognize change early and initiate gradual adjustments. Neither globalization nor the spread of modern communication technologies appeared overnight. And are turnarounds ever appropriate? Henry Mintzberg, who champions "managing quietly," rightly observes that after turning about you come back to exactly where you started and are looking the in the same direction as before.

Yet I also feel that "managing quietly" must not degenerate to "managing boringly," because leadership must always be inspiring. In this respect, I have to contradict Fred Malik again, who in a famous interview – perhaps with his own kind of provocation – has said: "Most managers are boring people. There is nothing else to report about them, as they lead an orderly life without affairs and scandals. I love boring managers. But they are never in the media, and they never go to talk shows." (Fred Malik in an interview: "Even board members should sometimes ride the subway," in the *Frankfurter Allgemeine Zeitung*, November 14, 2004, p. 35).

A middle ground must be found between leadership that patronizes, and leadership that incapacitates. Both force the employees into the role of the child or the victim, suffocating both personal responsibility and independent action from the outset. People should have a choice as to what adventures and challenges they want to face and at what speed.

3.2.11 Leading Means Inspiring People

Outstanding leaders spark something in other people. They pass along the passion that burns in them and kindle it in others through their words, enthusiasm and commitment. They do not have to push or pull their employees; they make them into true comrades. Energy, perseverance, determination and self-confidence are inspiring and motivating and are key characteristics of good managers. Perseverance, self-confidence and believing in a common goal is characteristic of successful "captains."

An example is Artur Fischer, founder of the Fischer group. In 1949 he had his first successful ingenious idea and invented a magnesium flash device. And another 5,800 other patents followed, including the world famous and ubiquitous gray dowel pins. Swabian ingenuity coupled with entrepreneurial vision made the small company into a worldwide group. But Artur Fischer was not driven by the money or the fame, which can be sensed by anyone who has met him. It is the desire to act, the joy of thinking and the fun of tinkering. What doesn't exist yet is simply invented. Today, at the age of 92, he is still announcing new patents. He is a prime example of intrinsic motivation and contagious passion.

Manfred Kets de Vries also believes the enthusiasm of leaders is a factor that distinguishes successful from less successful companies: "These companies keep their employees happy. The employees like to perform their duties, and their joy is contagious: happy employees make for happy customers. Bad tempered people can hardly inspire customers. The leaders play a key role when it comes to a good working climate" (de Vries 2002, p. 68). Top companies are characterized by a lively, strong corporate culture and internalized values. They all work together on a vision and think in systems. This "glue" is supplied mainly by well-functioning, differentiated information networks. In short: They are in love, with themselves, with their employees, with their "thing" and their company.

In order to "kindle" employees' drive and to keep them, there is a both simple and effective method – appreciation. Appreciation has always been shown too rarely and this is still the case today, although we have at least recognized the importance of the "human factor." Especially in economically difficult times in which we all must stand together, praise and appreciation are important. But at critical stages, the leaders often keep "tight" and give the employees a feeling of being replaceable. The result is that while most employees may identify themselves with their work, they no longer identify themselves with their employer. They can no longer answer the question: "Why am I working here?"

A CEO once said: "A company is after all a risk community." Risk, because it can become risky. Community, because managers and employees are all in the same boat. In our seminars we occasionally assess what motivates employees and what motivates leaders separately. And often the participating executives are amazed that the same things such as appreciation, meaningful work, and opportunities for development are named.

The problem is not simply that there is too little praise, but that if there is praise, then it is even wrong. General, superficial praise in the form of worn-out, blanket phrases is hypocritical and impersonal, and it destroys confidence and motivation. Sophisticated, personal feedback in direct conversation with the employee is required. And we should not only appreciate what they have already contributed, but should also listen to their ideas about the future.

Peter F. Drucker even went so far as to consider the promotion and inspiration of employees as a requirement for managers: "A supervisor owes it to his organization to deploy the performance potential of each of his subordinates as productively as possible. But even more, he owes the people, among which he occupies an elevated position, to achieve their highest possible performance with his help" (Drucker 1967, p. 149).

When executives have the charisma to create an irresistible vision and to create plans showing how to make that vision real, then they create meaning, they forge cohesion between themselves and other people in the company, they create a group feeling and they stimulate the collective imagination that connects people and allows them to dream. One such a charismatic dreamer is Ingvar Kamprad. The Swede had the vision of manufacturing furniture that would be affordable for ordinary people. Recently, he personally opened the first Ikea store in Moscow. Today, everywhere in the world people can fulfill their dreams of a lovely home, with the goods arriving in the distinctive blue and yellow containers. In almost every country in the world, his employees are singing in unison: "We are Ikea."

Yet it is not enough to announce an electrifying vision with drums and trumpets – they must be communicated and lived out time and again. The emotional glue that keeps the staff at all levels and the whole company together must be continually renewed; otherwise it becomes brittle and everything falls apart. If the company's ideology is really in the hearts of its staff and not just in its brochures, it can gain cult status and beat any competition.

The contagious passion of outstanding leaders is not just a flash in the pan. It burns persistently and nothing can extinguish it. Such leaders are characterized by an extraordinary determination, which is not diminished by setbacks or obstacles. Reinhold Messner had to turn back many times before finally reaching the peak to stand on Mount Everest, the roof of the world. This will and the conviction of the vision's rightness will radiate to all others and inspire them.

3.2.12   Leading Means Loving People

The previous chapters have shown that leadership always and everywhere has to do with people and is represented (from the perspective of the manager) in a variety of relationships within the magic triangle "self – employees – organization." Leading means feeling, an insight that is now reaching more and more active managers, scientists and consultants. I will go a step further and concretize this "feeling": leading means loving people.

A provocative statement, I know. You may be asking yourself "What has tough management got to do with love?" or think: "Love is part of my private life, not part of my job." And many executives share these views. They are experienced, master their tools and are perfectly familiar with the technical and business aspects of their company, but they are reluctant to show emotions and risk making themselves appear vulnerable to others. But exactly that is what the employees want to see and feel, for only this will make the boss credible and trustworthy for them.

3.2.12.1 Money or Love?

This is not a question for me: both belong together, at least in a company. The term "ability to love" might initially sound strange in the economic context, but love and power are not as far apart as we at first assume. Ability to love as a leadership skill has, as I understand it, nothing to do with sentimentalism or an addiction to harmony, but rather with certain basic values that make organic growth possible. Not by acting on command, but stemming from an inner drive, and therefore stable and sustainable.

The term "ability to love" should not be misunderstood, because it's not about intimate feelings or emotional dependency, but involves traits such as truthfulness, respect, decency and fairness to the employees. Love has a lot to do with the capacity for curiosity, affection, openness, integration, inner calm, care and awareness, actual interest, conflict resolution, common struggles, intensive contact and trust (see Höhn et al. 2003, p. 47 ff.).

Generating organic growth in a company requires a certain kind of leadership. This must ensure that gravity is stronger than the centrifugal forces working on employees. The ability to love is therefore important for four characteristics of personal leadership skills: inner conviction, contact, appreciation and resource orientation. These principles are not just rhetoric for fair-weather pursuits. They are also and especially valid when costs are being cut and even when layoffs are imminent.

Showing appreciation for employees does not mean that layoffs are impossible. And if it is determined that layoffs have to be made, a leader can stand up for their people but can hardly prevent them losing their jobs. Leaders can, however, implement job cuts in a fair way, decently and in keeping with a "culture of separation." This means that the executive makes a clear decision, informs the parties concerned as soon as possible, and potentially also organizes outplacement help and/or career counselling for them.

3.2.12.2 Philanthropists

The ability to love is directly related to good leadership and economic success. First of all, a good leader likes, knows, and accepts himself or herself. A person who loves himself/herself, radiates the necessary confidence and possesses a charisma and strength of character that spark enthusiasm in others. A leader must also love the people with whom and for whom he or she works: supervisors, employees and customers alike. He or she has to empathize and possess considerable emotional and social intelligence. Based on the leader's knowledge of his or her own person, "life charter" and beliefs, it is possible to better understand others, respond adequately, resolve conflicts productively and transform negative interpersonal energies into positive ones.

At the same time, the leader is not a family therapist and should be wary of providing his or her colleagues with "therapy." It is not the leader's task to change people or to intrude on their minds and characters, but to achieve solid results and meet business goals. You can always work on yourself and your own image, but not the others.

As a manager I always have to ask myself whether I am actually willing to accept the other party as an individual person and to acknowledge that they live according to their own screenplay of life. As Drucker claimed, "Understanding the people with whom one works and on whom one depends is the first secret to effectiveness. It is important to use their strengths, their values and their ways of working" (Drucker 1990b, p. 257).

But this is anything but easy in practice and requires an instinct for the appropriate level of closeness and distance. A manager once told me once: "I often find it a difficult balancing act to be a leader and at the same time to respect my employees as fellows. I have to maintain a clear position towards my employees in order to avoid any false fraternization. So I just had a bad experience with a female employee, who was disappointed because she first thought I was such a nice guy, and then I expected performance from her."

3.2.12.3 Appreciation Is Priceless

Those who get too little positive feedback and hear either empty words or nothing from their boss will resent it and feel worthless and misunderstood – and are consequently less effective and less thorough. It is little wonder then that 70% of German workers simply work "by the book." And the only response many executives can think of is to tighten control – which is exactly the wrong thing to do, as it only accelerates the downward spiral of motivation.

With the flattening of hierarchies traditional rewards, such as being promoted to a higher position, are gone. Managers can however show their employees recognition, appreciation and attention by other means that are not based on money or status, but on their personal contribution, and are therefore incentives for the future:

the employee is given the opportunity to determine their next project themselves. They are given more time to work on their favorite project. Or they can take part in education and training programs, and more. In working to promote employees' self-esteem and identification with their work, it is crucial that performance is clearly communicated, both internally and externally – and not that the boss collects all the praise for the work that his or her subordinates have done.

Peter F. Drucker especially emphasized this aspect. He felt that there are four prerequisites for meaningful human relationships: communication, teamwork, self-development and the development of others (see Drucker 1967, p. 107). From this perspective, managers are the trustees of their employees' resources. In many companies, however, there is hardly any real contact. Though there are many discussions, conferences and meetings, most of them fall under the category of "plenty of talk, but precious little content." Often this is mainly due to leaders' hesitation to make binding commitments and failure to truly open themselves to the other party.

It is about recognizing the other party as a person and developing an idea about what drives them. Here, dealing with emotions is extremely important. Therefore, the technical level is often reduced to a minimum in our systemic leadership seminars. We want the managers to develop a feeling for what is going on at the subconscious and unconscious levels, and not just stop at the surface. It is primarily the leader who determines the working environment and controls interactions and communication within the team.

Whoever knows how the other person is doing can much better deal with him or her, thus strengthening personal contact. This also includes expressing feelings. Once this level of contact has been established and each party can be certain of being treated with respect by the other, "negative" emotions such as anger can be addressed and discussed openly. A leader must provide his or her employees with both room to grow and a sense of security, which involves challenging and supporting them on the one hand and listening to and respecting them on the other. This in turn has a lot to do with having a positive view of people in general.

The relationship between leader and led, however, is always a balancing act: admiration can quickly turn to worship, just as criticism can devolve into senseless acts of rebellion. But if both the leader and his or her staff are aware of these dangers, a solid start in moving towards a different corporate culture has been made. A great deal of relationship management is required from leaders – this is and will remain true. Nevertheless, it is also fair to expect good employees to be able to gain attention for themselves and their ideas. I have often noticed that employees are very quick to complaint about the leadership not being suitably accessible. Of course this is often true, but did these employees try to put themselves in the leader's shoes, and have all possible means of communication been tried? Making excuses is an easy trap to fall into.

3.3   Conclusion: Leadership as Lifestyle

As previously stated in this work, good, successful, effective and relationship-oriented leadership means to me designing a world that others want to belong to. This requires more than a convenient toolbox of principles, rules and leadership styles. Leadership is not just another job, nor is it a job for everyone. Leadership is not something that can be done from 9 am to 7 pm, then hung on a hook until the next day.

Leadership, which goes beyond traditional management and is in keeping with the conditions and requirements of the modern world and modern people, is more than that – it is an attitude, a calling in life, and a lifestyle. It can be learned, but you have to bring with you the necessary qualities and abilities; otherwise communication training, presentation seminars and personal coaching will be useless.

Those who want to lead – not rule – must value, like, protect, and respect people, and must take them as they are, because there are no others. People cannot be administered or managed, but only led. A leader with the necessary social skills can be recognized less by how they handle customers and colleagues, and much more by how they treat their own employees, as well as the porter, the staff at the cafeteria or their driver. In this regard, possessing good social skills does not mean "being social" or indulging in an abundance of social niceties. Executives are not highly paid social workers; they are qualified relationship managers.

What Reinhard K. Sprenger has described as the "fully automatic air conditioning for the company," i.e., a solution that creates a positive mood and a pleasant business climate at the touch of a button, remains a dream (or a nightmare). Genuine and confidence-inspiring empathy, the ability to love, and a passion for people can be seen when leaders approach those they lead with humility and respect, conveying to them a sense that they make an important and meaningful contribution and are just as much a part of the whole as the leaders themselves. Trust, mutual recognition of performance, a shared goal of getting the most out of available resources, and the inner desire to travel down the path together – all of these aspects form the basis for sustained growth.

Chapter 4
More Than Just Talking or: The Instruments of Systemic Leadership

We do not remain good if we do not always strive to become better.
Gottfried Keller

In the previous chapters, I have taken you on a journey through the lessons of leadership. First, we explored what specific requirements apply to leadership to in the twenty-first century (Chap. 1). Then we looked at the existing management approaches and assessed the extent to which they can guide us in today's day-to-day work (Chap. 2). On this basis, I then illustrated how systemic leadership, an integrative approach and as such my preferred one, works and how each leader can succeed in creating a world that those they lead want to belong to (Chap. 3).

The following, final section will focus on pragmatically determining how the ideas and approaches presented can be implemented in management practice. I would like to present a modern leadership development model that especially addresses the issue of relationships. I would also like to reassess a number of well-known and lesser-known management tools in the light of this relationship-oriented approach and show what really matters in the application of these "means to an end." And thirdly, I would like to consider the issue of how leadership can be quantified and assessed – an aspect that is heatedly debated in light of the dawning recognition that the quality of leadership is ultimately the key driver for a company's success.

4.1 Can Relationships Be Learned? A New Approach to Leadership Development

Successful managers are unique, distinctive personalities, and there is no simple recipe for good leadership that could be taught in seminars or on the job. But ideally leadership development can help leaders to find and optimize their own inimitable style of leadership, to become aware of their own idiosyncrasies, weaknesses and strengths – i.e., their life statements – and to develop a feeling for people, situations and their attendant requirements.

D.F. Pinnow, *Leadership - What Really Matters*, Management for Professionals,
DOI 10.1007/978-3-642-20247-6_4, © Springer-Verlag Berlin Heidelberg 2011

Leadership is most successful when it combines mastery of the tasks involved and a leadership personality that can move the people working at the company. There are the leaders that sow seeds of growth. And this is only sustainable if the manager also acts according to ethical and moral principles. These aspects, together with appreciation, resource orientation, inner convictions and an ability to make contact are the necessary conditions for effective and systemic leadership. And allow me to say it once again: the effectiveness of leadership stands or falls with the systemic thinking and acting on the part of the leader. That is ultimately the personal insight that I wish to contribute to the leadership debate with this book.

4.1.1   Typical Factors That Disrupt Modern Leadership

A modern approach to leadership development must start with the right learning areas. If we consider the complexity of today's leadership, it has much to do with organizing cooperation that spans national borders, geographic regions and time zones. And unfortunately leaders often have to deal with a number of cooperation-related disruptions, e.g. in the form of demoralizing framework conditions.

If the leadership of a team or cooperation in a team is not working, usually one – or more than one – of the following 13 problems is to blame. If a leader succeeds in recognizes these factors, he or she can get the exchange of information back up and running by moving the decision-making process forward and restoring the effectiveness needed for cooperation.

1. Communication problems
   More than one person speaks at the same time. The others cannot understand what was said. Group members who are less assertive and glib and speech are not given a chance to speak and refrain from putting forward their arguments. As a result, information is lost.
2. Authority problems
   One group member will be listened to more because he or she ranks higher in the hierarchy. The boss is always right, even if he or she knows nothing about the problem at hand. More refined social skills, forcefulness personalities, and sometimes even physical appearance often mask a lack of expertise, information and arguments. Inappropriate factors gain influence and hamper or taint group decision-making.
3. Relationship problems
   Relationship problems between the group members mean that information and arguments are not listened to or taken into account. Relationship problems are transferred to the content level. This happens along the lines of the inner logic: "I don't like the other person. Therefore I will ignore or underestimate their factually sound arguments, just because they come from them."

4. Decisions

   Because no previous thought was given to which choices are more important than others, wrong or inadequate decisions are made. Or the priorities are wrong: too much time is invested in relatively unimportant decisions, which does not leave enough for the important ones.

5. Rules

   The group has not found the appropriate rules of procedure for the resulting problem. Problems with seating plans, speaking rules, powers of the group management, decision-making modes, time, etc. can have a substantial influence on practical teamwork.

6. Expressing dissenting opinions

   Members of the group are not ready to express views that differ from the majority opinion; and, if such views are expressed, are not ready to deal with them appropriately. Often, therefore, great ideas are ridiculed and shouted down by the "cheap and normal minded." No one any longer has the courage to use their potential for imagination and creativity to solve problems. There is a lack of willingness to participate constructively and to show ego strength.

7. Courage to likelihood-based decisions

   Given a plethora of analyses, the group cannot find the courage to make a likelihood-based decision. For most problems, there are good pro and contra arguments. As such, decisions nearly always include an element of risk that simply has to be accepted.

8. Time pressure, performance pressure and competitive pressure

   There are problems because the group itself is under such severe time, performance and competitive stress that they are not able "to see the forest for the trees." Especially in high-risk decisions with long-term effects, this can be disastrous.

9. Ratio of task roles and maintenance roles

   The ratio of task and maintenance roles in the group is not good. Frequently, goal-oriented task roles receive more attention than the necessary maintenance roles. This leads to frustration, since private needs and special interests cannot be satisfied. The willingness to cooperate in finding a group of solution suffers.

10. Systematic and intuitive working style

    The group is dominated by so-called "systematic" people, who always try to find a logical system for a solution, or by playful, more pragmatically oriented "intuitive" people. Yet some problems can only be solved quickly and well through the good interplay of both types.

11. Conflict resolution

    The group avoids conflict resolution. Since the good group dynamic must not be compromised, the members are anxious to avoid arguments, information and opinions that might result in a conflict. But conflicts can be conducive to better group decisions.

12. Underwhelmed or overwhelmed

    The group or individual group members have taken on a task that does not fit their skills, inclinations and abilities. They will respond to being underwhelmed or overwhelmed with resistance and by "dropping out" of the solution-finding process.

13. Identity

The group has not yet found its identity, i.e., the group is not yet sufficiently interesting to the members for everyone to fully commit and be able to identify with group decisions.

My colleagues and I have seen these thirteen disruptive factors time and again in our work with executives. The list could of course be extended, but my goal here is not exhaustiveness. I do however believe it makes good sense to always keep in mind the range of possible problems associated with so-called "soft" factors.

Leadership is not child's play, "management by"-style techniques are out, and executives are not overpaid craftsmen. I think we need new ways to clarify the importance of this issue. One such way has been suggested the Dutchman Joep P.M. Schrijvers: in his book "The Way of the Rat," which was voted management book of the year in the Netherlands, Schrijvers unveils in an amusing way the usual power games in modern companies – and shows how to best protect yourself from them (see Schrijvers 2004).

Yet readers often choke on their laughter when they read Schrijvers' not merely cynical advice. A bittersweet sample: "I deliberately use here the terms preferred by military leaders: the company as an advancing unit in which all internal rivalry and autonomy is shut off, unless it serves to accelerate the achievement of the company objectives (...). Any unifying language and staging is nothing more than calculated 'good behavior,' which hides the differences between 'mine' and 'yours' (...) Most professionals know their own interests: they want a certain position, to get into this or that salary group, have a certain standard of living, a lot of money for their winter vacation, to eat in this or that restaurant and every now and then a sabbatical. The interests of the company as a whole occur only sporadically on such lists" (Schrijvers 2004, p. 40 ff.).

There is certainly some truth to Schrijvers' statements, because sometimes those who rely on fair play truly are the ones who end up playing the fool. Being shown the machinations of the "rats" in the company by the author, readers learn much about what rocky shoals they as leaders have to look out for, and what rules and moves they have to master to do so.

And sometimes being a leader has little do with ivory towers of morality. As far back as the early twentieth century, Max Weber not only investigated the forms of legitimate rule but also distinguished between the ethics of attitude and the ethics of responsibility (see Weber 1919). The ends (of companies) hardly suffice to justify any means necessary, but responsibility also has many faces. And that means that, in some cases, as a leader I must also make harsh decisions to guarantee the desired results. This is not a call for making backhanded deals, but a reminder that executives must at times defend their values tooth and nail. Not although, but precisely *because* they want to lead systemically and successfully. Systemic thinking executives are not naïve, something I feel it is important to mention.

4.1.2 Creating Structures for Learning and Development

Executives in the German-speaking countries invest much less time in strategic than in operational issues, as a recent study confirms. Only 39% of their time is devoted to managerial strategy (see Frankfurter Allgemeine Zeitung, February 24, 2003). And doesn't sustainable learning belong to a leader's strategic and long-term strategic thinking? This point applies not only to the led, but also to the leaders themselves.

Sometimes after a promotion in a company the rumor goes around: "The company has lost another great expert and gained another bad leader." And often these cynics are right, because many managers take insufficient care of their employees and their development. The aforementioned poll presented the following breakdown of the time needed for individual activities: 34% of their time was spent dealing with their own specialized managerial roles. 21% went into planning and direction. The managers surveyed felt on average that 17% of their working time sufficed for employee motivation. Other tasks included providing information to employees and customers (14%) and solving conflicts (12%).

The managers also felt that technical and social skills are equally important. However, only 14% considered social skills something that can be learned. In my eyes, the last statement is practically a declaration of bankruptcy, not to mention the fact that it is simply wrong. The existing predispositions formed by the environment and through education and socialization are very relevant, but through targeted training and coaching, managers clearly can develop valuable social skills. The fact that according to this investigation nearly nine out of ten executives believe they cannot learn social skills leads me to the following conclusion: managers are afraid of "soft" subjects and therefore tend to quickly fire employees because of their alleged incompatibility with the team.

4.1.2.1 Bastions of Leadership Development

New leadership development faces a two-pronged challenge: firstly, structures for the development of leadership have to be created, and secondly, the companies and their advisers have to prepare the right leadership content. Let us first consider the structures:

Jack Welch or "Neutron Jack," the former CEO of General Electric, was a controversial figure; he was also very successful. One thing he achieved like no other: he trained his own executives and coined the phrase: "First people, then strategy." And he founded the pioneering corporate university called Crotonville, where he held courses. In addition, under his leadership General Electric developed a unique culture based on strong performance, but also on the observance of the company's values. There was an annual review of whether the objectives were met *and* the "GE Values" upheld. This was even taken so far that, if goals weren't met, human resources development stepped in; but if the values were violated, the manager in question had to leave the company.

The idea of a "corporate university" comes – like so much else – from the USA. The first such institution in Germany is the Lufthansa School of Business. Later companies like Bertelsmann, DaimlerChrysler and Merck followed suit. Basically, it is about connecting the learning process with the company's strategy, corporate culture and the internal change management. It was also an effort to breathe life into the new mega-phrase "knowledge management." In the meantime, there are hundreds of these company-owned universities.

Admittedly, some companies only changed the name of the responsible department; the learning philosophy and classrooms for the employees stayed the same. After all, "corporate university" sounds much more impressive than "human resources development." But I have the impression that the corporate universities have at least sensitized companies to the subjects of leadership development and human capital issues. Meanwhile, after the initial wave of founding these universities (especially in the context of the cost-cuttings in the last few years), disenchantment followed. The issues, however, remain highly relevant, and I warn against throwing out the baby with the bathwater.

It is interesting to observe: whenever in recent years a major German company was looking for a training program for its top executives or for a partner for its corporate university, then it often turned to one of the leading business schools in Europe or the USA. Topping the list were always the same names: the IMD in Lausanne, INSEAD in Fontainebleau, the London Business School, the Harvard Business School, and the Wharton Business School. These companies invited the big names, hoping to receive a wealth of suggestions from the "gurus." And this was often very successful. For example Manfred Kets de Vries, whom I hold in high esteem, is both a professor at INSEAD and leadership coach.

However, I also wonder if universities with their traditional teaching methods (lectures, case studies and group work) always deal closely enough with relationship-oriented leadership issues. For all their considerable professionalism, I believe that in addition to the traditional topics such as strategy, delegation and finances, it is especially important to reflect the perspective of the leaders themselves and to develop corresponding methods for self-perception and self-control.

4.1.2.2   Learning the Right Way

In this context keep we must bear in mind that adults learn differently than children and adolescents; after all, executives are usually over 30 and strongly established individuals. Therefore lecture formats are not always suitable for sustainable learning. I advise using the rule of thumb that an adult retains:

20% of what he or she hears,
30% of what he or she sees,
70% of what he or she talks about, and
90% of what he or she personally does.

For this reason, the seminars, the Academy offers are always experiential and behavior-based, and they strongly relate to the participants' current problems. If we at the Academy make concepts for our internal development programs, we place the emphasis on a complementary approach that takes into account several elements at the same time: seminars, project work, learning partnerships among the participants, the involvement of the top management as a sponsor and of senior executives as mentors, and above all, a detailed clarification of what we want to achieve at the outset.

It is important to us that the organization commissioning us has the opportunity to contribute its own culture – and thus its past – without in the process clinging to that past and blocking change. It is helpful if HR development managers and executives are on board and take part by actively marketing the joint program in internal newsletters and on their intranet. Thus additional attention, appreciation and momentum are gained, which our trainers can in turn use in the seminars (see Höhn and Rosenberger, Management & Training 6/2002, pp. 22–25) (Fig. 4.1).

A topic that had a boom a few years ago is e-learning. Virtual platforms for networking leaders, experts and knowledge were created to allow them to learn on their own, regardless of time and location. Companies like IBM, but also others, have provided good role models, e.g. with instruments such as "Learning Labs," "Collaborative Learning" and the "Coaching Simulator." We now know that only "blended learning," the combination of conventional seminars and web-based learning, works best. This approach is now complemented by elements where administrative transactions and internal process steps can also be taken by

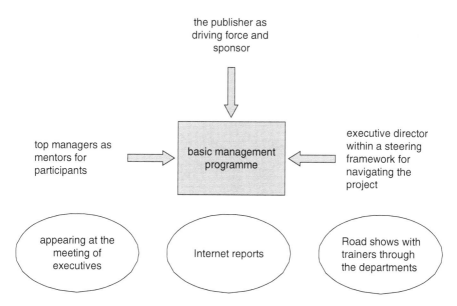

Fig. 4.1 An example for learning processes in the media industries (*Source*: Höhn and Rosenberger 2002)

managers themselves, with the aid of computer systems. This can significantly improve efficiency on a daily basis. Cisco Systems' "Self Service Manager" offers a wealth of illustrative material. Numerous tools – from data updates for employees, ranging from individual payments to team assessments – provide facilitate work and expedite processing. In short, the management development must always be close to the strategic and operational work of the leader, or else it loses its effect.

4.1.2.3   The Next Generation in the Pipeline

An important contribution in this regard has been supplied by the Americans Ram Charan, Stephen Drotter and James Noel, who have worked for large corporations such as General Electric, Philip Morris, and Citibank (see Charan et al. 2001). The three authors show how their companies optimally develop managers in-house. The starting point of their considerations is the fact that it is not important to train executives for certain qualities and abilities. Rather, it is a question of supporting them in the critical phases that each must go through by means of appropriate measures. The transitions from one leader to the next are especially important, as the requirements of the new job are taught and trained. Only in this way will the company's "leadership pipeline" always be sufficiently well stocked.

Essentially the three management experts identify six critical passages on the way from the expert to the chairman or chairwoman of the board:

From Managing Self to Managing Others – from specialist to team leader
From Managing Others to Managing Managers – from team leader to supervisor, with executives of your own
From Managing Managers to Functional Manager – from supervisor to department head (such as head of marketing or human resources)
From Functional Manager to Business Manager – from department head to director of a business unit, profit center or subsidiary
From Business Manager to Group Manager – from head of a business unit to director of several business units in the same region or sector
From Group Manager to Enterprise Manager – from director of several business units to chairman or chairwoman of the board

At every turn there are three central aspects of leadership that should be actively influenced by development and coaching activities:

requirements and associated skills
time-related requirements for certain management functions and associated new priorities
values and norms, i.e., what is relevant for leaders on this specific level (Fig. 4.2)

By way of example, there is a difference between leading experts and leading managers. As a "manager of managers," I have to make sure that I do not interfere with their daily business. At the same time, I have to ensure that the executives assigned to me perform their actual management tasks and not the work of the

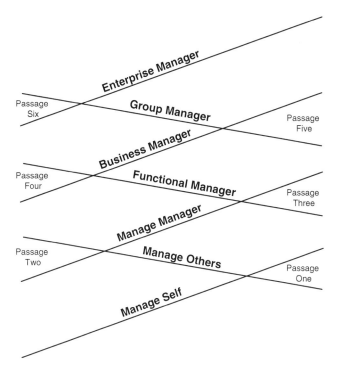

Fig. 4.2   Critical career moves for senior executives in larger organizations (*Source*: Charan et al. 2001)

specialists. The typical and major "manager of managers" role is to make the employees understand the corporate strategy. According to Charan et al. at this point the following four core tasks of leadership are most important and have to be on the manager's agenda: selecting and training the team and the department heads; demanding real leadership activities for this target group; (re-) distributing resources between departments; managing the interfaces between departments; and managing those between your own and other areas of the company (see Charan et al. 2001, p. 51 ff.).

As soon a as a leader works on an incorrect level, it negatively affects the layers above and below them, leading to stagnancy. If a team leader cannot delegate and does everything himself or herself, it is demoralizing for the professionals in their team. At the same time, the manager of the team leader fails, as the former has not properly supported the latter. This may have fatal consequences: these signals are received within the company – and suddenly other executives feel consciously or unconsciously encouraged not to comply with their job requirements.

In these new leadership development models, it is extremely important that all activities are carefully monitored. According to a study by the Federal Institute for Vocational Education and Training 85% of German companies expect that it will become more important to better determine training needs and to consistently monitor the long-term success of the training. That is easier said than done, but the discontent is growing. The news magazine Focus recently pointed out: "Companies do not want to spend more money for lax seminars or discussion groups with an uncertain benefit" (see Focus 10/2004, pp. 184–185).

How can benefits be guaranteed in practice? Three examples illustrate this: the mobile phone company Vodafone's executives were recently sent to the seminars to act as observers. In addition, supervisors should keep track whether and how their staff implement new knowledge in practice. At the consumer goods group Henkel, employees need to pass a computer-aided entry test before they can attend a seminar. And the insurance provider Gerling is currently discussing the introduction of an electronic diary to document the success of the seminar.

One thing is certain: though a simple questionnaire after the seminar can show that the participants (subjectively) are satisfied with the contents presented, this does not necessarily mean that they actually learned or understood what was taught them, let alone that they can apply it.

4.1.3   Insights: Systemic Seminar Practice

After these remarks on the structural conditions of the new leadership development models, I would now like to provide some rough ideas on how seminar content can be shaped:

The Academy offers practice-based systemic leadership seminars. These seminars focus on the key skills, tools and features of systemic and interpersonal leadership as well as self-awareness, personal responsibility, interpersonal skills, openness and trust, group dynamics, vision, work, conflict management, change management and conducting employee interviews, simultaneously working on the respective issue and at the relationship level.

Managers should take the idea of lifelong learning seriously and work constantly on their self-perception and relationship management. There are seminars and coaching on topics such as reflecting on your own leadership behavior, integrating your personality and leadership style, as strategies for difficult leadership situations, and communication.

4.1.3.1   From the Symptoms to the Causes

The Academy teaches management tools and enhances participants' leadership personalities, allowing them to both upgrade their methodological toolbox and refine their personal skills.

Our trainers and process consultants function primarily as "supporters" in the development of independent problem solutions by managers and employees. Thus, the CEO who initially gave the consultant the task of just motivating the team develops the insight to ask: "How can I as the CEO prepare our business for the future together with my managers and employees?" And in the end not the symptoms are processed, but the causes.

The principles of effective development work are, firstly, a comprehensive clarification of the task, which is important to ensure the transfer into practice. Here relationships are detected and analyzed and the causes, symptoms and real problem structures are identified. This usually happens in discussions with several company representatives on site. The second principle concerns the involvement of stakeholders. This is the opposite of the standard approach, which presents finished solutions, as expert consultants usually do. Focusing early on the participants' fears and concerns activates them and creates energy for the change work. By receiving individual and concrete feedback, participants experience a sense of "we are listened to."

The third objective is to overcome "thrust and suction forces," as my colleague Hubert Hölzl once put it so nicely. Situations are resolved, both internal and external trends are analyzed together, and a vision is developed. In this context, and on the basis of future perspectives (trends), the current strengths and weaknesses of the participants are considered. Thus the actual work is integrated. The fourth principle is that any effective development work requires "travelling companions with energy, endurance and desire." Yet humor is also important.

4.1.3.2   Corporate Theater and Fishbowl

To demonstrate the diversity of working with a systemic approach, in the following I will present some methods that we frequently use at the Academy, which need to be combined with an approach specifically tailored to the needs of the target group. Although these methods are practiced by coaches and consultants, they are to some extent also suitable for managers who want to keep their department or their company on their toes. However, interested managers should consult with the Academy or other experts about possible risks and side-effects. Sample methods include:

Trance and sitting in a circle without any "protective" tables. The only thing the executives have to do is listen. In a monotonous voice the consultants talk about an intellectual journey through upcoming workshop days, taboos, fears and apprehensions, verbalize any reservations and risks and then go into the content. In this way, the typical superficial courtesies and manners that you encounter in business are quickly left behind. In the next step, issues are focused on, e.g. what kind of thoughts and feelings did I have here today? Am I really willing to accept my share of responsibility for the impending change process? What is my role in my team, my area, my company? How direct is the communication within the company? How clearly and constructively are conflicts verbalized?

Fishbowl. The customer and consultants form an inner circle of chairs. The external managers sit in an outer circle and do nothing but listen, thereby sharpening their perception. The consultants have an interview with the client who both senses their respect and feels the freedom to truly act as a person. The conversation is conducted as if it took place behind closed doors. The talks deal with the necessary requirements for the customer's development, but also about openly discussing existing taboos, stereotypes and feelings. In a further step the circle can be extended by one or more employees from "the outside," who can then also talk frankly. With this method, potential "fear cultures" can be discovered on the one hand and, on the other, can be defused through direct communication.

Participant's initial poster. On a sheet of flip chart paper there is a task description that asks the participant to list their expectations, but also gives them an opportunity to introduce themselves: "When I think of my leadership skills, (a) I can ... very well; (b) ... is particularly important to me; (c) my stumbling blocks are ...; (d) my leadership motto is ...; (e) in this seminar I want to try to ..." On the basis of these questions, each participant creates their own personal poster, which they then present to the entire group.

Organization setup. This method should be used only by experienced trainers. The idea is to create a living sculpture that appeals to many senses and illustrates the hidden motives, effects and relationships. The parties represent themselves (or are represented by a group member) and learn about how they are perceived by others. Who is in the center? Who is on the edge? Who is bent over? Who appears to be dynamic? Who is looking at whom? This exercise shows how a group of people appears as a whole.

Art exhibition. On the walls of the room there are numerous bulletin boards, labeled with central questions about the participants' expectations of and their own contributions to the success of the workshop. Participants do not receive a glass of champagne (as they would at an art exhibition), but a pencil. Participants walk, read, write, add, underline – and thus create an inspiring atmosphere and a great deal of energy, and in the meanwhile spontaneous conversations develop between participants who previously hardly knew each other.

Vision work and corporate theater. What will the ideal company look like in 2050? Participants develop their own ideas, with no limits. In small groups, the leaders have the task of choosing a single perspective and represent their businesses quite differently for a change: as a pantomime, song, sketch, drama, thriller, love story or comedy. Thus, new creative ways of communicating with others in the company can be discovered and the colleagues can be experienced in a completely different way. It is also possible to run the theater in several acts: while the first act should be about "Our cooperation, yesterday and today," the second should show "Our cooperation starting from tomorrow." In the end some numbness and old conflicts might well dissolve in a laugh.

Nonverbal marketplace. Each participant faces a favorite opponent in the company and maintains eye contact with them. In a calm voice, the consultant throws in certain phrases from the outside to sharpen their perceptions: What do I really perceive about the other? What exactly does the other person do that makes me feel like I do? What "blind spot" of mine does he or she touch on unconsciously? What would happen if I told them exactly what is going on inside of me when they do this or that? What are the synergies between the two of us that could arise for the benefit of us and our company?

Confrontation meeting. When opposing camps or subgroups are clearly identified at a seminar, one can soften and sometimes even dissolve the roles and stereotypes by putting these groups – for example office service and field service – into separate rooms, where they answer the following questions: How do we see ourselves – strengths and weaknesses? How do we see the others – strengths and weaknesses? How do we think others see us? Then each group presents the results on a flip chart. The result is, as my colleague Alexander Höhn once put it, an "equally self-confident and self-critical self-assessment and external assessment." Moreover, the "secret knowledge" about the views of others is ultimately made transparent. After such a confrontation, which is also an effective instrument for conflict management, the groups should begin to cooperate. For example this can happen by improving ideas that are to be developed, explained, clarified and provided with an implementation timetable.

Generally, at the end of each seminar concrete measures and responsibilities should be defined. Perhaps learning partners can call each other in between workshop dates to ask about the progress of projects. At the beginning of the next seminar (if there is one) you can ask the following questions: What has changed? What still needs improvement? What do I want to have achieved by the follow-up meeting? Regardless of the details, the principle that applies here is: actions speak louder than words.

4.2   Tools as Means to an End

I have to admit, when executives ask me for tools, I am always skeptical at first, because all too often they expect patented recipes, cure-alls and ready-made checklists.

Leadership is more than that, and it requires a feeling for the fine line – between the individual and the system; between the physical and relational level; between authority and cooperation; between power and influence, between past and future; between intellect and emotion; and between clarity and ambiguity. The sum of these fine differences flows into systemic leadership. Therefore tools often divert attention from these key dilemmas of leadership.

Still, I believe that – within clear limits and under the conditions stated – you can acquire useful tools and techniques, which are described in the following section. Perception, contact and communication are important, because strong leadership is composed of these elements. Accordingly, tools such as the employee interview, feedback and coaching will be prominent. Two instruments (target-setting processes and delegating) concern the question of how leadership can create results, and how much time and what conditions are prerequisites. Two other instruments I will introduce focus on issues of interpersonal dynamics: conflict management and team development.

All of these instruments can overlap. Thus, a leader can also solve conflicts in a staff meeting. In addition, for example a feedback on mutual perceptions can be integrated into a meeting about goal negotiations. It is important that a manager looks sees tools for what they are: means to an end – good leadership. No more and no less.

A 2003 study by the Academy showed that for 85% of the respondents the talk between leader and employee is the most common tool of leadership. Thus, the oldest and probably (at the first glance) most obvious tool takes the top position, above the modern Balanced Scorecard and 360-degree feedback, which are difficult to implement in practice, although they are praised in theory by many consultants (see Academy Study 2003).

Especially under unstable conditions, it is less about the methods, but more about the people, their strengths and weaknesses that decide on the welfare of the company's human resources management, culture and viability. It fits into this picture that German companies mainly rely on teamwork besides the conversations. Management by objectives, management by target agreements, therefore, takes third place in the ranking. Even coaching seems to be enjoying much more popularity than the Balanced Scorecard, as an enormous process of change will be needed before this complex and interlocking system of corporate leadership is truly established.

By relying mainly on instruments such as annual interviews, coaching and team meetings, German executives prefer a management style that essentially relies on moods, feelings and nuances. The only question is whether this kind of contact is seriously practiced. Management tools that are based on dialogue and empathy always employ the leader in a double function: as an ad hoc conversation partner and as an emotional barometer. The (annual) employee interview may be the oldest and most rudimentary management tool – but it is not the easiest. While all leaders can talk, only a few know how to lead a goal-oriented conversation, something you don't learn at universities.

However, in this result I see a major problem or misunderstanding: many leaders underestimate the amount of time and attention that this form of leadership demands. For example, coaching is more than just a private crisis intervention that takes place every few months. A sound coaching program lasts 2 years, as coaching is an ongoing process. Later I will come back to discuss whether coaching can or should ever be done by the person's immediate supervisor – or whether it is better to have a third party (a consultant, another manager) conduct it.

4.2.1 The Employee Interview

Allen E. Ivey once said: "The communication between individuals is too important to be left to chance" (Ivey, 2001, p. 11).

Nothing can make interpersonal communication as lively as a personal interview. It allows a rapid exchange of ideas to gain new insights from mutual impulses; to effectively represent thoughts through your choice of words, tone of voice, facial expressions and gestures; to arrive at quick results and – not least of all – to form positive relationships with other people.

The personal interview is particularly well-suited to building trust, without which close cooperation is unthinkable. However, talking and discussing take time. Executives are constantly under time pressure and thus often try to replace meetings with employees with less time-consuming communications (letters, telephone calls, faxes and emails). If the distance between headquarters and the workplace of the employee is very great (a long road trip), the broad use of these means of telecommunication cannot be avoided for economic reasons. However, these technological alternatives must not lead us to neglect personal communication.

As important as the employee interview is, it can actually become counterproductive if it is not properly prepared for and implemented. Specifically, the following recommendations for a successful employee interview can be helpful:

Choose the right time and the right place. An interview shortly before the end of the working day is ill-advised.

Inform the employee well in advance about the purpose of the conversation.

Set the goal at the beginning of the conversation.

Put yourself in the employee's situation.

Take every employee seriously – especially if you feel superior to them.

Make sure that you give the employee sustained attention (not only at the beginning).

Involve the employee in the conversation and shape it like a dialog (ask open questions, explore opinions, solicit proposals, take expressed feelings seriously, listen).

Provide information in the correct "dosage" and with a view to the needs of your counterpart.

Present the most important issues very clearly, and place them well (e.g., at the beginning or end of a message).

Write down the results of the conversation, in particular the measures agreed upon.

Before concluding the conversation, ask the employee for their opinion and final assessment.

4.2.1.1   A Question of Preparation

After these introductory remarks I would like to take a look at the different stages of an employee interview: it starts with the preparation; after that the initial conversation follows, then the actual interview, the close, and as the last step, the summary and follow-up work.

What must be considered in order to prepare an employee interview? A good leader cares about inviting the employees ahead of time. Surprise dates should be taboo. If necessary and available, a conversation manual and/or an assessment scheme should be handed to the employee at the same time. In addition, the manager should inform the employee of the date, the content and purpose of the meeting and ask them to prepare for their part. Of course, the executive must ensure beforehand that an undisrupted conversation is possible – especially phone calls are problematic. Finally, all relevant documents, for example, guidelines and evaluation forms, have to be compiled. This includes creating your own list of questions. Only very few executives can react spontaneously and always ask the appropriate questions.

The supervisor should also consider what questions the employee might ask him or her prior to the interview. Possible questions are: What do you expect from me in the next six months? How is our company and our department going to develop? Why did you evaluate my performance as (good/average/poor) in this category? What career options do I have?

To clearly answer these or similar questions, the manager should consider the following points before the meeting: What are the employee's strengths and weaknesses? What proportion of the departmental and divisional goals can I delegate to the staff? What factors influenced their behavior and performance in the assessment period positively or negatively? What does the employee's "personal development plan" look like? What measures are needed in order to boost their qualifications?

In order to come to as objective a classification of the employee (if objectivity is feasible) as possible, it is useful to honestly answer the following questions: Am I approaching my employee unbiased? Do I have prejudices against him or her? Which results in the past have led to these prejudices? What impact do my personal attitude, my inner script, and my subjective perception have on my assessment of the employee's skills?

The interview should always be oriented on the employee. The employee should do the bulk of the talking, and the supervisor should only direct with questions, listen quietly, respond to the arguments of the employee, summarize the main points briefly and then signal to the employee that they are being listened to and understood. In addition, the manager should state the objectives and, if appropriate, explain their own desires if they deviate from those of the employee.

In summary, one can distinguish between the following areas of preparation: the content, the organizational, the methodological, and the psychological and mental preparation.

Content preparation. In order to conduct a thoroughly fact-oriented conversation you have to first collect all the relevant information associated with the occasion of the discussion and seek to clarify the situation; then you can set the desired objectives. Planning objectives makes it easier to lead successful and time-efficient discussions. It also makes it easier to later evaluate the talk's success. When planning the goals, the following five questions need to be answered:

What are the main goals that I want to achieve?
What are the secondary objectives that should also be pursued?
What intermediate goals could there be?
Are there alternative goals?
What negotiating limit should I set for myself?

On the basis of the objectives it has to be considered what arguments can be used. Here the manager should also examine the counterarguments to be expected on the part of the employee and whether he or she responds appropriately. In addition, it can be quite useful to determine the order of arguments in advance, taking care that not all of the most powerful points come at the beginning. Such considerations, however, are not about programming the flow of conversation. Flexibility is always necessary: a conversation can always take unexpected turns, and the manager has to respond spontaneously.

Organizational preparation. This aspect concerns the answers to six questions: Who participates in the conversation? Where am I leading the conversation? When am I leading the conversation? How much time will the conversation take? Which documents and tools (e.g. soft drinks) are needed? Which seating arrangement makes sense?

Unprepared or poorly prepared talks disrupt communication on the rational and factual level, as well as on the emotional relationship level. You may experience the following problems:

There will be misunderstandings, for example due to bad acoustics, distractions or poor timing.
The message is not taken seriously because the conversation is held "on the fly."
Talks can be provided additional "weight" by including written documents.
The conversational atmosphere is too "cold" due to an overly sober environment.
The employee feels devalued: The boss is sitting in a comfortable executive's chair, while the employee has to sit on a hard visitor's chair.

For a productive discussion, it is particularly bad if it is conducted under time pressure. Psychology plays an important part. For example if we speak quickly, we can easily give the impression that we want to get the conversation over with quickly. Thus we put – quite unintentionally – our partner under pressure. As a result, he or she withdraws and refrains from expressing thoughts that may be very informative.

Also, the time of the interview must be chosen carefully by the manager. Longer meetings just before lunch or just before closing time are not in the interests of employees, whose attention capacity is not ideal at these times.

Methodical preparation. It is useful to reflect on the probable progression of the conversation. For this reason, we should first clarity what type of conversation partner we have to deal with. We may already know them from other encounters and know what reactions they tend to have. How can we get them in a positive mood? What interests and preferences do they have? The methodical preparation also includes everything I mentioned before about the questions the employee might ask. The important thing is to be in a position to anticipate these questions.

Psychological and mental preparation. At least for important discussions, we should pay attention to our own mental state. Positive thinking leads to success. It's hard to heed this principle if you are a negative mood with regard to the occasion or the other person – or if you are overworked. Self-motivation is appropriate in such situations. This also includes reconsidering your negative attitude towards your conversation partner. If you fail to make this mental turnaround, it is advisable to transfer the meeting to another person or to cancel or postpone it.

After carefully preparing the conversation, you can start. The employee has entered the office – now what? There is no universal recipe. The opening of the meeting depends on the setting, experiences and expectations of you and your employee. Whether you use general topics (family, travel, vacation, etc.) to open the meeting or you get to the point at once depends on the situation and should be adapted to the personality of the employee. In both cases, it is important to articulate goals early in the conversation. It is also important to create a good atmosphere by carefully choosing your words and adopting a humble demeanor. The employee should feel secure, on equal footing and free to "open up."

The third phase is the longest, namely the employee interview, which concerns "the true matter." Here, keeping the following success factors in mind can help:

The conversation should be kept factual and friendly.
The employee should have sufficient opportunities to speak.
Monologues on the part of the manager are inappropriate.
The manager should not interrupt the employee.

The employee should first have the opportunity to take initiative and state where they see their own strengths and weaknesses. The manager may inquire by asking why.

Only after this step should you confirm or correct the employees' self-assessment.

Criticism should be constructive and in the "I" form and should never focus on the employee's personality or be in "you" form.

The manager should admit his or her own shortcomings and seek alternative solutions. The best solution is one proposed by the employee himself/herself.

Following important points you should ask whether you have been properly understood.

Conflicts and "sore points" should be openly discussed and not swept under the rug – ensuring this happens is the manager's responsibility.

Problems should not be immediately assessed, but first analyzed objectively with reference to the causes.

Open questions are important: What do you think? What do you suggest? How do you like that?

The manager should identify possible solutions and provide assistance.

You should also double check that the employee has understood exactly your opinion on a particular goal or a particular measure. Work on the worst-case scenario assumption that communication mostly fails.

During the conversation the personal characters of both the supervisor and the employee always play a role. Try to recognize moods intuitively and direct them by paying close attention to both yourself and the other party.

The next phase of the interview is a good close. This should primarily include a summary of the key issues: What issues were raised? What goals were determined? Where was agreement reached, and where do opinions still differ? Should a superior be included in the case of disagreement? Where is the focus for next year compared to this year? What measures have been defined, and what timeframe?

After the employee has left the room, the manager's work is not done. You must now attend to a good follow-up on the conversation, so that the outcome can be implemented in a sustainable way. Any individual actions with colleagues or supervisors need to be coordinated. The HR department must likely be informed. And the employee should receive a written copy of the minutes. In addition, the manager must write down the dates of future progress checks in his or her own calendar.

The success of a conversation is reinforced – or is even made possible to begin with – only if it is properly evaluated. Here the manager should review the factual implementation of the goals agreed upon and at the same time perform a psychological analysis.

The implementation substantially includes the agreed-upon operational activities and – when appropriate – planning follow-up contacts (continuing discussions, written confirmations, thank-you letter, etc.). The psychological analysis, which is unfortunately often left out, deals with the behavior of the conversation partners. The manager should answer the following questions:

Have I achieved my aims for the conversation?

What was good, what went wrong?

How did I behave? Did I respond to the interests of my conversation partner? Did I show them appreciation and respect? Did I let them make their point?

How was the atmosphere? How did I influence it?

What impression did the partner probably get from me?

What impression and what new insights did I get from them during the conversation?

What should I consider for the next talk with this partner? What are their interests, needs and desires?

What did I learn from this conversation for me? What should I do better in the future?

How are staff meetings evaluated by experienced professionals? At a committee meeting of the Academy (see Höhn et al. 2003) a colleague expressed: "In practice many employee interviews are very tense, with the employee thinking: 'Now you sit down and the big boss tells you what kind of person you are.' The fact that it is necessary to institutionalize these interviews just shows how difficult it is for managers to make real contact in the company."

Another panelist added: "All of the tools are ultimately about creating a space where one can say the things that otherwise vanish in the maelstrom of the modern business world. It is about taking the time to leave the hard facts behind and to talk about how the cooperation is really working: where there is trouble, what is good and what is not so good, where are taboos and sacred cows that impede work, or when it is time to celebrate successes. With a bit of routine, and when trust has been created, it is perhaps possible to resolve bilateral conflicts within the team in public."

In any case, the initiative for an employee interview should come from the manager. He or she has to create the framework for this kind of leadership communication. That often banal things hamper the actual interview is simply a fact. As such, it should be natural to keep eye contact with the employee during a conversation. But it is not so easy to maintain constant eye contact, especially if you are not the one speaking. A colleague once told me: "For me it is a clear indication of the 'cultures of fear' prevailing in many businesses that the employees run around with their eyes down." And I believe he's right.

In the Handelsblatt, I read the following statement: "This is how annual interviews should not take place: bosses who have left the factual level have not understood the purpose of the instrument." And further: "Nor are these interviews to tell the employees once a year – as a tribunal – everything that has been building up, right in their faces." (Reppesgaard, Handelsblatt, August 19 2005). The author referred to a study by the management consultants Kienbaum, which observed that, especially in the DAX 30 companies, but also in medium-sized businesses, the annual employee interview "has developed from an obligation to an important human resource and motivational tool."

But there is the potential for a fundamental misunderstanding here: though of course it is not a tribunal, the purpose is nonetheless to frankly (though respectfully) communicate opinions. Of course you should not "stockpile" criticism, but sometimes everyday work life only allows us to address longer-term issues in this framework. And it goes without saying – this point is particularly important to me – that leaders must sometimes leave the objective level. This does not have to end in slamming doors, but a manager can only create a good atmosphere for discussion, if he or she works on both levels: the factual and the interpersonal. In other words: I will only get to know my employees as people if I am also willing to show myself as a person (with feelings, speculation, fears, etc.). Many executives may find that their behavior matches that described in the article above, but unfortunately this creates a false impression.

In many discussions, the partners each other's point – precisely because they are trying to stay on the objective level. This produces unfruitful discussions that drag on and on, leading to confusion and not to any productive results, and conflicts between the now even more frustrated partners can arise. These shortcomings can often be avoided if the topic of conversation is stated clearly, if the participants can and do prepare for the interview, if the conversation is controlled sensitively and consistently at the same time, if vague statements are clarified, and if all participants have sufficient opportunity and are encouraged to contribute their thoughts.

It is especially important to structure the conversation. Conversation partners who like to talk must be encouraged to come to the point and not to get sidetracked. It is equally important to address overly shy speakers. To achieve this, a conversation needs to be efficiently controlled. A tip based on my personal experience: when a discussion begins to wander off course, the person leading the conversation should simply ask the question: "What exactly is the subject we're talking about?"

4.2.1.2 A Question of Technique

The person asking the questions is who leads the conversation, and they can control it through the questions they ask. The person who asks questions retains the initiative and can steer the conversation in the direction he or she desires. Questions enrich and enliven a conversation. This is especially true for conversations in which issues are to be resolved and solutions are to be found. The results of such creative conversations depend largely on the quantity and also on the quality of the questions asked. Hence the truism: "The right question is already half the answer."

Many discussions suffer because not enough questions are asked. This can be due to a number of reasons: lack of knowledge about the productivity of questioning, habit, laziness, apathy, poor conversation routines, lack of opportunity, actual or perceived time pressure, insecurity and fear.

The last reason is of major importance. Those who ask questions show that they (presumably) don't know something. And lack of knowledge is often regarded as a weakness. Consequently, many managers are afraid of losing prestige by asking questions. Due to the unrealistic demands they place on themselves ("the boss knows everything"), they believe that in order to fulfill their leadership roles they must have answers, not questions.

However, by asking questions, you always receive additional information. Questions yield insights into the thoughts, opinions, expectations, hopes, fears and motives of others. They also allow you to participate in and profit from the knowledge and the creativity of others. However, conversations can also be harmed by incorrect questioning techniques. Therefore, I would like to define this point more closely:

A manager must first check whether a question about a certain topic is appropriate at all or whether it might distract from the real subject.

Then, a question should be formulated as clearly as possible and in a concrete way. Also, you should ask only one question at a time and wait for the answer first before you continue. In order to precisely connect further questions, you need to listen carefully to the conversation partner and give them your undivided attention. And the last basic rule is to always use the appropriate type of question.

Which types of question are there, and what are their advantages and disadvantages? The following section presents the five most common types of questions that a manager should know and master:

Closed questions. These questions are usually answered with "yes" or "no," but also with "I don't know." Here is an example: "Have you gotten to know our new colleague?" This question is not very communicative and it is more difficult to continue the conversation. The taciturn person interviewed will give his or her answer without further explanation. To continue the conversation, you need to ask further questions. Often, there is an impression of paternalism if a series of closed questions is asked – a feeling arises that this is an interrogation. Nevertheless: in certain situations closed questions also have advantages. They are simple and concrete, they are generally easily answered, and they get right down to the point.

Open questions. The answers to these questions can be formulated freely. Open questions are also known as W-questions because they usually start with a question word (Who, What, Where, When, Why, etc.). Again, an example: "What is your impression of our new colleague?" This question encourages communication. It calls for a longer response, usually results in more information and also expresses a greater interest in the communication and thus in the conversation partner himself/herself. On the other hand, open questions can overwhelm the other person or result in embarrassment.

Alternative questions. To answer this type of question, there is a choice between two alternatives. Example: "Should we meet with our new colleague this morning or this afternoon?" With such questions the decision-making process is simplified and accelerated, provided your conversation partner has a basically positive attitude towards the process. If they have a negative attitude it can easily lead them to feel they are being manipulated, which harms the relationship.

Rhetorical questions. These questions are asked without expecting any response. Example: "How nice that we've found an efficient new colleague. Isn't it?" This question includes the conversation partner and prevents the impression that a monologue is being held. On the other hand, your partner can feel they are being made fun of because no real answer is expected.

Leading questions. These are not real questions, because they "feed" the other party the desired answer. The questioner has already determined the response in advance, quasi knowing everything, and will not listen to anything else. Example: "You also find our new colleague very nice, don't you?" These questions can be useful when it comes to influencing others. But they do not promote open communication in order to clarify facts or develop new ideas.

Circular questions. This type of question is often used in systemic consulting. The aim is to gain new perspectives by asking creative questions. Example 1: Employee A is asked how the boss responds when Employees B and C have their usual argument at the monthly team meeting. Example 2: What does Employee A believe D thinks about the dispute between Employees B and C?

Systemic leadership is heavily strongly on creative questions: we can also ask paradoxical questions, such as: "Who would be interested in the project failing?" or "What do we have to do in order to prevent the success of the project?" We can ask "Assuming that…" questions like: "Assuming that Employee B sought to clarify his work duties, would this help or harm the climate in the team?" In these cases questions can help to develop exciting new scenarios that can become a breeding ground for long sought-after solutions.

The person asking the questions leads the conversation. I like to repeat this often-quoted maxim, because it is simply true. In a good employee interview, the superior asks incisive questions and the employee answers them. The shares of talking are distributed between manager and employee in the ratio 70–30%. Let me illustrate this again using an example:

Let's say it comes to a staff meeting on the subject of teamwork. The manager is interested in whether an employee considers himself/herself to be a team player.

First, the manager needs to know the criteria behind this assessment. Some points are evident: letting the conversation partner talk uninterrupted, actively listening, and showing respect for the opinions of others. Questions regarding these issues asked by the manager are: What is important for the cooperation in teams? What must be done in order to achieve a common goal as quickly as possible? What is the role of your group leader? How is a typical team meeting conducted? What do you like more and what less? An important note: be sure that you move from general to more specific questions. Only in this way can you proceed in a goal-oriented and solution-oriented way.

Finally, I would like to introduce the "Five Whys Principle" for the analysis of management problems. If you as a manager only have a vague notion of what is troubling your employees, you can use the "Five Whys" to find the reason for their behavior. By sequentially asking five different "why" questions the causal chain can be traced back to the true problem and real improvement can be achieved. Here is an example of a boss and a subordinate manager who is responsible for a high level of absence in his department:

Question 1: Why is the absence rate so high? Because the employees are dissatisfied with their work. They have the impression that their absence is not noticed.

Question 2: Why are the people dissatisfied? The employees are not challenged and they have the feeling that they are not given any responsibility for their tasks.

Question 3: Why do the people have no decision-making responsibilities? The manager refuses to share responsibility and is also constantly interfering in the employees' tasks.

Question 4: Why is the manager interfering so much? Since the manager has had bad experiences delegating decisions, he does not dare to give any responsibility to the employees.

Question 5: Why did the manager have bad experiences delegating? Because he was told to delegate tasks, but he was not given freedom of decision, the tasks were poorly completed. In addition, the department head failed to adequately inform his employees.

As a result, the manager's boss determines that the high rate of absence is due to the fact that there is no proper delegation.

4.2.2 Feedback Culture

Feedback – this is a buzzword used constantly in companies today. Apparently, everyone constantly gives everyone else feedback. But closer inspection shows that in most cases this "feedback" only consists of general assessments on the factual level. For me, feedback is something else, as I would like to briefly discuss below.

In cooperation based on trust, the partners understand and accept one another – and ideally even support and encourage each other. Whether or not this succeeds depends largely on how each perceives the other party's behavior and how the two appreciate each other. The better the parties know understand their relationship, the better the collaboration will be. It is especially important to identify and eliminate disruptions to interpersonal relationships that have been caused unknowingly. Often we distance ourselves from each other without explicitly talking about it; sometimes we do not even notice it ourselves.

To resolve problems of this kind, we need to give each other mutual feedback about our behavior from time to time. Here, the actual behavior should be in focus. Statements regarding presumed character traits or motives are less useful and often counterproductive. The feedback must not only include discussing "misconduct" but also recognizing "correct" behavior and encouraging such behavior. If it is obvious that the relationship level within companies is strengthened in this way, then the feedback culture also influences the corporate culture.

4.2.2.1 Understanding Situations and Structures

Situational feedback, which follows on each consecutive communication session, has to be distinguished from structural feedback, which deals with the entire cooperation. Yet in both cases the focus is on clarification, as the parties assess their past cooperation, their interpersonal relationships, and their feelings. In addition, the partners should also agree on which future improvements should be made in this regard.

In daily practice, we are often not sensitive enough, and at times we are even clumsy. Situational feedback is a spontaneous statement on an individual behavioral process that we consider wrong. We express our criticism more or less verbally, accompanied by the appropriate body language (a stern facial expression, frowning, finger-wagging, etc.). Sometimes criticism comes across too coarsely. This is especially the case when we lose our temper – and our criticism is correspondingly harsh: "Would you stop constantly interrupting me? Let me finish first!" And based on these statements, we expect that the other person will change their behavior as we wish. The results are often disappointing. Perhaps the other person will try to act as desired for the moment. However, this is usually not out of personal conviction, and is almost never long-term.

To make matters worse, personal relationships can suffer from tough criticism, thus making cooperation unnecessarily difficult. Where is the problem? It is not the feedback itself. On the contrary: in order to improve cooperation it is essential that we speak about previous behavior. This particularly applies for executives talking to their employees. The problem often lies in the inappropriate form of feedback.

It is therefore particularly important to also utilize structural feedback, i.e., regular and thorough discussions of the cooperation to date, in order to ensure productive and undistorted communications. Feedback should be given several times a year, e.g. in the context of employee interviews, where in my experience precisely this structural feedback is often left out. Reasons for this include a lack of insight concerning the value of feedback ("What is it good for?"), lack of time ("When am I supposed to do it?"), lack of practice ("What will the others think of me if I start doing it?") and bad experiences ("Why should I do it and embarrass myself again?").

4.2.2.2   A Wealth of Good Reasons

Why are feedback and a subsequent discussion so important for effective communication? Here is an overview of the main reasons:

We get to know ourselves and our partner. Feedback makes us realize how our behavior affects others.

We can better assess the effects of our behavior.

We recognize what is important for our cooperation.

Above all we see where there are pitfalls and obstacles to cooperation.

We talk about how we can improve our conduct and reduce disruptive factors.

We provide behavioral recommendations.

We encourage our partners to continue their "correct" behavior and to change their "misbehavior."

We become more secure with others. This particularly applies to employees and their behavior towards their superiors.

We are more responsive to the expectations and demands of others.

We recognize that we must adjust our expectations concerning others.

We do not keep all of our critical feelings towards others (disappointment, anger and frustration) bottled up, but speak about them. As such, we don't swallow our negative feelings, but instead rid ourselves of them (in a reasonable tone, and in a constructive manner).

We do not keep the other party in the dark with regard to their feeling that something is wrong with our relationship. By talking about this openly, communication becomes more relaxed.

We clear up misunderstandings that can quickly lead to conflicts.

The resultant benefits are obvious: the objective cooperation will be strengthened, interpersonal relationships will improve, motivation to work will be boosted, personal development is promoted, and the working atmosphere is also improved. In short: in order to improve the "what" aspects of cooperation, we must first reexamine the "how" aspects. Feedback thus serves as a guide to both the manager and the employee.

4.2.2.3   "I" Messages Instead of Tit-for-Tat

Feedback should be structured and received in keeping with the guidelines above. Unfortunately, this is usually not the case. Feedback often sounds too much like criticism or is at least perceived as such by the recipient. Lack of self-confidence colors our perceptions; we see hidden attacks even in benevolent advice. And we respond accordingly: with justifications or even tit-for-tat "back talk"; in any case, not productively. Thus, the purpose of the feedback is completely lost; in some cases, just the opposite effect is generated. The employee's behavior will remain unchanged, and the personal relationships will be further strained. To avoid this, feedback should be formulated as a suggestion and not as an attack – and should also be understood as such. Basically, feedback is a service – a friendly service. We should, therefore, be welcome it rather than getting angry.

In order for feedback to be understood the interpersonal relationship between the "sender" and the "receiver" must be in good shape. If this is not the case, obstacles and disruptions will have to be addressed first. The sender must be accepted as a person in his or her own right, and ideally should be recognized as an authority. Without this condition feedback cannot succeed.

Moreover, it is essential to suitably formulate feedback. Above all, make sure that you act sensitively. The "how" is just as important as the "what." Feedback should be expressed and presented clearly but benevolently, because the self-esteem of the partner can be easily harmed and is difficult to restore. If the feedback is perceived as unjustified criticism or as mere "venting," it not only affects your counterpart's receptiveness to suggestions, but it also strains your interpersonal relationship.

Feedback sounds less aggressive when it is formulated as an "I" message rather than a "you" message. Using the first form, I express the impact the other party's behavior has on me. Here is an example: Imagine one of those people who listen poorly and constantly interrupt others. It would be terribly clumsy if you said: "Please stop constantly interrupting me!" The right "I" message, however, might be: "I would like to finish. When you interrupt me, I can't express my thoughts clearly and I'm afraid that I'll forget important points."

Or take an employee who has not completed his assigned tasks. Usually, the reaction is: "You (!) need to do your work more conscientiously." The manager reacts in this way because he or she feels angry and frustrated, and wants to express that frustration. As a result, the employee submits (often only superficially) or rebels in the form of ignorance or defiance. In contrast, the corresponding "I" message would be something about how the employee's behavior makes the manager feel: "I find it exhausting to always have to remind you to do your work."

However the feedback is formulated – in the end it is mainly about its being clear and objective. If you speak impolitely, using an "I" message will not help anything. It is not so much what you say, but how you say it. How much caution is needed depends largely on the authority of the feedback giver and the sensitivity of the feedback recipient. For example, younger people should be especially careful when talking to older people.

However, beating around the bush out of sheer caution is just as wrong, and only makes things worse. Trivializing is another mistake ("It's not so bad, really."). For thick-skinned partners you may even need to be painfully clear. In any case, however, it should be noted: the feedback needs to be spelled out clearly. Finding the right tone for each individual is part of the practical art of leadership.

4.2.2.4 Channeling Your Own Feelings

From art to handicraft: managers have to observe only a few, simple rules of communication in order to establish a feedback culture in their company. Thus, criticism should always relate to the concrete behavior of others so that they really can change it. In addition, the feedback should be specific, include examples and be detailed in order for the other person to fully understand it. It has to aim at the matter, and not at the person.

It is also important to realize what triggers certain behavior. Do I feel offended? Do I feel angry? Am I sad? Though moral judgments should be avoided, emotions are allowed. Above all, the manager has to listen and not immediately "return fire" if he or she dislikes the other party's standpoint. Feedback should be simply left as it is, and we should thank our conversation partner for it.

In addition, (situational) feedback should be given as soon as possible after the situation in question. At the same time, the right opportunity should be chosen and the receptiveness of the other party needs to be considered. Feedback is always subjective and therefore "I" messages are highly recommended. Leaders must always remember, too, how they can include positive aspects in the feedback. And always keep in mind that feedback has two sides – what you want to convey, and what parts of your statement are received.

The provider of feedback may target actual behavior ("When I talk to you, you always talk so fast."), can address its impact ("I can't even understand you when you talk so fast."), or express feelings ("I have always the feeling that you want to get done talking with me as quickly as possible."). Within the framework of the rules described, the facets of the feedback can vary. It is dangerous however, when personal characteristics are cited ("I have the impression that you don't like talking to others."). In this case the feedback recipient may "close up" and fight back.

In my leadership seminars, we always offer the participants concrete language support:

Those who want to give feedback can describe their perceptions ("I have noticed..."), can talk about their feelings ("It makes me feel..."), or express their desires ("I would like..."). They can also combine something positive ("What I like/what I like about you is...") with more critical points ("What bothers me/what I would like to see more of in you is..."), and close with a specific request for the person in question ("Therefore, I would like you to...").

4.2.2.5 Feedback from the Bottom to the Top – Or 360 Degrees?

If the leader himself or herself is the recipient of feedback (and I hope he or she will be as often as possible), then they should consider the following: first ensuring your own capacity to accept feedback. Then you should listen well and actively, and ask questions in order to understand problems. You should also feel free to write down important points. In any case, you must avoid excuses and apologies. At the end of the feedback you should thank the other party and, if appropriate, encourage the other to continue giving you feedback.

Feedback can take place in several directions: from the executive to the employee, from executive to executive, but also from employee to executive.

For example the employees of Sun Microsystems evaluate the leadership of their superiors twice a year using multiple-choice questions, a voluntary and anonymous process. The 26 questions are answered online, and include: Does your boss treat you with dignity and respect? Does your boss formulate clear work instructions? Do they coach you sufficiently? Do they give feedback? Do they allow enough freedom of choice?" The HR manager of the company stated in an interview: "It's about improving leadership, not selecting leaders." The goal is also for executives to be capable of being criticized. And there are always surprises, because the external assessment will differ from the manager's own impression.

You may be wondering whether this feedback can also be given orally. I think this depends greatly on the maturity of the organization. In principle, these exchanges are also possible face-to-face. The executives of Sun Microsystems, however, argue that the online assessment is "much more objective and more open" than an interview with the boss. It is more objective this way because the assessing employee does not have to be afraid of the manager's reactions.

But it is important that the executive presents the results in a later review meeting and that there are visible effects for the employees. In this meeting, the manager cannot make excuses. They must above all only moderate and direct the talk by asking questions. At Sun Microsystems the three distinct strengths and weaknesses are primarily addressed in such a process. Those who are reluctant to have a direct confrontation with their employees may consult a mentor beforehand.

A particular form of situational feedback is the so-called "lightning round." It stands out for its brevity and is a useful tool. A leader of a team, department or division can use it in regular meetings. The process is simple but effective: "At the beginning of the meeting each participant describes, quite simply, how he or she feels at that moment and what thoughts just went through their mind. These statements are not commented on. Using this simple measure, we have strengthened the personal contact with each other and established a different kind of approach. (see Höhn et al. 2003).

Kets de Vries tells of the following episode: Two executives meet in the hallway. One says to the other: "The 360-degree feedback doesn't scare me, only the 360-degree feedback that comes after it." A catchy phrase, for in fact that is how overall feedback, also called 360-degree feedback, works, though only if the top managers are also brave enough to hear unpleasant things. I share the view of Kets de Vries that systemic training is necessary beforehand to ensure that the participants are willing to give and receive extensive and honest feedback. The method is primarily used in international companies like General Electric, Intel and Nokia.

Kets de Vries also reported that only about 10% of all executives can accurately assess their own behavior: two-thirds of the 90% majority overestimate themselves, while one-third underestimate themselves (see Kets de Vries 2002, p. 90). It is simply a fact that many leaders ignore their weaknesses and have no desire to explore their blind spots. Feedback sessions can help, which brings us back to the topic: the quality of leadership and a positive business development depend heavily on how a leader deals with himself or herself. *Quod erat demonstrandum.*

Essentially, all managers crave contradiction. They know all about the loneliness at the top. Open communication and open feedback would give them more certainty in their decisions. However, this rarely happens. And of course, this is not only the fault of the employees, but often of the leaders themselves: If my boss is not open, certainly I as his or her employee am not. Reasons for this are insecurity, cowardice and lack of information. Often there are even homemade taboos, involving thinking like: "I assume this isn't allowed – so it's not allowed." And it is precisely here that a feedback culture that is initiated at or at least supported from the top can help.

4.2.2.6 No Fear of Feedback

As such, the advantages of a feedback culture are obvious. And yet, it is only human that we are reluctant to hear about our own imperfections – however elegantly expressed. Two American HR experts put it this way: "Employees are terrified of only hearing criticism. For their part, executives are afraid their subordinates will respond to even the slightest criticism by being dismissive, getting angry, or breaking into tears. The result? Everyone keeps a low profile and says as little as possible" (Jackman and Strober, 7/2003, p. 78).

If we do not learn to overcome this fear, we stand in our own way. The tendency to shelter ourselves from feedback can have problematic implications: we deny trouble and do not face the reality, or postpone things due to insecurity. We respond with pessimism, self-sabotage, or jealousy – and thus we are ultimately harming not only ourselves but the entire organization. The example of jealousy shows this quite well: We like to compare ourselves to others. But this can be problematic if the comparison is dominated by greed, envy or distrust. People who are jealous tend to see their fellows in an overly positive light, and in so doing put themselves down.

Feedback is a good way to see things realistically and not to exaggerate your own shortcomings. Our own fear of feedback is often unfounded and becomes greater, the less we receive responses from others. Therefore I recommend the following: go to your superiors, to your subordinates and colleagues and tell them that you are actively seeking feedback. Ask questions about yourself and ask for specific examples in order to fully understand what is being said. Take responsibility for yourself by working to better assess your own effect on others.

4.2.3 Coaching

What is coaching? It includes an individual consultation and support by an external expert in a professional or private context. Coaching encourages clients to develop their own solutions. A coach should have psychological and business knowledge, as well as practical experience. Coaching takes place in several sessions and for a limited time.

Coaching is private consulting, in the context of the roles and responsibilities of a manager. Successful coaching expands the number of prospects and possibilities for action. Especially large companies that are undergoing massive restructuring after mergers or change processes currently depend more and more on coaching.

The reasons for a personal coaching can vary. Sometimes it is tricky to support management decisions, sometimes it is former employees who now have new roles as leaders, and often it is a personal learning process. Also, it may be about a leader who has to cope with resistance or obstacles. It always involves a degree of personal development and strengthening for the participant's day-to-day professional life.

As coaches, we pay attention to how things are connected: where and how inner beliefs, perceptions and behavior patterns develop, and the role of the corporate culture in that development. We help participants to activate their inner voices and help them to weigh arguments and emotions. To this end, we brake, accelerate and hold a mirror up to them, provide feedback, and invite them to try something new.

Coaching has nothing in common with monologues and didactic lectures. It involves working together intensively, makes participants thoughtful, extends their field of view, and clarifies and strengthens their personal solution-finding expertise.

A popular request made of executives is: "Act as a coach for your employees." I question this requirement. Why? Because I have the impression that many managers and consultants use this line because it sounds modern and chic, without applying in practice what coaching really is (see above). On the other hand I do consider it wise that a leader orient his or her thoughts and actions on the methods of a coach.

But it remains true that managers can never act as coaches in the true sense. While they may use coaching tools, such as circular questioning, a real coach needs to be independent. In short, a leader can never be a coach for his or her employees. The coach as a "functional entity" must therefore come from outside, as they must be unbiased and incorruptible. Here, only an external perspective can help.

The six steps of employee coaching are:

Presenting the problem. The employee tells his or her view.

Elaborating on the problem. The leader asks: Who else sees the problem as well? In what situations does it occur and when does it not? How has it been managed so far? How have you succeeded in coping with the problem so far? What should stay the way it is?

Developing new ideas. The wishful thinking scenario: what is bad about it? The worst-case scenario: what is good about it? How would you recognize that the problem had been solved? What would you have to do to make the problem worse?

Developing measures. From the findings of the analysis, the manager and employees develop proposals for change together. Each proposal is reviewed for its potential consequences. (What happens if...?) If the consequences are undesirable, then new measures have to be found.

Implementing the action. The employees give impulses, while the manager stays in the background. Important: small steps at the beginning, close monitoring of change, adaptation of the measures to the system.

Evaluating the action. What has changed? Does the problem still exist? Has it been replaced by a new one?

How does someone actually become a coach? Coaching is consulting in a dialog. A coach essentially knows no more than his or her client, but does know methods to allow the client to find the solution themselves. That sounds very simple – and that is why we find the term "coach" far too often on the business cards of freelancers. But be warned: offers from reputable advisors and those from charlatans cannot be distinguished at first glance. The term coaching is not a registered trademark, and there is no university degree in coaching, as topics such as "human nature" and "conversational skills" are hard to find in higher education. Instead, a private market for coaching courses has been established – and has become obscure, since it is difficult to separate the wheat from the chaff. Coaching covers many aspects: human resources issues, management issues, job and career issues, work-life balance, etc. As such, it is no surprise that among coaches, organizational consultants, communication experts, psychologists, educators and others are represented.

The only advice we can give to future coaches is to search for practical relevance. Only courses that offer the opportunity to watch experienced coaches at work or to gain your initial experience under the guidance of experienced coaches are worth the money. One of the greatest assets a coach can have is his or her own life experience. Don't worry: a coach must not have experienced or achieved more than anyone else; he or she must instead know how to deal with successful people and what pitfalls there are in coaching talks. And the coach must learn to hold himself/herself back over and over again, a challenge that reading books on leadership or attending conferences can't help with. Being able to truly help others is what makes this job so appealing. Entire organizations can be revitalized simply by skillfully interviewing people. And for managers it makes sense to integrate coaching elements into their work.

First of all, coaching means asking constructive questions. Constructive questions are those that encourage the employees to form their own concepts – solution-oriented and future-oriented. Here are a few practical suggestions for asking managers different questions in different phases of a coaching talk:

At the beginning of the interview. Providing this conversation proves useful in the end, how would you notice it? What would have changed? What would you take with you? What makes you feel that this is your problem? Who suffers most because of it? Who benefits most?
During the problem analysis. Who else sees the problem? In what kind of situation does it and when doesn't it occur? How has the problem been managed so far? What should stay the way it is? Did you do everything possible to solve the problem on your own? What has helped the most so far? When did this problem occur last? How do you explain the problem, how did it come about? Provided a miracle happened overnight and the problem disappeared, how would you notice the difference first? What else would change? What would be the best and what the worst consequence? What would you need to do in order to make sure the problem didn't become worse?

During the settlement process. When will person A have solved the problem? Who can help him or her? Should the problem prove to be unsolvable, who will most easily come to terms with it? Do you think that I can help you with it? How could I help best? How you can help me to help you? If we find a more appropriate explanation (than your current conjecture), will it affect the process in a positive way, or simply lengthen it? Concerning the wishful thinking scenario: what is bad about it? Concerning the worst-case scenario: what is good about it? How would you recognize that the problem is gone? What have you done to exacerbate the problem? Concerning all solution options: what would happen if...? If the consequences are undesirable, then find new measures.

At the conclusion of the discussion. Should we still have more conversations? Are you now more confident that you can help yourself? Should we end the coaching for now, and start up again when needed? What are your goals for next time?

It is important that at the beginning of the session the employee or the manager, who will be coached can explain in detail his or her view of things and listens to the coach in order to analyze the problem. On the basis of the findings of the diagnosis, the coach and coached develop proposals for change. Each proposal is reviewed for its potential consequences. The settlement process is done in dialog and aims in the first step at the development of new ideas and in the second at the development of new measures. Important factors: small steps at the beginning; closely monitoring the change; if required, adapting the measures to the system further. After coaching the measures are tried and evaluated in the next session. The assessment can be renewed on the basis of the following questions:

What has changed?
Does the problem still exist?
Has it been replaced by a new one?

4.2.4 Conflict Management

Conflicts between problems and opportunities – this sums up the handling of conflicts. Whether a factual conflict, a relationship conflict or a conflict of values – usually employees and managers vary between lamenting, acting, therapy and resignation. But these conflicts also have a positive side: we learn from each other, we encounter different views, and we are not so prone to jumping to the obvious solution. For change processes, conflicts are even essential, as only conflicts release the energy that is needed for change.

Conflicts are normal; they are part of everyday business life. How conflicts are resolved determines the morale of the employees and, taken in sum, the quality of the corporate culture. Dieter Frey once said: "Not the conflict is the problem, but the way it is handled" (Frankfurter Allgemeine Zeitung, May 4, 2005). Frey criticized the fact that there was no conflict culture in the business world. Many executives were either avoiding conflicts or provoking conflicts in hard times.

In principle, I agree with this analysis. To me it is important, however, that conflicts are not only perceived as normal, but also perceived as rewarding – as long as people deal with conflicts, as long as they deal with the true issue and do not withdraw. Yes, conflicts are essential. A 2002 study carried out by the Academy showed that teams tend to fail when they cover up conflicts; 90% of all executives surveyed agreed. Far fewer respondents (53%) believed that openly dealing with conflicts was critical for the failure of teams (see Academy Study 2002).

The prerequisite for good conflict management in companies is an anxiety-free communication culture. It must be possible to address any topic, without having to fear negative consequences. This also becomes evident from how leaders conduct critical conversations. In this example, I would like to more closely examine how conflicts can be dealt with.

As a prerequisite for a successful critical conversation four aspects should be considered: Leaders should praise, praise, praise – not only in the actual conversation, but in general. The appreciation of the criticized employee should always take priority. Mistakes must be viewed by managers and employees alike as opportunities. Finally, the feedback must always be acceptable for the employee.

Praise, praise, praise. Criticism is only acceptable if praise has been previously expressed. Therefore, never forget to praise your employees. This can be a little something in between ("Good idea; thanks!") or a larger issue (You mention the employee's completing their final project with praise in front of the entire department). A rule of thumb is that the relation between praise and criticism should be 4:1, so that criticism is not seen as a lack of appreciation. Give the management tool "praise" a try. Unfortunately, in our society criticism is much more common than a kind word. Break this cycle and praise whenever you notice something positive. By praising you can also make your own life easier. Performance that is achieved through pressure requires constant monitoring; performance that stems from employees' self-motivation does not need to be monitored. However, praise only what is truly worthy of recognition. False praise is often understood as a humiliation – or as the calm before the storm.

Appreciating the employee. Your employees' behavior is generally based on a positive intention for the person or group in question. This also applies to behavior that could be called a "mistake." If for example an employee constantly annoys you with stupid jokes and disrupts work processes, he or she may very well want nothing more than recognition and attention – and is willing to become unpopular in order to get it. You could remove the troublemaker or try to change them with pressure. However, it is more sensible to find out the real motivations for their behavior and to satisfy them by other means. If this troublemaker wants attention, you can give it to them by occasionally praising their work; then their troublesome behavior will stop all by itself.

Viewing mistakes as opportunities. Errors at work cannot be avoided. It shouldn't be any other way, because mistakes are always a chance to learn something more, to pick up new ideas and grow. The greatest inventions of mankind "happened accidentally" – they were in one way or another the product of errors. Only in cases of sabotage arc errors malicious. All other errors happen because of lack of knowledge (i.e., the manager would need to teach employees better or give them more time to practice), fatigue (i.e., the employees are overworked and new labor arrangements are needed) or routine (i.e., the staff is not challenged and needs a more interesting task). Perhaps the error was due to the environment: the workplace is too loud, machines are broken, the protective gear is defective, the ventilation is poor or the working environment is negative. As a manager, it is your job to investigate the causes of errors. There is always a degree of responsibility on the part of the leader. This should be kept in mind when preparing a critical conversation, so that you don't unfairly vent your anger on an employee.

Feedback must be acceptable. Criticism should always be mentioned soon after the disruptive behavior has taken place. Take advantage of this opportunity and do not postpone talking about problems. Otherwise the employee could get the feeling that mistakes can never be lived down. The criticism should always be related to behavior and not to the person of the employee; don't say: "You are an erratic person," but: "What strikes me is: recently you often come late to work." Be specific. Only in this way can the employee relate to your criticism. Never say "You are always late." or "You're constantly making mistakes"; identify the specific situation. "Yesterday the number of errors in your production was above average."

The following steps can help you to lead feedback sessions:

Preparation. Take the time to prepare some written notes before you start. Note your conversation goal. Make yourself knowledgeable about the background of the employee. Is he going through a divorce right now? Was she sick a lot lately? Has he done a good job before this incident? Be sure to find an appropriate time at which neither you nor the other party is under time pressure. You should not be disturbed during the conversation. Create a relaxing atmosphere and never engage in critical discussions "off the cuff."

Warm-up phase. When the employee arrives, first take care to create a relaxed atmosphere. This will not only help the employee but also you, because you will probably also be a bit on edge. Provide the famous cup of coffee or tea at the beginning. Look for a gentle introduction to the topic, so your conversation partner gets the chance to get used to the situation. Recognize the employee's positive qualities and talk about them, too. Remember what I mentioned earlier: praise and criticism must be in a healthy balance. Avoid using "yes, but..." sentences. Also, if you use praise only for tactical purposes, your conversation partner will notice it immediately.

Target/actual comparison. Mostly a critical discussion will take place when the employee's results differ from an expected goal. Use questions to lead the employee to recognize this difference himself/herself. Remember that the employee's behavior is normally beneficial. Only in this (individual) case did that behavior not lead to the goal. So the criticism should not be "blanketing," but always be related to this particular situation. If the employee retreats into stubborn silence or launches a counter-attack, it means you weren't sufficiently sensitive.

Develop new practices together. Allow your employee to participate in the decision-making process with regard to new behaviors. Only then will they have the commitment to change their behavior. Once again, emphasize their positive qualities and take these as a basis to start from. Do not lose sight of the goal here. But there will always be many paths that lead to the goal. Thus, not the behaviors that you might prefer are the best, but the behaviors that both match the qualities of the employee and lead to the goal. The responsibility for implementing the solution should remain with the employee.

Make clear agreements. You should make arrangements as to when to get together and to compare target/actual values again. Be concrete: agree on what has to be done and when. Here, too, leave the responsibility for your employee's behavior with the employee and work with questions instead of pressure. Objectives should be clearly defined, realistic and involve solid deadlines. And remember that great goals should be broken down into smaller mini-goals, in order to avoid overwhelming your employee. These mini-goals also make it possible to give feedback in a timely manner, which is in turn the prerequisite for the employee knowing what they have done wrong (or right) and what needs to be changed (or maintained). Remember that an employee will change their behavior only if they realize that doing so is beneficial for them. So when you talk about consequences, you should discuss not only the negative consequences (threat of dismissal, warning, an entry in their personal file, salary reductions, etc.), but also the positive ones: they may be given the chance to take on greater responsibilities, be assigned to new and interesting tasks, or receive a bonus.

Conclusion. At the conclusion of the critical discussion there should always be praise to ensure a positive end to the interview. You can thank your employee, for example, for the constructive conversation. Send your employee away with the feeling that you believe in them and their abilities, that you are confident they will solve the problem successfully. Give them the feeling that with this interview alone, they are already well on their way to beating the problem, because this is true. Let your employee feel that they were not in a critical conversation, but in a regular "staff meeting."

Of course, we cannot master critical conversations if we only have theoretical knowledge and know a few case studies. Without consistent training and systematic practice, this skill cannot be taken for granted in everyday leadership. We observe that executives fail time and again to consider the most basic rules. And this brings us back to the subject of the leader's personality. Leading means above all leading one person: yourself.

4.2.5 The Objective Agreement Process

Management by objectives is a well-known management tool; even Peter F. Drucker mentioned this issue. However, the idea is still not in use everywhere. Some companies continue to practice authoritarian leadership and use presence – rather than goals and trust. Objective agreements (i.e., agreements on objectives) can also be viewed systemically. Above all, I find this tool interesting because it allows us to combine hard and soft factors of corporate leadership. An old adage says: "If you know nothing about your destination, every path will look the same."

Allow me to begin with an example: in his 2002 book "Leadership," former New York mayor Rudolph Giuliani describes how he led and shaped the ungovernable city for nearly 8 years (see Giuliani 2002). Giuliani has been known worldwide based on his decisive action after the terrorist attacks of September 11th, 2001. In his autobiography he lists a number of guiding principles that were important to him. Some of them would seem banal:

Deal with first things first.
Prepare relentlessly.
Everyone is accountable all of the time.
Surround yourself with great people.
Promise little and deliver much.

These books are always naturally full of self-congratulation and justification. Still, by his personal example and through numerous anecdotes we can see the conflicting areas executives are often moving in. I found it particularly interesting that Giuliani had a sign with the words "I am responsible" put on his desk to constantly remind him of his own fundamental belief.

Literally, Giuliani writes, "Throughout my career I have stressed that account-ability and responsibility are the cornerstones of any activity in public administra-tion and that my administration owes accountability to those for whom we work. And this principle starts with myself."(Giuliani 2002, p. 88)

And Giuliani can be proud of the final balance – something that many top executives who write autobiographies cannot claim. Above all, what he achieved for the public safety of New York is worth mentioning: between 1994 and 2001 crime rates decreased by 57%. Breaking down this figure, murders were down by 66%, shootings by 75%, and car thefts fell by 68%. At the same time, the average time between an emergency call and the arrival of the police was reduced from 8.4 to 7.3 min.

Why do I describe all this in such detail? Because here two basic principles of objective agreements can be recognized very well. First, it is important that the correct criteria and metrics are used. Otherwise you produce endless statistics that aren't good for anything – except for those who maintain these data columns and thus secure their jobs. For the citizens of New York what is important is that they can now actually live more safely. The fact that the authorities previously measured their success by the number of arrests (instead of the actual decline of crime) is just another interesting anecdote described by the author. Second, Giuliani, who during his time in office also had his fair share of enemies, implemented these criteria and metrics consistently and enforced them. He himself was the constant initiator and the critical spirit. In short: if the leadership "takes it easy," this signal will rapidly spread, and the whole system will once more be called into question.

Another view on the issue of objective agreements is provided by Reinhard K. Sprenger. He describes them as "trust prosthetics" and sees them as an instrument born of peoples' distrust: "They were invented when they lost control, had no visual contact anymore, could not verify whether the other person was also fully committed. Or because they were dissatisfied with the performance of an employee, because they wanted to drive somebody, or because they wanted something in writing, to better reward and punish, or, vice versa, because it was believed to protect them from their superiors." (Sprenger 2002b, p. 133)

First of all, Sprenger is surely right when he points out that objective agreements are sometimes born out of distrust. I believe, furthermore, that they are not always applied with the necessary sense of calm, but rather in a technocratic way: the main point is that there are objectives written down in the documentation, which we can semi-reasonably measure. I agree with Peter F. Drucker that "management by objectives" leads to the alignment of individual and corporate goals and harmonizes them. In this sense I do not believe that objective agreements are not principally born of distrust.

In his writings, Sprenger also differentiates – that should certainly not be concealed here: firstly, he acknowledges that within limits objective agreements can also be useful. He also stresses that *how* these objectives have been established is of great importance, differentiating between three scenarios:

Whenever targets are imposed on the employees from the top down, you should be suspicious as to whether each employee is doing everything to achieve these goals.

Whenever targets are jointly negotiated and then agreed upon, the manager should trust the employees to find sensible ways to meet them, and trust that the objectives ultimately be achieved.

Whenever achievement is rewarded by a bonus it signals distrust and provisions are made for the non-attainment of goals.

One way or another, "objective agreements as a tool will never eliminate the problems of distrust." The reason is that objectives must be negotiated, agreed upon and reviewed – and this assumes that the relationship between manager and employee is serious and sincere. But this cannot be automatically assumed, says Sprenger. "Objective agreements don't bind workers; only trust can." (Sprenger 2002b, p. 134)

Here, I think that Sprenger throws out the baby with the bathwater. When there is a real possibility of establishing contact (and admittedly this can only be said about a minority of all relationships between bosses and employees), then it should also be possible to create an "honest" atmosphere in the target agreement process. Again, the tone makes the music. Under no circumstances should executives give up the goal of getting the most out of target agreement from the outset.

About Sprenger is right about another point. Since objective agreements with their rules and parameters need clear interpretations and good conditions, and markets are often rapidly changing, we need the room for such discussions between managers and employees. Because: "reality is richer than words." (Sprenger 2002b, p. 136)

And I would like to mention another point: In close connection with business agreements on objectives, strategies must be designed. The indicator of systemic leadership as I represent it here is that even this "hard" process need not always proceed only in ordered and conventional channels. So, managers should not always maintain the same rituals and strategy, for example their usually meeting in a horseshoe shape over PowerPoint presentations. There is another way: with theatrical performances and panels, with spray cans and wax crayons.

Once one of my colleagues commented on this: "In some strategy workshops the managers outline their visions for the future on a whiteboard. With their colleagues and without a voice recorder. What a process: publicly taking a stand and "spraying" their vision without having to consult endless strategy documents, not to mention the feedback of colleagues. The energies evident at such moments are impressive."

The regular target agreement interview is the main instrument to allow for a systematic dialog on objectives between managers at all levels and their employees. It is also the most important component of a comprehensive management approach that can be called "Leading by objective agreements." The contents of such conversations, which are held at least once a year, are objectives, behavioral objectives and personal development goals.

The purpose of these discussions is that the objectives, the planned results, are discussed and if possible a consensus is found. As such, we must distinguish between defined targets and objective agreements. As part of these meetings there is also a decision made with regard to the prioritization of the individual goals. Furthermore the measures to be taken should be defined in order to achieve the agreed-upon objectives, and possible trade-offs and solution scenarios should be addressed.

What is the benefit of objective (agreement) conversations? What arguments can be used? Here is a list for implementing this instrument:

Anyone who sets objectives and concentrates his or her forces; this concentration increases impacts, lowers costs and reduces execution times.

The sound planning of goals forces us to become aware of the current situation, the future scenarios, the opportunities and risks of the market, as well as the strengths and weaknesses of the company.

Target planning allows target progress checks, which reveal vulnerabilities and can trigger a learning effect.

Goals that are both ambitious and realistic challenge employees to deliver higher performance.

The employees and their expertise are actively involved with in the planning process.

Employees are encouraged to take personal responsibility.

The exchange of ideas and discussion between management and employees is encouraged.

Jointly agreed-upon targets increase the motivation to work, which is further enhanced as the planned objectives are achieved or even surpassed.

Management and employees will receive feedback on their previous behavior and thus become more aware of their personal and social skills.

The development of employees is systematically aligned with the company's goals. The cooperation between management and employees is improved.

This brief overview shows that everyone benefits from leading by objectives: the entire enterprise, the leaders and the employees.

The number of targets should be limited to what is feasible. Too many objectives can scatter the concentrating effect of target planning. In order for there to be an actual "agreement," the employees must not only have enough opportunities to contribute their own ideas, but also be invited and encouraged to do so. If executives enter into the process with unalterable objectives and are unwilling to negotiate, something has gone very wrong.

Employees will only fully accept targets if they are at least roughly compatible with their own personal goals and personal value system. Objectives gain additional momentum if they are transformed into images ("visions"). In addition, negative formulations should be avoided because they can be demoralizing. Instead of "Our discussions should not take so long," say "Our discussions are limited to one hour."

Well-formulated objectives must meet the requirements of the following "SMART formula":

Specific	$\Rightarrow$	What is to be concretely achieved?
Measurable	$\Rightarrow$	How can we tell that the objective has been achieved?
Challenging	$\Rightarrow$	Is the target a challenge?
Realistic	$\Rightarrow$	Is the target realistically achievable with our resources?
Terminated	$\Rightarrow$	When is the deadline for the goal?

If these requirements are not taken seriously, it can create major sources of interference in the concept of "leading by objective agreements."

4.2.6   Delegating

Delegating responsibility to employees is an important precondition in order for leadership to take place at all. Also, the aspect that leaders have to "unburden" themselves is relevant here. Delegating tasks also has the benefit of empowering employees.

The process of delegation is significantly influenced by the leadership values of the manager. For leadership values, Koestenbaum developed a model covering the four main dimensions of vision, courage, understanding, and a sense of reality.

Those who are forward-thinking and innovative, constantly keep in mind their long-term goals, and take clear action possess *vision*. Those who stand by their own opinions, take the initiative and accept responsibility when things seem to be difficult or controversial, demonstrate *courage*. Leaders are *understanding* if they are sensitive, open, honest and fair to others, and support their development. And they have a *sense of reality* if they take the constant changes in their environment into account.

Empowerment involves the daily implementation of these four dimensions of leadership behavior in our concrete behavior. Vision, coupled with a sense of reality, allows us to define ambitious and achievable goals and to reach them. In the leadership process, the leader communicates these goals to his or her employees and then provides them with the necessary resources and the necessary space. Providing this space takes courage and trust. Finally, the leader has to be able to assist his or her employees if they have difficulties achieving a goal.

Empowerment is thus a combination of target setting, self-reliance and support. This is the path that determines the success of a company.

Let me once again define delegating: delegating is the transfer of clearly delineated duties, needs and skills that are necessary to accomplish this task, along with the related responsibilities. Why should a manager delegate? He or she should do so in order to distribute tasks so as not to discourage employees and in order to encourage and challenge them, to train specialists and to take some of the burden off of himself or herself as leader.

Executives should also pay attention to the following points. Otherwise, delegating can backfire:

Delegating is not about getting rid of unpleasant tasks. That doesn't mean that you cannot delegate an unpleasant task to an employee in an emergency. But if you do, be sure to explain the situation to the employee, and do not always ask the same employee.

Delegating should go hand in hand with a careful consideration of an employee's personal development. That means you should think about where you want to encourage this employee and with which tasks you can do this best. Of course, the quality of their work also has also implications for its assessment on your part.

You cannot delegate leadership and management responsibilities.

Before a manager starts a delegating talk, he or she should also consider the following questions: What is the underlying objective? How can I describe the activity in simple words? What information and documents are required for the employee? What skills do I need to pass on?

When the conversation takes place you should discuss the following issues: What does the task look like? Why do I want this employee to take over the task? Is the employee willing to do the job? What is he or she still lacking (practice, training, etc.)? What is the time required for the task? How quickly do response, control and returns need to take place? What resources and information are available to the employee?

At the same time, the manager should consider what problems may result from delegating. On the part of the employee, these can include:

He or she feels overwhelmed, but does not say so.

He or she claims to be overwhelmed (though this is not true).

The employee truly does feel overwhelmed, and yet there is no way to relieve him or her from other tasks in the short term. The remaining employees are jealous because they were not asked to do it.

variant	I have decided ...	... and you may discuss with me
1.	... nothing at all	... whether something is to be done
2.	... that something is to be done	... what is to be done
3.	... what is to be done	...when, how, where and by whom it is to be done
4.	... when, how, where and be whom it is to be done	... my reasons for my decisions
5.	... everything	... consequences that follow from this for you
6.	... everything	... nothing at all

Fig. 4.3 How to delegate (*Source*: Schwarz 2005)

The employee has to give up on the (uncompleted) task, even though he or she is able to complete it (reverse delegation).

On the part of leaders, there is a risk that they want to do everything themselves and cannot "let go." Another difficulty might be that no true delegating takes place, because the manager constantly interferes and does not extend trust to the employee. Lastly, the delegating talk might not have been through enough, as a result of which the employee does not exactly know what they are supposed to do.

Using a delegation scale can help to assess the specific situation and the respective level of delegation (Fig. 4.3).

4.2.7   Developing Teams

Teamwork is popular and widespread, but it does not run itself. Effective collaboration can only succeed if there is clarity on the relationship level. Forming a team is never the solution to a problem, but the first step on a long road. A survey of 376 executives working in teams shows where the stumbling blocks are on this journey: communication problems, an unclear definition of the task and unexpressed conflicts (see Academy Study 2002).

A team's composition is critical to its success. Meredith Belbin (see Belbin 1996) distinguished between eight typical team roles that people consciously or unconsciously assume because of their personality traits and behaviors when they cooperate with others: the "plant," the implementer, the monitor evaluator

(=observer), the teamworker, the coordinator, the shaper, the resource investigator and the completer finisher. In German teams, according to my observations, the monitoring, coordinating and delegating roles are represented disproportionately, while innovators who can come up with unique and creative ideas, monitor evaluators and completer finishers are far too rare. It is the mixture that makes the difference, but only in very rare cases does the selection of team members follow the Belbin typology. In most cases it is simply based on technical expertise, hierarchical structures, or on mere availability.

4.2.8   Phases of Team Development

Anyone who wants to understand teams needs to understand their dynamics. Different phases of good team development can be distinguished. Following the pattern "Forming – Storming – Norming – Performing," there is first an orientation (forming) phase for the individuals who are to cooperate. In this phase the participants are polite, friendly, distant, and in the truest sense of the term "socially acceptable." They are careful and wear masks; their true selves are only partially visible. The next phase of the conflict (storming) is characterized by the participants becoming impatient and beginning to challenge each other (more subconsciously than consciously). Personal animosities and antipathies become visible, and emotions are no longer hidden. The participants are confronted with conflicts (see Lewin 1947).

Then it comes to the stage of imposing order (norming), in which relationship conflicts are identified and resolved if possible. However, "I" still overshadows "we." But the participants try to return to working on substantive issues. Roles and rules for cooperation are defined and the team gets started. Only after these stages is a working group complete, and only then can the phase of integration and performance begin (performing). In this phase, even hidden conflicts are discussed openly and emotions are revealed and lived out. There is feedback and confrontation, and a "we-feeling" is created. In other words: if a group tries to avoid the critical "storming" phase, then it will likely never be a true team and will remain unable to integrate.

A word on leading teams: basically, the executive has to distinguish between task and maintenance roles, and show them depending on the situation. Task roles are for example taking the initiative to define goals, proposing ways to coordinate ideas, or giving structure. Maintenance roles are for example encouraging others and showing supportive behavior, handling conflicts without creating "losers," working to involve all participants, to integrate opinions, and to allow open communication.

I see three fundamental success factors for teamwork:

The variety of personalities: often, friendly relationships among the members is considered an ideal basis for teamwork – this is a fallacy, because a team needs diversity and variety not only in technical respects, but also in terms of personalities. If you are alike, you cannot complement each other.

Clearly defining the task and setting rules: a team leader must not only set targets and deadlines, but also define the rules of the game. Who will be informed when? When is what decision made and how? Good teams begin their work by defining these rules. Members will need a space where they can discover that open conflicts are not deadly and that it is much better to deal with them creatively and passionately, instead of through intrigue and "underground." Only if every team member knows that the joint effort is beneficial not only for the business but also for their own development, will they really get involved.

A good team leader: in many companies teams fail because they lack a leader. One of the myths of management says that teamwork and leadership are opposites. Effective teams need clear leadership, a person who sets the direction and the framework and who takes responsibility. The task of a good team leader is to manage the moods of the group members, to control and use them, without letting go. The building of teams and working groups is not a license to lead in a laissez-faire style – just the opposite is true.

Managers can only form a working group into a powerful team if they manage to heed these three success factors, link the task to the personal development of the team members and simultaneously create an emotional and inspirational social atmosphere. "Power teams" are characterized by an open and authentic relationship, which involves considerable controversy and regular feedback. Conflicts are not swept under the carpet, but are the point of departure for further improvements in the interest of finding the best solution.

4.3 Can Good Leadership Be Measured?

In calm seas, the ship and its outstanding engineering are praised; but when a storm develops, all eyes turn to the captain in the hopes of receiving instructions and signals. Leadership is never unimportant, but in times of crisis there is a growing awareness of its importance. Yet the newly awakened interest in the "leadership factor" is anything but blind worship.

At the same time, in recent years companies have become increasingly interested in being able to estimate the value of their own "human capital" and to measure it more accurately. Management is only one of many components. Initiatives such as the Human Capital Club (see www.human-capital-club.de) or approaches such as the Balanced Scorecard (Kaplan and Norton 1996) reflect this interest (Fig. 4.4).

Combining these two trends, the question is whether good leadership can be measured – and if so, how? Purists would say that good leadership is a prerequisite and is always measured by the results. However, it is impossible to clearly link good results to a single cause. So – is good leadership measurable? In closing this work, I would like to pose this question, and to answer it – within certain limits.

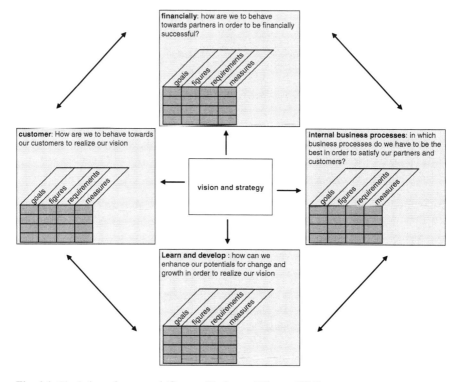

Fig. 4.4 The balanced scorecard (*Source*: Kaplan and Norton 1996)

Salary, bonuses, decisions, communication and leadership styles – suddenly all of these topics are at the center of interest, and are often criticized. More and more people are wondering: what is good leadership worth? What part does leadership play in the company's profits? What impacts can leadership have? Does leadership make a difference? In the U.S., consultants have developed a suitable calculation method: similar to the measure of success "return on investment" (ROI) there is now the measure of the "return on leadership" (ROL), which is intended to provide information on the profitability of corporate leadership.

How important is leadership as a business success factor really? The consulting firm Hewitt Associates divided 320 U.S. firms into two groups, those with single-digit and those with double-digit growth rates. It is interesting that more than 70% of the top 20 companies have in-depth policies for the selection, development and salary of executives. Among the less successful companies only 38% have such an approach. It is also interesting to see that all of the top 20 companies use the performance evaluation as a natural tool for career planning.

In companies with less economic growth, only 64% use the evaluation. The "return on leadership" (development) would seem to be demonstrable. Unfortunately, it has not yet gotten around to many German companies that investing in leadership requires more than just lip service. The head of human resources at L'Oreal, Oliver

Sunday, said: "The leadership development is often very time consuming, but the effort is rewarded with young but already experienced international business management graduates." And he seems to know what he's talking about: L'Oreal was voted the best European employer in 2003 (see Handelsblatt, October 22, 2004).

However, the ROL is too simplistic, because personnel do not work according to the pattern "command received – performance – result." Even if leadership cannot be measured, it can certainly be felt. Good leaders know they can shape systems only if they understand themselves as part of those systems and their inherent powers. Even outsiders can quickly see what impact a manager has on the daily routines of the employees: whether they act only on instructions or on the basis of trust and appreciation. Is the fear of losing their job their motivation to work, or is it the belief that there is more than just the salary that is worth working for?

Does the leader know what his or her employees need, what motivates them, and what moves them? Do the employees feel that their leader is in contact with them? An important indicator is whether both sides are not just talking about results, but also about possible and actual ways to achieve them. An important factor is that all employees know which potentials make them valuable, which potentials still are waiting to be discovered, and which ones can be trained. If appreciation and trust determine the climate, then mood signals will be perceived by all parties in good time before paralyzing fear and distrust can develop.

Precisely because these factors cannot be assessed with hard figures, but only intuitively, the measurement of success for managers begins in themselves, in their personalities, values and motivations. And that is the approach of the seminars on "systemic leadership" at the Academy.

4.4 Conclusion: Achieving Customer Satisfaction with Leadership Tools

"A good leader has to make himself or herself superfluous." This was the slogan a few years ago. In the meantime, we know that good leadership makes a difference. The return on leadership is there, although it is not easily measurable. However, this should not lead managers to underestimate the issue. On the contrary: its importance can hardly be emphasized enough. Perhaps it will help in this regard to once again refer to the father of all management gurus: Drucker believed that the success of a company – and its leadership – cannot ultimately be measured by internal criteria, but only by the satisfaction of its customers (see Drucker 2000). And smart leaders have long-since recognized just how right he was.

Chapter 5
Conclusion or: Where the Road Is Leading

No future can make up for what you have missed in the present.
Albert Schweitzer

As I have explained several times, in my opinion leadership means creating a world that others are glad to be part of. I am convinced that in the future the "soft" factors of leadership will continue to grow in importance because of their immense impact on companies' economic success. If the change in the management development and leadership in companies' everyday work is effective – we know that course corrections of large ships always take considerable time and space, so for large corporations it will be visible only after a few years – then there will be a different understanding of leadership than today. And due to increasing internationalization and digitalization, Germany is experiencing a salutary push that will eliminate the last vestiges of the "imperial" tradition of leadership – towards networking, trust and emotional intelligence.

Essential management tools will always belong to the equipment of a good leader, and we must work to improve these tools further and to adapt them to new requirements. Their application should be taught not only in theory but be based on learning by doing – much more than it is today – and should not begin (or end) at the executive level, where any mistake can have disastrous consequences for the entire organization, precluding long-term learning. To this extent, I agree with Malik concerning his complaint about the lack of practical training of leaders and I place my hopes in the future.

But good training is not enough. Choosing future managers should no longer primarily be based on their IQ but also their EQ. Authenticity will be more important than a particular type of leader, and self-management and relationship management skills must become more important than a stack of business school degrees. Yet the fact that "soft" factors are gaining credence does not mean a relapse into a cuddly "we all love each other" mentality. When I provocatively claim that leading also means being able to love, I am talking about hard work. This involves truly accepting yourself and the people around you and promoting their strengths in order to enable them to take on personal responsibility and self-

D.F. Pinnow, *Leadership - What Really Matters*, Management for Professionals,   237
DOI 10.1007/978-3-642-20247-6_5, © Springer-Verlag Berlin Heidelberg 2011

determination, as well as letting them go and trusting in their individual performance and intrinsic motivation to perform; further, it means exercising power as a
leader, providing guidance and serving as a role model while remaining remain
humble – and all of this requires courage, effort, continuous learning, self-criticism,
conflict resolution skills, stamina and strength; leadership is performance.

And this performance will be essential in the coming years and decades, which
will be characterized by fiercer global competition. Many executives who have
become lost in the dizzying heights of the upper echelons forget all too quickly
and too readily that their performance is measured in results – not in hours worked,
not in vacation days accumulated over the previous years, and not in the hectic
bustle that ensues when they rush through the departments of "their" company.

New models will be developed as a means to measure the "return on leadership"
in hard figures, making it quantifiable and calculable. I doubt that these
efforts will be successful, but if they serve to raise awareness among executives
and shareholders, employees and managers, of the relevance and benefits of a
relationship-oriented approach to leadership that truly appreciates the "human
resource," then I have nothing against the development of such models.

Let me conclude this book with ten central theses:
The ideal manager does not exist.
Leadership begins with yourself.
Leadership is primarily self-management and relationship management.
Leadership is a constant learning process.
Leadership means loving people.
Leadership can be learned, but certain leadership traits are prerequisites –
    especially initiative and empathy.
Leadership requires the integration of individual needs and organizational
    objectives.
Leadership is the combination of management and guidance.
Leadership can – to a limited extent – be measured.
Leadership is an issue for our millenium.

References

Books, Papers and Articles

Bartlett, C. (2003). Standpunkt: Christopher Bartlett, *Campus Management Band, 1*, 425–427 (Frankfurt/Main).

Bartlett, C. A., & Ghoshal, S. (2000). *Der Einzelne zählt. Ein Managementmodell für das 21. Jahrhundert.* Hamburg: Hoffmann und Campe.

Baumgarten, R. (1977). *Führungsstile und Führungstechniken.* Berlin/New York: de Gruyter.

Belbin, M. (1993). *Team roles at work.* Oxford: Butterworth-Heinemann.

Belbin, M. (1996). *Managementteams.* Wörrstadt: Erfolg und Misserfolg.

Bennis, W. (2003). Standpunkt: Warren Bennis. In *Campus Management, Band 1*, 199–201 (Frankfurt/Main).

Bennis, W., & Nanus, B. (1985, 1996) *Führungskräfte. Die vier Schlüsselstrategien erfolgreichen Führens*, New York: Campus Verlag, München: Heyne.

Berglas, S. (2003) Führungskräfte-Coaching. Wenn der Trainer falsche Tipps gibt. *Harvard Business Manager, 1*(S.), 98–105.

Blake, R. R., & Mouton, J. S. (1980). *Verhaltenspsychologie im Betrieb. Das neue Grid Management-Konzept.* Düsseldorf/Wien: Econ-Verlag.

Boyens, F., & Gerhardt, T. (2003). Mit Worten und Taten Vertrauen schaffen. *Harvard Business Manager, 12*, 100–105.

Bruch, H., & Ghoshal, S. (2004). Drache und Prinzessin. *Wirtschaftswoche, 32*, 62–65.

Buckingham, M., & Coffman, C. (2001). *Erfolgreiche Führung gegen alle Regeln – wie Sie wertvolle Mitarbeiter gewinnen, halten und fördern.* Frankfurt/Main: Campus Fachbuch.

Campus Management Band 1, Frankfurt/Main (2003a).

Campus Management Band 2, Frankfurt/Main (2003b).

Charan, R., Drotter, S., & Noel, J. (2001). *The leadership pipeline: How to build the leadership-powered company.* San Francisco: Jossey-Bass.

Clarke, B., & Crossland, R. (2003). Die Kommunikationskluft überwinden. *Executive Excellence, 53*, 8–9.

Csikszentmihalyi, M. (2004). *Good business: Leadership, flow and the making of meaning.* London: Penguin.

de Vries, K. Manfred: dysfunctional leadership, instead, *Working Paper Series*, 1–11.

de Vries, K. (2002). *Manfred: Das Geheimnis erfolgreicher Manager: Führen mit Charisma und emotionaler Intelligenz.* München: Financial Times Prentice Hall.

de Vries, K. (2004). Manfred: Chefs auf die Couch. *Harvard Business Manager, 4*, 62–73.

Doppler, K. (1999) Dialektik der Führung – Opfer und Täter

Doppler, K., & Lauterburg, C. (2002). *Change management: Den Unternehmenswandel gestalten*. Frankfurt/Main: Campus Verlag.

Drucker, P. F. (1942). *Die Zukunft der Industriegesellschaft*. Düsseldorf: Econ.

Drucker, P. F. (1956). *Die Praxis des Managements*. Düsseldorf: Econ.

Drucker, P. F. (1967). *Die ideale Führungskraft*. Düsseldorf: Econ.

Drucker, P. F. (1984). *Erfolgreiches Management in Krisenzeiten*. München: Heyne.

Drucker, P. F. (1999a). Die Kunst, sich selbst zu managen. *Harvard Business Manager, 5*, 9–19.

Drucker, P. F. (1999b). *Management im 21. Jahrhundert*. München: Econ.

Drucker, P. F. (2000). *Die Kunst des Managements*. München: Econ.

Drucker, P. F. (2004). *Was ist Management? Das Beste aus 50 Jahren*. München: Econ.

Fayol, H. (1916). *Administration Industrielle et Générale*. Paris: Dunod.

Fiedler, F. E. (1967). *A theory of leadership effectiveness*. New York: McGraw- Hill.

Flaherty, J. E., & Drucker, P. F. (1999). *Shaping the managerial mind*. Düsseldorf: Jossey-Bassv.

Galford, R., & Seibold-Drapeau, A. (2003). Die Feinde des Vertrauens. *Harvard Business Manager, 5*, 96–106.

Ghoshal, S., & Bartlett, C. A. (2003). Mythos globaler manager. *Harvard Business Manager, 11*, 84–102.

Ghoshal, S. (2003). Standpunkt: S Ghoshal, *Campus Management, Band 1*, 220–222 (Frankfurt/Main).

Ghoshal, S. (2004). Die strategische Ressource Mensch. *Handelsblatt, 16*.

Gloger, S. (2004). Systemische Organisationsberatung. Eine irritierende Leistung. *Manager Seminare, 72*, 62–71.

Goffee, R., & Jones, G. (2001). Warum sollte sich jemand gerade Sie zum Chef wünschen? *Harvard Business Manager, 6*, 50–61.

Goleman, D. (1996). *Emotionale Intelligenz*. München: Hanser-Verlag.

Goleman, D. (1999a). *Der Erfolgsquotient*. München: Hanser Verlag.

Goleman, D. (1999b). Emotionale Intelligenz – zum Führen unerlässlich. *Harvard Business Manager, 3*, 27–36.

Goleman, D. (2000). Durch flexibles Führen mehr erreichen. *Harvard Business Manager, 8*, 27–38.

Goleman, D., Boyatzis, R., & McKee, A. (2003). Die Gefühlslage des Chefs – sie bewirkt Wunder oder Unheil. *Harvard Business Manager, 3*, 75–87.

Gosling, J., & Mintzberg, H. (2004). Die fünf Welten eines Managers. *Harvard Business Manager, 4*, 46–59.

Graen, G. (1976). Role-making processes within complex organizations. In M. D. Dunnette (Hrsg.), *Handbook of organizational psychology* (pp. 1201–1246). Rand McNally College Pub. Co: Chicago.

Guliani, R. W. (2002). *Leadership – Verantwortung in schwieriger Zeit*. München: Bertelsmann.

Guserl, R., & Hofmann, M. (1976). *Das Harzburger Modell. Idee und Wirklichkeit und Alternative zum Harzburger Modell*. Wiesbaden: Betriebswirtschaftlicher Verlag Gabler.

Handy, C. (1993). *Understanding organizations*. London: Penguin Books.

Handy, C. (1995). *Die Fortschrittsfalle. Der Zukunft neuen Sinn geben*. Wiesbaden: Gabler.

Handy, C. (1996). *Gods of management: The changing work of organizations*. New York: Oxford University Press.

Handy, C. (1999). *Gute Egoisten: Die Suche nach Sinn jenseits des Profitdenkens*. München: Goldmann.

Harvard Business Review (2001) Breakthrough leadership: It's Personal, Special Issue, 12.

Harvard Business Manager. (2004). Was gutes Management ausmacht. *Führung Spezial, 4*.

Harvard Business Manager. *Führung und Organisation, 8*.

Harvard Business Manager. Führungskräfte- und Personalentwicklung, Band *1, 2*.

Heifetz, R. A., & Linsky, M. (2002). Wie Topmanager Krisen überleben. *Harvard Business Manager, 6*, 18–32.

Heinen, E. (1998). *Betriebswirtschaftliche Führungslehre. Grundlagen, Strategien, Modelle*. Wiesbaden: Gabler Verlag.

Hersey, P., Blanchard, K. H., & Dewey, J. E. (1996). *Management of organizational behavior: utilizing human resources.* Prentice Hall: Upper Saddle River.

Herzberg, F. (1959). *The motivation to work.* New York: Wiley.

Herzberg, F. (2003). Was Mitarbeiter in Schwung bringt. *Harvard Business Manager, 4,* 50–62.

Hilb, M (Hrsg.). (1998) *Management der Human-Ressourcen. Neue Führungskonzepte im Praxistest.* Neuwied/Kriftel: Luchterhand.

Hinterhuber, H. H. (2005). *Leadership.: Strategisches Denken systematisch schulen von Sokrates bis Jack Welch.* Frankfurt/Main: F.A.Z.-Inst. für Management.

Hinterhuber, H. H., Friedrich, S. A., & Krauthammer, E. (2001). Leadership als Lebensstil. *Frankfurter Allgemeine Zeitung, 30,* 33.

Höhn, R. (1980). *Führungsbrevier der Wirtschaft.* Bad Harzburg: Verlag für Wissenschaft.

Höhn, A., Pinnow, D. F., Rosenberger, B. (Hrsg.) (2003) *Vorsicht: Entwicklung! Was Sie schon immer über Change Management und Führung wissen wollten.* Leonberg: Rosenberger Fachverlag.

Höhn, A., & Bernhard, R. (2002). Unternehmens-coaching – ein Praxisbeispiel Nachwuchs fördern bei Hubert Burda Media. *Management and Training, 6,* 22–25.

Huy, Q. N. (2002). Ein Loblied auf die mittleren Manager. *Harvard Business Manager, 2,* 72–81.

Jackman, J. M., & Strober, M. H. (2003). Keine Angst vor Feedback. *Harvard Business Manager, 7,* 78–87.

Jumpertz, S. (2003). In turbulenten Zeiten führen. *managerSeminare, 71*(11–12), 36–43.

Kanter, M. (1998). *Rosabeth: Bis zum Horizont und weiter.: Management in einer neuen Dimension.* München/Wien: Hanser.

Kaplan, R. S., & Norton, D. P. (1996). *The balanced scorecard.* Boston: Harvard Business Press.

Katzenbach, J. R. (1998). Muss auf der Chefetage ein Team agieren? *Harvard Business Manager, 3,* 9–17.

Kieser, A., Reber, G., Wunderer, R. (Hrsg.) (1995). *Enzyklopädie der Betriebswirtschaftslehre.* Handwörterbuch der Führung, Band 10, Stuttgart: Schäffer-Poeschel.

Kim, CW., Mauborgne, R. (1997) Warum rücksichtsvolle Chefs erfolgreicher sind, *Harvard Business Manager: Führung und Organisation, 8,* 17–26.

Königswieser, R., & Exner, A. (1999). *Systemische interventionen.* Stuttgart: Klett Cotta.

Kotter, J. P. (1989). *Erfolgsfaktor Führung.: Führungskräfte gewinnen, halten und motivieren.* Frankfurt/Main: Campus-Verlag.

Kotter, J. P. (1996). *Leading change.* Boston: Harvard Business School Press.

Kotter, J. P. (1999a). *On what leaders really do* (3rd ed.). Boston: Harvard Business School Press.

Kotter, J. P. (1999b). *Wie Manager richtig führen.* München: Hanser Fachbuch.

Kotter, J. P., & Heskett, J. L. (1993). *Die ungeschriebenen Gesetze der Sieger: Erfolgsfaktor Firmenkultur.* Düsseldorf: Econ.

Kotter, JP (2004) Mit Ideen und Konsequenzem gegen den Zynismus. *Handelsblatt, 7.*

Kouzes, J. (2002). *The leadership challenge.* San Francisco: Jossey-Bass.

Kouzes, J. (2003). Standpunkt Kouzes. In *Campus Management Band, 1,* 148–150, Frankfurt.

Kratz, H.-J. (1999). *Delegieren – aber wie?* Offenbach: Gabal.

Kühl, S. (2003). Die Grenzen des Vertrauens. *Harvard Business Manager, 4,* 112–113.

Kühl, S., Schnelle, T., & Schnelle, W. (2004). Kooperation: Führen ohne Führung. *Harvard Business Manager, 1,* 112–80.

Lemper-Pychlau, M. (2001). Führung mit offenem Visier Das Lernziel "Authentizität". *Personalführung, 12,* 20–25.

Lewin, K. (1947) *Frontiers in group dynamics, i. Concept of group life: social planning and action research,* New York.

Luhmann, N. (1984). *Soziale Systeme.* Frankfurt: Suhrkamp.

Luhmann, N. (2000). *Organisation und Entscheidung.* Wiesbaden: Westdeutscher Verlag.

Maccoby, M. (1977). *Die neuen Chefs.* Reinbek: Rowohlt.

Malik, F. (1984). *Strategie des Managements komplexer Systeme. Ein Beitrag zur Management-Kybernetik evolutionärer Systeme.* Bern/Stuttgart/Wien: Suhrkamp.

Malik, F. (2003a). *Führen, Leisten, Leben. Wirksames Management für eine neue Zeit.* Stuttgart/ München: Campus Verlag.

Malik, F (2003b) Wider den Reduktionismus, *Campus Management Band 1*, 266–269 (Frankfurt/ Main).

Manzoni, J.-F. (2003). Heikle Themen geschickt ansprechen. *Harvard Business Manager, 2*, 73–81.

Maslow, A. H. (1943). *A theory of human motivation, psychological review*, New York.

Mayo, A. (2003). Humankapitalrechnung. *Campus Management, 1*, 440–443.

McClelland, D. C., & Burnham, D. H. (2003). Macht motiviert. *Harvard Business Manager, 4*, 84–95.

McGregor, D. (1960). *The human side of enterprise*. New York: McGraw-Hill.

Mintzberg, H. (1999). Profis bedürfen sanfter Führung. *Harvard Business Manager, 3*, 9–16.

Mintzberg, H. (2003). Standpunkt Mintzberg. *Campus Management, Band 1*, S.44–46 (Frankfurt/ Main).

Mintzberg, H., Ahlstrand, B., & Lampel, J. (2002). *Strategy Safari: Eine Reise durch die Wildnis des strategischen Managements*. München: Redline Wirtschaft.

Moss, K. R. (1989). *When giants learn to dance*. London: Simon and Schuster.

Müller, U. R. (1997). *Machtwechsel im Management*. Freiburg: Rudolf Haufe Verlag.

Müller, H.-E. (2001). Wie Global Player ihre Mitarbeiter führen. *Harvard Business Manager, 6*, 16–26.

Neuberger, O. (2001). *Das Mitarbeitergespräch*. Leonberg: Rosenberger Fachverlag.

Neuberger, O. (2002). *Führen und führen lassen: Ansätze, Ergebnisse und Kritik der Führungsforschung*. Stuttgart: Lucius und Lucius.

Nicholson, N. (2003). Keine Angst vor schwierigen Mitarbeitern. *Harvard Business Manager, 4*, 22–37.

Peters, T. J., & Robert, H. W. (1982). *In search of excellence*. New York: Harper and Row Publishers Inc.

Pinnow, D. F. (1999). Wechsel? *Management Guide 2000, 9* (Bad Harzburg).

Pinnow, D. F. (2000a) Führen Fühlen, *Management Guide 2001, 9* (Bad Harzburg).

Pinnow, D. F. (2000b). Woran erkennt man einen Leader? *Management Guide 2001, 9* (Bad Harzburg).

Pinnow, D. F. (2001a). Zu wenig Zeit für Beziehungen. *Personalwirtschaft, 11*, 14–19.

Pinnow, D. F. (2001b). Ich – Team – Organisation. *Management Guide 2002, 9* (Bad Harzburg) Frankfurter Allgemeine Zeitung.

Pinnow, D. F. (2001c). Führen und fühlen. *Frankfurter Allgemeine Zeitung* 10–12.

Pinnow, D. F. (2002a). Teamarbeit in deutschen Unternehmen. *Personalwirtschaft, 11*, 6–7.

Pinnow, D. F. (2002b). Führen – Lieben – Wachsen. *Management Guide 2003, 9* (Bad Harzburg).

Pinnow, D. F. (2003a). Führen – Macht – Sinn. *Management Guide 2004, 9* (Bad Harzburg) 3.

Pinnow, D. F. (2003b). Return of leadership. *Management Guide 2004, 9* (Bad Harzburg) 6–7.

Pinnow, D. F. (2004a). Führen in Verantwortung. *Management Guide 2005, 9* (Bad Harzburg).

Pinnow, D. F. (2004b, July 2). 100 Tage Einsamkeit. *Frankfurter Allgemeine Zeitung*.

Pinnow, D. F. (2004c). Leadership 2004: Führen im Gespräch. *Personalwirtschaft, 1*, 6–7.

Pinnow D. F. (2005). Entscheidungen treffen. *Management Guide 2006, 8* (Überlingen/Bad Harzburg) 8–9.

Probst, G. J. B., & Gomez, P. (Hrsg.) (1991). *Vernetztes Denken: Ganzheitliches Führen in der Praxis*, Wiesbaden: Gabler.

Prusac, L., & Cohen, D. (2001). Soziales Kapital macht Unternehmen effizienter. *Harvard Business Manager, 6*, 27–37.

Reiter, L., Brunner, E., & Reiter-Theil, S. (Hrsg.) (1991). *Von der Familientherapie zur systemischen Perspektive*, Berlin/Heidelberg: Springer.

Reppesgaard, L. (2005, August). Jahresgespräche sind meist eine Farce. *Handelsblatt*.

Rieckmann, H. (2003). In turbulenten Zeiten führen. *managerSeminare 71*, 11–12.

Rosenkranz, H. (1990). *Von der Familie zur Gruppe zum Team. Familien- und gruppendynamische Modelle zur Teamentwicklung*. Paderborn: Junfermann-Verlag.

Rühli, E. (1996). *Unternehmensführung und Unternehmenspolitik*. Bern/Stuttgart: Haupt Verlag.

Satir, V. (1988). *Meine vielen Gesichter: Wer bin ich wirklich?* München: Kösel-Verlag.

Satir, V. (2002). *Selbstwert und Kommunikation*. München: Verlag J. Pfeiffer.

Sattelberger, T (1991) Die lernende Organisation. Konzepte für eine neue Qualität der Unternehmensentwicklung. Wiesbaden: Gabler.

Schrijvers, J. P. M. (2004). *Das Ratten-Prinzip.: Mit List und Raffinesse erfolgreich sein*. München: Goldmann.

Schwarz, G. (2005). *Die 'Heilige Ordnung' der Männer.: Hierarchie, Gruppendynamik und die neue Rolle der Frauen*. Wiesbaden: VS Verlag.

Seiwert, L. J. (2002). *Das neue 1x1 des Zeitmanagement*. München: Redline Wirtschaft.

Senge, P. M. (1996). *Die fünfte Disziplin. Kunst und Praxis der lernenden Organisation*. Stuttgart: Klett-Cotta.

Shope, G. N. (2003). Talente gezielt fördern. *Harvard Business Manager, 6*, 79–89.

Simon H (2003) Integrative strategie, *Campus Management, Band 1*, 277–281 (Frankfurt/Main).

Sprenger, R. K. (1999). *Mythos Motivation. Wege aus einer Sackgasse*. Frankfurt/Main: Campus Verlag.

Sprenger, R. K. (2000). Führung und Kooperation in der globalisierten Wirtschaft. *Personalführung, 12*, 18–24.

Sprenger, R. K. (2001). Führung muss neu gedacht werden. *Personalführung, 6*, 82–83.

Sprenger, R. K. (2002a). *Das Prinzip Selbstverantwortung. Wege zur Motivation*. Frankfurt/Main: Campus Verlag.

Sprenger, R. K. (2002b). *Vertrauen führt. Worauf es im Unternehmen wirklich ankommt*. Frankfurt/Main: Campus Verlag.

Sprenger, R. K. (2003a). Mitarbeiter brauchen Freiheit. *Harvard Business Manager, 4*, 107–111.

Sprenger, R. K. (2003b). Der sichere Weg, Zweiter zu werden, *Handelsblatt, 11*.

Sprenger, R. K. (2004a). Feiern sie feste. *Handelsblatt, 8*.

Sprenger, R. K. (2004b). Vom Mythos der guten Führungskraft. *Handelsblatt, 8*.

Staehle, W. H. (1989). *Management: Eine verhaltenswissenschaftliche Perspektive*. München: Psychologie Verlags Union.

Taylor, F. W. (1913). *Die Grundsätze wissenschaftlicher Betriebsführung*. München: Oldenbourg.

Thommen, J.-P., & Achleitner, A.-K. (2001). *Allgemeine Betriebswirtschaftslehre*. Wiesbaden: Gabler.

Tushman, M., & O'Reilly, C. (1988). Unternehmen müssen auch den sprunghaften Wandel meistern. *Harvard Business Manager, 8*, 78–89.

Ulrich, D. (1999). *Strategisches human resource management*. München/Wien: Hanser Fachbuchverlag.

von Foerster, H. (2002). *Einführung in den Konstruktivismus*. München: Piper.

von Rosenstiel, L. (Hrsg.). (2003). *Führung von Mitarbeitern: Handbuch für erfolgreiches Personalmanagement*. Stuttgart: Schaeffer-Poeschel.

von Schlippe, A., & Schweitzer, J. (1999). *Lehrbuch der systemischen Therapie und Beratung*. Göttingen: Vandenhoeck & Ruprecht.

von Schulz, T. F. (2003). *Miteinander reden. 3 Bände*. Reinbek bei Hamburg: Rowohlt Verlag.

Vroom, V. H., & Philip, W. Y. (1973). *Leadership and decision making*. Pittsburgh: University of Pittsburgh Press.

Wagner, G. G. (2003). Besserer Nachwuchs für das Management. *Harvard Business Manager, 3*, 108–109.

Watzlawick, P. (2004). *Wie wirklich ist die Wirklichkeit? Wahn – Täuschung – Verstehen*. München: Piper.

Watzlawick, P., Beavin, J. H., & Jackson, D. D. (2000). *Menschliche Kommunikation. Formen, Störungen, Paradoxien*. Bern: Huber.

Weber, M. (1919). *Wirtschaft und Gesellschaft*. Köln/Berlin: Kiepenheuer & Witsch.

Weber, M. (1972). Wirtschaft und Gesellschaft. Grundriss der verstehenden Soziologie, Tübingen (pp. S. 140 ff).

Weinert, A. B. (1998). *Organisationspsychologie*. Weinheim: Ein Lehrbuch.

Wiersema, M. (2003). Auf die Auswahl kommt es an. *Harvard Business Manager, 6*, 58–70.

Wunderer, R. (1997). *Führung und Zusammenarbeit. Beiträge zu einer unternehmerischen Führungslehre*. Stuttgart: Schäffer-Poeschel.

Wunderer, R. (1999). *Mitarbeiter als Mitunternehmer. Grundlagen, Förderinstrumente, Praxisbeispiele*. Neuwied/Kriftel: Luchterhand.

Wunderer, R. (2000). Unternehmerische Kompetenz: Aufgabe auch in eigener Sache. *Personalführung, 8*, 58–60.

Wunderer, R. (2002). Führe global und lokal. *Personalwirtschaft, 9*, 40–45.

Zohar, D. (2003). Spirituelles Kapital, *Campus Management, 2*, 50–53.

Studies

Akademie-Studie. (1999). *Warum Veränderungsprojekte scheitern*. Bad Harzburg: Akademie für Führungskräfte der Wirtschaft.

Akademie-Studie. (2001). *Beziehungsweise, Führung und Unternehmenskultur*. Bad Harzburg: Akademie für Führungskräfte der Wirtschaft.

Akademie-Studie. (2002). *Mythos Team auf dem Prüfstand*. Bad Harzburg: Akademie für Führungskräfte der Wirtschaft.

Akademie-Studie. (2003). *Führen in der Krise – Führung in der Krise? Führungsalltag in deutschen Unternehmen*. Bad Harzburg: Akademie für Führungskräfte der Wirtschaft.

Akademie-Studie. (2004). *Zur Leistung (ver)führen. Leadership und Leistung in deutschen Unternehmen*. Bad Harzburg: Akademie für Führungskräfte der Wirtschaft.

Internet

Conger, J. (1996). *Can we really train leadership*? URL: http://www.strategy-business.com.

Dobiey, D., & Wargin, J. J. Führung in der digitalen Ökonomie: Management und Leadership. URL: http://www.galileobusiness.de/artikel/gp/artikelID-90.

Frey, D. Auf dem Weg zu Spitzenleistungen: Unternehmen als Center of Excellence. URL: http://www.lmupd.de/kongress/kongressource/pdfs/frey.pdf.

Habbel, R. W. (2001). The human factor: nurturing a leadership culture. In Faktor Menschlichkeit. URL: http://www.strategy-business.com.

Kongress. (2003, June 26). Leadership meets University. URL: http://www.lmu-pd.de.

Mintzberg, H. (2001). Why I hate flying, and other tales of management. URL: http://www.strategy-business.com.

Mohn, R. (2000). Neue Ziele in der Welt der Arbeit. In: Menschlichkeit gewinnt, S.153–196. Download-Dokument neuezieleweltderarbeit.pdf. URL: http://www.competence-site.de/personalmanagement.

Probst, G. J. B. Veränderungen im Unternehmen: Führen statt Verwalten. URL: http://www.knightgianella.ch/D/d-DOWNLOADS/d-PDF/d_leadership/LS-1-2000.pdf.

Rosenstiel, L. V. Change Management – Mitarbeiter für Veränderungen motivieren. URL: http://www.lmu-pd.de/kongress/kongressource/pdfs/rosenstiel.pdf.

Rüegg-Stürm, J. (2003, April) Kulturwandel in komplexen Organisationen. pdf-Dokument Diskussionsbeitrag 49. URL: http://www.ifb.unisg.ch/.

Simon, H. (2001). Freiheit und Sinnstiftung: Führung im 21. Jahrhundert. URL: http://www.competence-site.de.

Sprenger, R. K., & Heuser, U. (2001, June 25). Online-Debatte "Führung neu denken?" URL: http://www.changeX.de.

URL: http://www.competence-site.de/personalmanagement.

URL:http://www.handelsblatt.com/pshb/fn/relhbi/sfn/buildhbi/cn/GoArt!200014204614,776841/SH/0/depot/0/.

The Author

Associate Professor Daniel F. Pinnow, CEO of the Academy for Leadership in Überlingen, Germany is one of the most famous experts in leadership and management science in German speaking countries. He is associate professor of leadership at the Capital University of Economics and Business in Beijing, China and lecturer for leadership and human resource management at the Technical University of Munich. As a pioneer in systemic leadership in Germany, Pinnow combines his extensive leading and managing experiences with traditional management theories, organizational psychology and family therapy.

Pinnow earned a master's degree in economic sciences from the University of Cologne and a master's degree in social sciences. Throughout his studies he focused on psychology and organizational sciences. The experienced management trainer and leadership coach has been on the board of directors of the Cognos AG, one of Germany's biggest private providers for further education and gained deep leadership experience as top manager within international companies such as EADS and E.ON Ruhrgas AG.

In addition to his bestseller 'Leadership – What really matters' (Führen – Worauf es wirklich ankommt, 5th edition in 2011), which was additionally published in China as one of the first German management books, Pinnow has been publishing numerous papers and books on leadership, human resource management, and ethics.

Daniel F. Pinnow lives in the region of Lake Constance, Germany.

He can be reached through the Academy for Leadership www.die-akademie.de and through his personal Web site www.daniel-pinnow.de.